SAVORING
THE HAMPTONS

*Discovering the Food and Wine
of Long Island's East End*

by SILVIA LEHRER

RUNNING PRESS
PHILADELPHIA · LONDON

Cover and interior design by Amanda Richmond
Typography: Aperto, Lomba, and Memoir.

Running Press Book Publishers
2300 Chestnut Street
Philadelphia, PA 19103-4371

Visit us on the web!
www.runningpresscooks.com

TABLE OF CONTENTS

ACKNOWLEDGMENTS

WHERE DOES ONE BEGIN TO THANK THE COUNTLESS PEOPLE WHO PLAYED A meaningful role in the creation of this book? Let me try:

To Jason Allen Ashlock, my brilliant entrepreneurial agent, for his ongoing commitment to shape this book and bring it to fruition.

With deep thanks to Arlene and Alan Alda. In both of your very hectic lifestyles Arlene, you managed to keep the messages on track. And to Alan's thoughtful foreword that set the context of this book.

To Geoffrey Stone, my most amenable and patient editor, who always managed to find a solution to some, and at times many, perplexing problems.

To the team at Running Press: Chris Navratil, publisher, Craig Herman, marketing director, Bill Jones, art director, Amanda Richmond, senior designer (for the beautiful pages), Seta Zink, senior publicist, and the wonderful sales and support staff.

To Karen Wise, named one of the top ten wedding photographers in the country, she approaches her subject in the most natural way and with appreciation for her gorgeous photography.

To emeritus professor Dr. Leslie Kanuk, for her fine moral judgment, wise counsel, and warm friendship.

To Roman Roth, award-winning winemaker and vintner whose wine philosophy and wine suggestions are detailed throughout this book.

To Elizabeth Andoh, cookbook author and culinary educator whose friendship and effective guidance helped me to pursue my dream.

To Shirley O. Corriher, food scientist and author for her food wise assistance.

To Linda Slezak, who has been my eyes and ears on the North Fork of Long Island.

To literary agent Sarah Jane Freymann and her husband, college professor Steve Schwartz; to Anne Hargrave, art curator and wine enthusiast; to Dariele Watnick of Once-Over Organizing; to Tom Swinimer, technical wizard; to Elizabeth Schneider, cookbook author and consultant; to Geraldine Pluenneke, contributing writer; and to Patricia Zamoyska and Debbie Pitts for their unwavering support and encouragement.

To my many students whose close friendships have been a big plus in my life: I thank most sincerely and affectionately Dozie Sheahan, Janet Whelan Postma, Hank Ferlauto, and Lisa Tamburini for the timeless hours spent chopping, dicing, slicing, cooking, and offering advice on presentation for the picture perfect photos. And to Barbara Freiberg, Linda Slezak, Lilia and Michael Collins, Linda and Rob Leahy for their talented assistance in testing recipes—friends and foodies all!

And finally to my husband, Fred, whose cooking leaves much to be desired but who has an uncanny sense of taste. He will stop to think while eating then may offer a suggestion to make the dish even better!

FOREWORD

We first met Silvia Lehrer over French pizza. We didn't know there was such a thing, but apparently in the south of France they reached across the border at one point in history, tossed some dough in the air, and when it came down, it had a French flavor all its own.

We came to know about that interesting transformation in a cooking class we took with Silvia about twenty-five years ago. Then, a couple of years later, we went with her on a glorious trip through Italy where we ate the food of several regions and then settled down in Florence to learn a few things about Italian cooking in the kitchen of her friend Giuliano Bugialli.

Through all of this, Silvia showed an insatiable curiosity about good food, the places where it evolves, and the chefs who creatively cook with it: the same curiosity she shows in this book.

Food, of course, starts in the earth, and the growing conditions in a particular place can determine a lot about the food's flavor. But, it's also the people who live on that patch of earth and the culture they've developed that makes the food taste the way it does. The ingredients that grow in a region and the taste for flavors and combinations of flavors that develop among its people—and the studious, imaginative chefs who mix and re-mix those elements—make for dishes you don't find anywhere else.

Silvia has explored the food and culture and chefs around the patch of earth where she lives and she's found a signature, a fingerprint, that's very much of the place.

The area she's explored is called the East End of Long Island. Long Island sits in the ocean off the coast of New York like an alligator with its tail pointing west and its open mouth facing east. The top of this open mouth is called the North Fork, and the lower jaw is the South Fork. It's a hungry alligator, and the two jaws are separated by enough water to create a diverse food environment. It's the home of the Hamptons, where people come from all over the world every summer, many of them to settle down for winters, too. There is an interesting intersection here of history, geography, cultures, wineries, and creative chefs. Exploring the elements of the land around her has led to this fascinating book. It will give you pleasure while you read it, while you cook from it in the kitchen, and when you bring its bounty to the table.

The art of preparing food that touches something in you when you eat it is something Silvia Lehrer has spent a lifetime learning. And her ability to teach others how to accomplish that same bit of magic has been a gift to the rest of us.

Food may be the original gift of our species, as it is for others. Ants feed one another, birds fly home to the nest with nourishment for their young, and mother's milk is a universal first meal for most mammals. For us humans, food connects us in more ways than we can count. We grow it together, often cook it together, and then sit down in the ritual of eating it together (a ritual that may be on the decline in some families, sadly). We celebrate milestones over meals, and the meals themselves often celebrate the culture we come from. The food we eat identifies and affirms our kinship. Wherever we go in the world, one of the first questions we often are asked is, "Do you like our food?" The implication is if you like our food, you'll like us, because, in a way, our food *is* us. To know and love a people's food is the first step in warming to the people themselves.

In these pages, you'll meet the people of this island who keep the bees, dig the clams, grow the zucchini, and tend the chickens and turkeys and goats, along with the gifted chefs who have taken the flavors indigenous to this land and mixed them in ways that will be sure to warm you.

Turn the page and get to know them.

—ALAN ALDA

INTRODUCTION

Savoring the Hamptons focuses on the bounty and the beauty of the part of Long Island known as the Hamptons. There is simply no place like it. The Hamptons is not one place, but rather a necklace of seaside towns and villages on Long Island's South Fork, stretching east from Westhampton to Montauk, where a stately lighthouse guards over the meeting of the Long Island Sound and the Atlantic Ocean. On the North Fork stretching East from Riverhead to Orient Point—Riverhead or the "Head of the River" is where the Peconic River flows into the Great Peconic Bay, a beautiful body of water that separates the North and South Forks. It is a lush farmland that rolls out between the bay and the ocean and combines the best of what the land and sea offers. It explores the unique blend of produce, seafood, people, and beauty of the East End of Long Island.

The local people, who have lived here on both forks for generations while farming or fishing, along with the many others who come to enjoy resort living, have defined the area by its individual towns. A decided loyalty and pride among our diverse population of locals—fisherman, academicians, artists, writers, farmers, and celebrities—has resulted, giving the entire region an air of distinction.

The Hamptons, of course, has an undeniable cachet. The media's extensive attention to it brings forth new crowds each season. They come for many reasons, the most prominent being the sheer physical beauty of the area, both naturally and architecturally. Start the list with our beautiful beaches and their white sand dunes, the seemingly endless rows of clipped green hedges and ancient trees that surround Gatsby-like mansions, the beautiful homes that rise up along the coastline. Add the sprawling green farm fields, hidden ponds and bays, the pull of the ocean tides, the endless horizon, and the unique light that has drawn artists here for decades.

And, finally, there is the food. I have been so inspired by the quality of the food that I found myself writing an entire book about it.

For more than eighteen years, my husband and I have lived in Water Mill, a tiny hamlet in the township of Southampton. I still get a thrill while driving through our picturesque villages past historic windmills and windswept fields. Our home here has become for us an escape into rural quietude, a break from the hectic activity of running a demanding business.

In the early nineties, after more than a dozen years of teaching and directing cooking classes at my own cooking school and specialty table-top shop, Cooktique in Tenafly, New Jersey, I began to give cooking classes and write a weekly cooking column for a popular newspaper on the East End. As a Hampton year-rounder, the setting became my well-spring, helping me create new and diverse recipes based on my classical training abroad and in the United States, more than thirty years of hands-on teaching, and working with some of the finest artists in the culinary world. Through the years celebrity chefs, such as Jacques Pepin, Giuliano Bugialli, Paula Wolfert, Martha Stewart, Elizabeth Andoh, Maida Heatter, Nicholas Malgieri, and Madeleine Kamman, have graced my teaching kitchen.

The ever increasing awareness of regional cooking, the freshness and uncompromising quality of ingredients, and the abundance of availability on the East End are the inspiration for the recipes in this book. Life on an island revolves around the seasons, and this cookbook reflects that aspect of Long Island life with its four sections—spring, summer, autumn, and winter. Flavor, nutrition, and balance have always guided my cooking, and, because of my location, I have the ability and pleasure of using the season's finest produce and seafood while pursuing all three guidelines.

Within each of the four sections I introduce personalities of the East End, in both food and places, with interviews and brief histories of farmers, fishermen, farm stands, and wineries. The North and South Forks of Long Island boast several full-fledged wineries, such as the celebrated family-owned Paumanok Vineyard in Aquebogue on the North Fork. Improved production techniques and friendly weather have led to consecutive years of excellent grape production, and the vineyards are now yielding mature vines. Long Island wines have come of age and are receiving well-deserved press in major publications. While most of the vineyards are on the North Fork, the South Fork certainly holds its own. A visit to Christian Wolffer's stylish Wolffer Estate Vineyard in Sagaponack is magical. The saffron-colored, European-style building, housing state-of-the-art technology is surrounded by fifty acres of gently rolling hills.

Regardless of the season, food and entertaining are always big in the Hamptons. Pricey fundraising benefits along with glittering bashes abound during the "season"—a period formally defined as the days between Memorial Day and Labor Day, but now stretching long before and well after these holidays. Frequent parties fill up the calendars of those willing and able to socialize during the season. These glimpses into the life of both the North and South Forks are interspersed among the many recipes for appetizers, salads, entrées, and desserts that center on the local flavors of the area.

Life is never simpler than after the summer season ends, when the big soirées and clambakes fade into memory and the kids go back to school. The year's loveliest weather accompanies the Hamptons International film festival in October when international film celebrities grace our shores. Many of the residents volunteer during the weeklong event, creating a brief rush of "high summer" excitement before winter descends.

Yet, it is the winter holidays—a special time for friends and family, gatherings and celebrations—that bring timelessness to the East End. With snow falling and fewer restaurants and stores open, it is like living in the Hamptons of fifty or sixty years ago. The open spaces—the very reason many residents came here in the first place—seem more boundless, and the streets are blissfully empty, except perhaps on weekends.

Many wonderful new restaurants have sprung up in the towns and along the highways of the South Fork. It was only natural that theaters, museums, galleries, and mini-malls evolved in the various towns, such as the Parrish Art Museum, a venerable institution in Southampton aglow with incredible art displays and fascinating lectures to accompany them; the Bay Street Theater in Sag Harbor, where distinguished playwrights offer original works; the Westhampton Beach Arts Center, where one can enjoy local theater and cabarets, as well as art films; and Guild Hall in East Hampton, whose continuing efforts to bring artists and writers to the local public have added a significant dimension of culture and social activities to the area throughout the year for visitors and residents alike. Cocktail and dinner parties frequently revolve around these events each season.

Separated by the Great Peconic Bay from the South Fork, one will find a quiet beauty and modest charm to the bucolic landscape of the North Fork. Agriculture is alive and well on the North Fork, with its sprawling vineyards and farm fields. The beautifully preserved Zachariah Hallock House in Jamesport is a living museum where everything is exactly as it was, including a working wood-burning stove in the kitchen. Although the town is called Jamesport, the area is known as Hallockville. Zachariah Hallock, a captain in the Revolutionary War, built the house and purchased much of the land surrounding it, which includes bed-and-breakfasts that exist there today; docent tours are available at the museum. There is a children's camp at the museum where the children experience a genuine working farm to churn butter, connect in an agricultural lifestyle, and ride antique tractors. TAIST, which stands for The Arts In Southold Town, is an organization that brings in cultural dance and concert events with professional artists to the community. Farm-to-table annual dinners are held outdoors in summer with locally sourced foods donated by the local farmers.

Whatever the season, Long Island's East End, just like its food, is vital and delicious. It is my hope that the recipes and remembrances on the following pages let you taste and savor the pleasures of the Hamptons' local flavors wherever you live.

Savoring the Hamptons in
SPRING

When the sun's rays become more prevalent, 'round late March into April, well after the calendar's official notation of the first day of spring, a wonderful feeling wells up within me. It is a time when bright yellow forsythia and clumps of daffodils begin to flower and farmers are moving their seedlings from the greenhouse to the open fields.

There is a great deal of anticipation in the air as the summer crowds begin to return in mid-spring to this easternmost tip of Long Island. Farm stands throughout the region open at a quickening pace, and the ever-growing interest in local, sustainable, and organically grown foods is reflected by the attendance at local farmers' markets on both the North and South Forks. Here local artisans assemble to offer the great variety and quality of local ingredients we have here on the East End.

When bundles of asparagus spears stand tall on supermarket shelves, they have the stamp of early spring written all over them. Whether asparagus are thin or plump doesn't matter. What does matter is that it is fresh with firm stalks and dry compact tips. Asparagus is low in calories and high in nutrients. When roasted over high heat, its natural sugars caramelize to intensify its flavor. An elegant combination of asparagus and mushrooms is a delectable springtime treat for Asparagus Flan with Mushroom Ragoût, or Risotto with Asparagus, Green Beans and Mushrooms from your local mushroom grower.

An Assembly of Peas is a sweet treat of the season. Sorrel used to be grown in home gardens, as the herb was difficult to come by. Today you will find the leafy herb at local farm stands and farmers' markets in spring. Sorrel has an appealing yet acidic sourness but mellows when cooked to a purée and served with a quick sauté of salmon or sandwiched between a crisp Potato Tart.

Every season has a specialty, and spring is the season of delicate flavors. It is the season of fits and starts, one day a basket of peas or baby spinach will arrive at farm stands; on another day perhaps asparagus will show up. These are just some of the ingredients to be showcased for the season's flavors to shine through.

IT'S A MATTER OF TASTING
Touring the Local Wineries

A TRIP OF LESS THAN ONE HUNDRED MILES FROM MIDTOWN MANHATTAN takes you to the wine country on the North Fork of Long Island. It is like entering another time and place, perhaps the French countryside, where a Sunday drive to the country is a tradition.

The wine country on the East End of Long Island, an area known for its farming community and beautiful beaches, has grown into an urbane wine region. A roadside marker on the North Fork—"Welcome to the Long Island Wine Country"—greets guests as they enter to spend a day or a weekend touring the vineyards, tasting the wines in state of the art or rustic tasting rooms, and meeting the people who live and work at the wineries. Most wineries are open year round, seven days a week—and it's so easy to drive from one winery to the next. While both the North and South Forks boast several celebrated full-fledged wineries, most wineries are concentrated on the North Fork—an area that, happily for the grapes and the people who grow them, has remained unhampered by suburban sprawl. Charming country inns complete with excellent dining rooms, seaside restaurants, and a plethora of bed-and-breakfasts are interspersed through the attractive landscape.

Long island wines have been defined by talented winemakers learning to work with their own terroir. Improved production techniques and the favorable maritime climate have led to consecutive years of excellent grape production, and the vineyards are now yielding mature vines. Long Island wines have come of age and are receiving well deserved press in major periodicals. We often hear that wine is food and indeed it is. Here on the East End, we have the luxury of growing a diversity of food and pairing the local wines to complement it.

ROMAN'S WINE PAIRING RECOMMENDATIONS

CHOOSING THE APPROPRIATE WINE TO PAIR WITH FOOD CAN BE A DAUNTING challenge. But don't be afraid because it's not that difficult. If possible, cook with the wine you plan to drink and just follow some simple guidelines—but most of all trust your own taste and the result will be great. With a little bit of luck, your dining and wine pleasure will be enhanced when the food, the wine, and that always important element for success—ambience—match perfectly, creating a heavenly experience. Actually the East End of Long Island, with its abundance of great produce and amazing wines, is considered as close to heaven as one can get on earth.

Here are some simple food and wine pairing tips:

· Fun food with fun wine: A zesty gazpacho with a rose or a blended white wine.
· Simple food with simple wine or simple food with great wine: Serve a less complex wine if you just want to keep everything easy and casual, but serve a great, more complex wine if you want to allow the wine to take center stage.
· Complex food with simple wine or great wine: you may want to have a simple palate cleanser or a great wine pairing that matches the food's intensity.
· Spicy food with soft, aromatic (semisweet) wine: a sweet Riesling or Gewürztraminer will do the trick.
· Sweet food with an even sweeter wine, such as a late harvest/botrytis or an ice wine.

All the wines I have suggested in this book are from very reliable wineries on the East End and are based on my recent tastings. I encourage you to first taste the wines and especially the new vintages. Vintage variations change according to the climate and other variables. A new vintage may change the style of wine from the last vintage. It also will give you an indication how bold or tame to be with your food seasonings and what specific ingredients to emphasize. *Remember that wine should always enhance the food.*

Tasting is the way to become a master of wine and food parings. Someone has to do it! Enjoy!

—Roman Roth, winemaker at Wolffer Estate Vineyard in Sagaponack

SHIITAKE MUSHROOM CAVIAR

MUSHROOMS ARE AN EARTHLY DELIGHT. A MOCK CAVIAR IS MADE FROM FINELY CHOPPED mushrooms sautéed with garlic and shallots. I use shiitake and oyster mushrooms from Open Minded Organics mushroom company in Bridgehampton. In season, the mushrooms can be found at local farm stands and farmers' markets.

YIELD: ABOUT 1 CUP

¼ pound shiitake mushrooms, stems removed

¼ cup oyster mushrooms

2 tablespoons extra-virgin olive oil

1 large shallot, finely chopped

2 garlic cloves, finely chopped

Kosher salt and freshly ground black pepper

2 tablespoons chicken stock (see page 335) or low-sodium canned

1 tablespoon finely chopped fresh flat-leaf Italian parsley

1 tablespoon snipped fresh chives

Rinse the mushrooms in a colander under a spray of cool water. Transfer to a clean kitchen towel and pat dry. Finely chop the mushrooms with a knife or in a food processor. If using a food processor, be careful not to overprocess.

Warm the oil in a 12-inch nonstick skillet over medium-low heat and then add the shallot and the garlic. Sauté for 1 to 2 minutes, until tender but not brown. Add the mushrooms and cook, stirring occasionally, until barely tender, about 5 minutes. Season with salt and pepper to taste. Increase the heat to medium high, add the chicken stock, and cook, stirring, until the liquid has evaporated. Add the parsley and chives, stir to mix, and remove from the heat. Prepare the caviar up to two days ahead. Refrigerate, covered, in a suitable container. When ready to use, transfer the caviar to a serving bowl, bring to room temperature, and serve with crackers or crostini (see page 99).

SUN-DRIED TOMATO TAPENADE WITH CHÈVRE CROSTINI

BE SURE TO USE OIL-PACKED SUN-DRIED TOMATOES FOR THE FLAVOR TO FULLY DEVELOP. When developing this recipe, I used the goat cheese chèvre from Catapano Dairy Farm in Peconic on the North Fork. The tapenade may be refrigerated for up to a week in a suitable container.

YIELD: 8 TO 10 SERVINGS

1 small shallot, coarsely chopped

4 ounces sun-dried tomatoes packed in oil, finely chopped (about ½ cup)

Zest of 1 lemon

2 tablespoons capers, rinsed

Freshly ground black pepper

3 to 4 tablespoons extra-virgin olive oil

Crostini (see page 99)

2 ounces chèvre

Black Greek olives, for garnish (optional)

Combine the shallot, sun-dried tomatoes, lemon zest, capers, and pepper to taste in the work bowl of a food processor fitted with the steel blade and process to mix. With the processor running slowly, pour enough olive oil through the feed tube to moisten the mixture. This can be prepared ahead and refrigerated in a suitable container.

When ready to serve, top each crostini with a thin layer of goat cheese and a dollop of the tapenade. Arrange on a platter, garnish with olives, if using, and serve.

SPRING GREEN SOUP

THIS INSPIRED SPRING SOUP IS FROM THE TUSCAN CITY OF LUCCA. TINY PIECES OF LEEK, green onion, carrot, and fava beans float like jewels in the clear broth. Leeks are a sandy vegetable and should be washed very well.

YIELD: 8 SERVINGS

2 large leeks, root ends trimmed

3 thin carrots

1 bunch spring onions or scallions

$^2/_3$ pound fresh fava beans

1 tablespoon unsalted butter

2 tablespoons extra-virgin olive oil

7 to 8 cups chicken stock (see page 335) or low-sodium canned

Kosher salt and freshly ground black pepper

Dill sprigs or fresh marjoram leaves, for garnish

Trim the ends and remove the dark green leaves from each leek and discard. Cut the leeks in half lengthwise and rinse under running water to remove any grit and sand. Soak the leeks in fresh water for 10 to 15 minutes. Drain, dry, and cut crosswise into thin slices. Set aside.

Peel and trim the carrots and then slice thin. Trim the spring onions or scallions of any bruised areas on the green stems and the root ends and slice thin. Shell the fava beans and drop them into boiling salted water for 1 minute (any longer and they will be mushy). Drain and rinse under cool running water to stop the cooking. Remove the outer skin of the fava beans and discard. With a paring knife, split the outer skins and slip out the beans with your thumbnail. This step can take a bit of time, but it is worth it. (Beans with their skin on are tough and bitter.) Set aside.

Melt the butter with the oil in a large $5^1/_2$ quart saucepan over medium heat. Add the leeks, carrots, and spring onions. Sauté the vegetables for 4 to 5 minutes, stirring occasionally. Pour in the stock and bring to a boil over high heat. Season the soup with salt and pepper to taste. Reduce the heat to medium low and simmer briskly for 20 to 25 minutes. Add the fava beans, taste for seasoning, and simmer for 2 to 3 minutes longer. Serve hot, garnished with dill sprigs.

The soup can be completely prepared up to 2 days in advance. Refrigerate, covered, and when ready to serve, bring the soup to room temperature and reheat before serving.

THE AMERICAN HOTEL
Sag Harbor

THE AMERICAN HOTEL IS A SMALL BOUTIQUE HOTEL IN HISTORIC SAG HARBOR. It is located in a landmark building that was built in 1846 at the height of the whaling era. Today, Ted Conklin, one of the leaders of the Slow-Food movement on the East End of Long Island, runs this charming hotel and restaurant that is highly regarded by locals and visitors alike. The restaurant's award-winning, inventive fare is led by the talents of British-born chef Jonathan Parker.

Chef Parker was professionally trained in London and the French Riviera. He was initially inspired by his grandmother's Sunday roasts and Yorkshire pudding, and her classic English desserts. In fact, she was a professional cook.

Jonathan came to the states with his American-born wife and worked at Le Bernardin and Rafael's in New York City. The menus at the hotel change with the seasons and are grounded in American-French classical tradition. Jonathan brings to the table his strong connection with fish and shellfish and a blend of creative dishes from France, Italy, Asia, and the United States focusing on local and imported ingredients.

The four separate candle-lit dining rooms with exquisitely set tables, laden with silver and crystal, offer a warm and elegant dining experience. The bar area, with its cozy fireplace, is a special place to be on cold winter evenings. The hotel is open year-round and dinner is served seven nights a week.

SCALLOP CEVICHE FROM THE AMERICAN HOTEL

THE AMERICAN HOTEL IS A SMALL, HISTORIC BOUTIQUE HOTEL IN THE HEART OF SAG HARBOR, New York, where executive chef Jonathan Parker offers this piquant do-ahead ceviche.

YIELD: 6 SERVINGS

12 ounces diver scallops

$1/2$ to $3/4$ teaspoon diced Serrano chile

$1/2$ cup diced red bell pepper

3 tablespoons diced poblano pepper

2 tablespoons diced red onion

1 tablespoon chopped fresh cilantro leaves

Juice of 1 large lemon

Juice of 1 large lime

2 tablespoons extra-virgin olive oil

Pinch of cayenne

Kosher salt and freshly ground white pepper

Remove the side muscle attached to the scallops and discard. Rinse and pat the scallops dry with a paper towel and then cut into $1/4$-inch dice. Place in a mixing bowl. Add the chile, bell pepper, poblano pepper, onion, cilantro, lemon juice, lime juice, oil, cayenne, and salt and pepper to taste and stir to mix. Allow to marinate, covered, in the refrigerator, for 4 to 6 hours or overnight. After 1 or 2 hours, taste the ceviche to adjust the seasonings as necessary.

To serve, spoon the ceviche into fluted scallop shells placed on a bed of julienned cucumber or into lettuce-lined martini glasses with toast crisps.

RAGGED EGG AND SPINACH SOUP

WHEN SCRAMBLED EGGS ARE BEATEN INTO HOT BROTH, THE EGGS SHRED INTO "RAGS."
The name derives from Straciatella, meaning rags in Italian. Adding spinach gives the soup an appealingly robust flavor. One of the first signs of spring is the welcome of the crinkly green leaves of spinach.

YIELD: 6 SERVINGS

1 pound fresh spinach

2 garlic cloves, peeled and left whole

2 tablespoons extra-virgin olive oil

Kosher salt and freshly ground black pepper

1/8 teaspoon freshly grated nutmeg

6 cups chicken stock (see page 335) or low-sodium canned

2 eggs, lightly beaten

1/3 cup freshly grated Parmigiano-Reggiano cheese

Remove the coarse stems from the spinach and discard any blemished leaves. Rinse the spinach thoroughly in several changes of lukewarm water to remove the sand and grit. Drain and gently pat dry in a clean kitchen towel. Transfer the spinach to a cutting board and coarsely chop the leaves.

In a 10 to 11-inch skillet with a lid, sauté the garlic cloves in the oil over medium heat until golden brown, about 3 minutes; discard the garlic. Put the spinach in the skillet and coat with the garlic-infused oil. Cover the pan and simmer for 2 to 3 minutes. Uncover and simmer, stirring frequently, to evaporate the moisture in the pan. Season to taste with salt and pepper and the nutmeg. This can be done up to a day ahead to this point and refrigerated in a suitable container.

Pour the stock into a large saucepan. Bring to the edge of a boil over medium-high heat and then reduce the heat to medium low and briskly simmer the spinach for 2 to 3 minutes.

Meanwhile, in a small bowl, beat the eggs until frothy and then stir in the cheese. Add a small amount of the simmering stock to the eggs and whisk to temper the mixture. Return the egg mixture to the stock and stir vigorously for 1 to 2 minutes or until the egg looks as though it has been torn into little flakes. Adjust the seasonings if necessary. Serve at once with additional cheese passed at the table, if desired.

LEEK AND SORREL VICHYSSOISE

VICHYSSOISE IS A CLASSIC LEEK AND POTATO SOUP SERVED CHILLED. HERE SORREL, A BOUNTIFUL local herb from the field, is added to give the soup its lemony characteristic. The soup benefits from do-ahead preparation whether served hot or chilled.

YIELD: 6 SERVINGS

2 large leeks

2 tablespoons unsalted butter

1 onion, finely chopped

Kosher salt and freshly ground white pepper

1 pound boiling potatoes, peeled and cut into 1/2-inch cubes

6 cups chicken stock (see page 335) or low-sodium canned

1/2 pound fresh sorrel, stems discarded, leaves rinsed and coarsely shredded

1/2 cup heavy cream

Snipped chives, for garnish

Trim the ends and remove the dark green leaves from each leek. Cut the leeks in half lengthwise and rinse under running water to remove any grit and sand. Soak the leeks in fresh water for 10 to 15 minutes. Drain, dry, and cut crosswise into thin slices.

Melt the butter in a large saucepan over medium heat. Add the leeks and onion and sauté until tender, 7 to 8 minutes. Season with salt and white pepper to taste. Add the potatoes and stir to mix. Add the stock and simmer for 16 to 18 minutes, or until the potatoes are tender. Stir in the sorrel and simmer for 1 to 2 more minutes. Taste and adjust the seasoning if necessary.

Purée the soup in batches in a blender or with an immersion blender directly in the saucepan until the mixture is smooth. If serving warm, return the soup to a clean saucepan, add the cream, and simmer until heated through. Do not allow the cream to boil. Ladle into soup bowls and garnish with snipped chives. The soup may be prepared up to two days ahead and refrigerated in a suitable container until well chilled. Serve cold, garnished with chives.

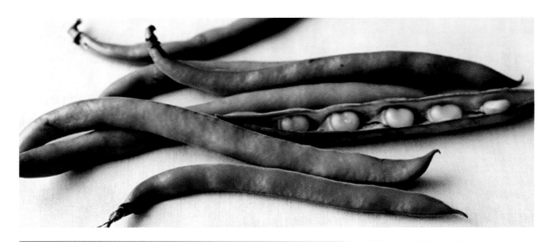

FAVA BEAN AND MOZZARELLA SALAD

THIS INSPIRED TUSCAN SALAD INCORPORATES FRESH SEASONAL FAVA BEANS FOR A TASTE of spring. Shell the beans, blanch in boiling salted water, and then slip off their heavy skins for a tender salad. This salad is best prepared ahead. Letting the salad sit for a few hours or a day allows the flavors to develop.

YIELD: 6 TO 8 SERVINGS

2 pounds fresh fava beans

2 garlic cloves, finely chopped

$1/2$ pound mozzarella or Pecorino, cut into small dice

2 tablespoons fresh marjoram or $1/2$ teaspoon dried oregano

Zest of 1 lemon

2 to 3 teaspoons freshly squeezed lemon juice

3 to 4 tablespoons extra-virgin olive oil

Kosher salt and freshly ground black pepper

Remove the fava beans from their pods. Bring a large pot of salted water to a light boil and drop the beans into the water. Cover the pot and return to a boil. Cook the fava beans until tender, 2 to 4 minutes, depending on size. Drain in a colander and rinse with cold water to stop the cooking. With a paring knife, split the outer skins and slip out the beans with your thumbnail. This step can take a bit of time, but it is worth it. (Beans with their skin on are tough and bitter.)

Place the garlic, mozzarella, marjoram, lemon zest, lemon juice, oil, and salt and black pepper to taste in a mixing bowl and stir to mix. Add the fava beans and toss gently to mix. Taste and adjust the seasonings if necessary. Prepare up to one day ahead for the flavors to mellow. Transfer to a serving bowl and serve at room temperature.

SATUR FARMS
Cutchogue

"FORTY OR FIFTY YEARS AGO, THERE WERE SIXTY TRUCKS BRINGING PRODUCE from the North Fork every day into New York City. Over the course of the next two generations we lost the farming industry on the East End of Long Island," said Eberhard Müller, formerly the executive chef of the celebrated French restaurant Lutèce in Manhattan. Today, Eberhard Müller and his wife, Paulette Satur, are the proprietors of Satur Farms in Cutchogue on the North Fork of Long Island.

After completing his traditional European apprenticeship in the Black Forest of Germany, Eberhard worked at Alain Senderen's L'Archestrate in Paris, a Michelin three-star restaurant. When he arrived to work at the World Trade Center four years later, in 1985, he scoffed at the lack of quality of ingredients.

Paulette Satur grew up on a dairy farm in central Pennsylvania, earned a BS in horticulture from Pennsylvania State University and an MS in plant physiology from University of Arizona. She then moved to New York City and, hearing about the wine region on the North Fork of Long Island, decided to move there to work for Hargrave Vineyard. She then continued her wine interests by joining a New York City wine importer-distributor.

"Eberhard had just taken over at Lutèce when he got his New York Times three-star review," said Paulette. "Soon after, I invited a friend to have dinner at Lutèce for her birthday. The wine sommelier said to Eberhard, 'The wine salesperson from Martin Scott Wines is here having dinner, I think you may want to meet her,' and so he came out to the table and didn't leave," they said in unison. The relationship soon evolved beyond business, and they were married on Christmas day in 1996. In 1997, they bought an eighteen-acre farm, and, although Eberhard was still at Lutèce, he and Paulette started farming in 1998. "We grow all the ingredients that can be grown on the North Fork and that are important to restaurants, chefs and even home chefs, meaning everything from asparagus to zucchini. We also have good relationships with local farmers, for instance, Latham and Wickham Farms on the North Fork grow our tomatoes," said Eberhard. Paulette responded with, "Satur Farms specializes in leafy salad greens: mesclun, baby spinach, wild arugula, mâche, and so much more."

Satur Farms takes pride to keep their farms sustainable by cover cropping, proper PH management, and balancing minerals in the soil with trained supervisors in the field. Surely they have filled the gap between farmer and chef to bring a variety of quality produce to the table.

SPRING GREENS WITH ROASTED GARLIC VINAIGRETTE

THIS RECIPE WAS INSPIRED BY A SALAD THAT SCOTT CHASKEY OF QUAIL HILL FARM OFFERED at a slow food dinner. The fresh crisp, colorful greens are an explosion of flavor with the piquant roasted green vinaigrette. Roast the garlic ahead; they will keep for about a week in the refrigerator. Make extra—they'll keep!

YIELD: 4 TO 6 SERVINGS

$^1/_3$ cup extra-virgin olive oil

4 to 5 large garlic cloves, peeled and sliced paper thin

Kosher salt

$1^1/_2$ teaspoons Dijon mustard

3 large roasted garlic cloves (see page 334)

2 to 3 tablespoons red wine vinegar

Freshly ground black pepper

8 cups fresh mixed greens (such as arugula, mâche, radicchio), washed and spun dry

Preheat the oven to 325°F.

Warm the olive oil in a small saucepan over medium low and add the sliced garlic. Cook until the garlic is lightly golden and crisp, $1^1/_2$ to 2 minutes. Remove the garlic with a slotted spoon and drain on paper towels; reserve the infused oil. Sprinkle the garlic chips with salt to taste and set aside.

Pour the reserved garlic oil in a small mixing bowl and when cool, add the mustard and squeeze the roasted garlic pulp from the skins. Mash the garlic into the oil and mustard with a fork and slowly whisk in the red wine vinegar. Season with salt and pepper to taste.

Place the salad greens into a bowl and dress with enough vinaigrette to coat the leaves. Divide equally onto four to six salad plates and top with the garlic chips.

TUNA TARTARE WITH AVOCADO SALAD

WHEN DANNY CORONESI OF COR-J SEAFOOD IN HAMPTON BAYS AFFORDED ME A LARGE PIECE of "toro," the belly of fresh tuna used primarily for sashimi, I prepared the following recipe with delicious results. You may prepare it for a salad as below or serve in a bowl to spread on crackers for an appetizer.

YIELD: 4 TO 6 SERVINGS

FOR THE TUNA TARTARE

5 ounces sashimi-quality tuna belly

1 teaspoon grated fresh ginger

1 large scallion, thinly sliced (light green and white parts)

2 teaspoons sake (Japanese rice wine)

Zest and juice of $\frac{1}{2}$ large lemon or lime

$\frac{1}{4}$ teaspoon kosher salt

$1\frac{1}{2}$ teaspoons dark sesame oil

FOR THE SALAD

2 ripe avocados

Pinch of red pepper flakes

Zest and juice of 1 lime

1 tablespoon extra-virgin olive oil

Kosher salt and freshly ground black pepper

4 to 6 large leaves of Boston lettuce, washed and spun dry

Parsley sprigs, for garnish

For the tuna tartare, thinly slice the tuna and then stack the slices and mince. Combine the tuna in a bowl with the ginger, scallion, sake, lemon zest and juice, salt, and sesame oil and stir to mix. The tartare can be prepared up to several hours ahead. Refrigerate, covered, in a suitable container until ready to serve.

For the salad, halve the avocados, remove the pits, and scoop out the flesh with a large spoon. Coarsely chop the avocados, transfer to a bowl, and season with the red pepper flakes, lime zest and juice, olive oil, and salt and pepper to taste. Toss to mix. Place a large lettuce leaf on each of four to six salad plates. Equally divide the avocado mixture over each leaf and top with the tuna tartare. Garnish with parsley sprigs and serve.

NOTE: For ease of slicing freeze the tuna belly for 20 minutes.

COUNTRY FARM STAND SALAD

WHEN ROADSIDE STANDS ARE BURSTING WITH YOUNG TENDER SALAD GREENS AND HERBS IN spring, the salad bowl takes a whole new approach.

YIELD: 4 SERVINGS

2 to 3 cups selected salad greens, such as lamb's lettuce, arugula, curly endive, and/or young spinach

$1/2$ cup coarsely chopped fresh mixed herbs such as, basil, tarragon, and mint

3 tablespoons extra-virgin olive oil

Kosher salt

1 tablespoon tarragon vinegar

3 scallions, thinly sliced (white and light green parts)

2 tablespoons sunflower seeds

Wash each kind of salad green separately in a salad spinner and spin dry. Wrap in paper towels to absorb any excess moisture. Wash and dry the herbs, taking care not to damage them. Arrange the leaves and herbs in a loose pile in a large, wide salad bowl.

Carefully toss the greens with the oil to coat the leaves evenly. This can be done up to 10 minutes before adding the vinegar. Place about one-third of a teaspoon of salt into a tablespoon measure and fill the tablespoon with the tarragon vinegar. Stir the salt into the vinegar and pour over the salad. Carefully toss again while arranging the leaves to their best advantage to balance color and texture. Sprinkle the scallions and sunflower seeds on the greens and serve.

ROASTED ASPARAGUS

ROASTING AT A HIGH HEAT CARAMELIZES THE NATURAL SUGARS AND INTENSIFIES THE FLAVORS of vegetables. The inspiration for this recipe came from Johanne Killeen and George Germon's *Cucina Simpatica*.

YIELD: 6 SERVINGS

1 pound fresh asparagus

1/4 cup extra-virgin olive oil

2 to 3 teaspoons kosher salt, or more to taste

1 to 2 tablespoons unsalted butter (optional)

Preheat the oven to 425°F.

To prepare the asparagus, break off the tough woody ends where they naturally bend. With a paring knife, peel away the tough points along the end of the spears, leaving the tender ones at the top. Rinse well and then pat dry with a paper towel.

Pour the olive oil and salt onto a baking sheet. Coat the asparagus with the oil and salt. You can prepare the asparagus to this point and then reserve them in the refrigerator until ready to cook. Bring them to room temperature before roasting.

When ready to serve, roast the asparagus in the upper third of the oven until the spears are tender when pierced with the tip of a knife, 10 to 12 minutes, depending on their thickness. Remove from the oven. Add the butter, if using, to melt over the asparagus.

With tongs, transfer the asparagus to a serving platter and pour the pan juices over them.

ROASTED SPRING ONIONS WITH VERJUS

SPRING ONIONS ARE ONIONS THAT ARE PULLED OUT OF THE GROUND WHEN THEIR TOPS ARE still green. They have a definite bulb with the same concentric formation as "dry" onions. Onions pulled before the bulb has formed are scallions. Roasting the onions with the verjus imparts a delicious tartness.

YIELD: 4 TO 6 SERVINGS

1 bunch spring onions, about 4 large

Kosher salt and freshly ground black pepper

2 tablespoons fresh thyme leaves

3 to 4 tablespoons extra-virgin olive oil

3 tablespoons verjus (unfermented grape juice)

Preheat the oven to 400°F.

Trim and discard the lengthy green leaves of the onions. Slice the onions crosswise into thirds. Arrange in a single layer on a baking sheet lined with parchment paper. Sprinkle the onion slices with salt and pepper to taste. Add the thyme leaves and olive oil. Pour the verjus over the onions.

Roast the onions for 35 to 40 minutes, until lightly browned and tender. Some outer rings may blacken, which can be discarded. The onions may be roasted up to one day ahead. Refrigerate in a suitable container and serve at room temperature.

AN ASSEMBLY OF PEAS

SELECT THE FRESHEST MIX OF SPRING PEAS FROM YOUR FARMERS' MARKET FOR A SWEET taste of the season.

YIELD: 4 TO 5 SERVINGS

$^{1}/_{3}$ pound snow peas

$^{1}/_{3}$ pound sugar snap peas

$^{1}/_{3}$ pound sweet peas

1 to 2 tablespoons unsalted butter

Kosher salt and freshly ground black pepper

1 cup loosely packed chopped fresh herbs, such as basil, mint, and/or chives

Trim and remove the string from the snow peas and sugar snap peas; remove the sweet peas from their pods.

Bring a large saucepan of salted water to a boil. Add the peas and cook until barely tender, about $2^{1}/_{2}$ minutes. Drain, shake dry, and return to the pan. Place over medium heat and stir in the butter and salt and pepper to taste. Cook for about 2 minutes longer. Add the herbs and stir to mix.

SMASHED YUKON GOLD POTATOES WITH ROASTED GARLIC

BUTTERY YUKON GOLD POTATOES ARE THE PERFECT CHOICE FOR CHIC, SMASHED POTATOES.

YIELD: 6 SERVINGS

1 roasted garlic head
  (see page 334)

2 pounds Yukon Gold
  potatoes

Kosher salt

1½ tablespoons extra-
  virgin olive oil

Freshly ground black pepper

Preheat the oven to 350°F.

Squeeze the roasted garlic from the head and mash into a purée. Scrub the unpeeled potatoes under cold running water to remove all traces of soil and cut into quarters. Place in a large pot and add enough cold water to cover by about 2 inches. Bring to a boil and add 2 to 3 teaspoons of salt. Simmer briskly for 16 to 18 minutes, or until the potatoes are tender when pierced with a knife.

Drain the potatoes and return to the saucepan. Smash them with an old-fashioned potato masher until still a bit coarse. Add the roasted garlic purée and olive oil and season with salt and pepper to taste. Stir with a large fork and serve hot.

THE GREEN THUMB
Water Mill

RAYMOND HALSEY AND HIS WIFE, PEACHIE, WITH THEIR FOUR ADULT CHILDREN, Patti, Johanna, Billy, and Larry, are the eleventh generation to work the farm as their ancestors have done since 1644. The Green Thumb is an organic farm, fully certified since the early 1980s. Thomas Halsey, originally a colonist from New England who settled in Water Mill, began farming on the East End of Long Island in the 1600s, when the earth was naturally organic and continued to be until the Second World War, when chemicals and pesticides came into use. The Green Thumb used pesticides through the mid-seventies at a time when the Halsey boys, now grown, persuaded their father to allow them to go organic. Larry and Billy began by purchasing one hundred thousand earthworms to re-indoctrinate beneficial nutrients and aerate the soil, along with their commitment to natural farming practices, such as crop rotation, composting, and biodynamic preparation to keep the soil balanced naturally.

"Farming is so deeply rooted in the family, and, unless you're a farmer, you really can't understand the connection to the land," said Johanna Halsey. She also referred to the local farmers and neighbors, "who are the best of the best even though they are not necessarily practicing biodynamic farming like crop rotation, but nevertheless, practice commitment to the soil."

Unique to the area is a perfect mix of silt, clay, and sand designated by the U.S. Department of Agriculture as "Bridgehampton Loam." Most farmers in the early days were potato farmers, and Long Island became one of the most important potato producing regions of the North American coast. Raymond Halsey was a potato farmer until he and his wife realized the retail potential of running a farm stand. By giving up part of the land to a variety of vegetables, they started The Green Thumb, the first farm stand in the area, in the 1960s, when their four children were very young.

That summer was a success at the farm stand, and Raymond Halsey started to experiment with many different kinds of vegetables and herbs. In 1968 he had a huge greenhouse from Holland assembled on the property. The vegetables that were sold were always young and fresh. In 1968 they built a larger Green Thumb farm stand and now use the original stand as a walk-in cooler out back.

The Green Thumb harvests more than three hundred varieties of organic vegetables, herbs, and fruits. Like all farmers, the Halsey family embraces the seasons and looks forward to spring's new asparagus peeking out of the ground, the first strawberries of summer, the new leafy greens and heirloom tomatoes fresh from the vine, the corn and cantaloupe, and the beautiful colors of autumn when all manner of winter squash gush from the ground.

Billy, Larry, Patti, and Johanna meet every week through a good part of the year to brainstorm new ideas and to hash things out in this multifaceted business. They have plans to build a high tunnel, an even larger greenhouse to basically grow a variety of tomatoes, a crop that could be problematic due to weather. Whether it be planting, production, and harvesting or working the greenhouses or the farm stand, it is a tribute to this special family's legacy to continue in the family tradition.

Property values on the East End of Long Island referred to as "The Hamptons" have soared. To preserve the land and to keep farmers farming, John v.H. Halsey, a ninth cousin of the Halsey siblings, founded and incorporated the Peconic Land Trust in 1983, a not-for-profit, tax-exempt organization dedicated to conserving Long Island's working farms.

PURPLE SPROUTING BROCCOLI

"WHAT IS THIS?" I ASKED JOHANNA HALSEY OF THE GREEN THUMB ORGANIC MARKET IN WATER Mill as I held up a banded bunch of branches topped with a supply of tiny purple sprouts. "It's purple sprouting broccoli," she replied. I took this "new to the area" vegetable and treated it with a classic Italian technique for cooking broccoli. When I prepared it for two Italian foodie friends, they exclaimed, "This is even better than broccoli rabe." The vegetable's early spring season is brief, with a limited window of time to enjoy it.

YIELD: 4 TO 6 SERVINGS

1 bunch farm-fresh purple
   sprouted broccoli

1 tablespoon kosher salt

2 to 3 tablespoons extra-
   virgin olive oil

1 to 2 cloves garlic, sliced
   into thin slivers

Pinch red pepper flakes

Freshly ground pepper
   (optional)

Cut the base stems of the broccoli and discard. Rinse thoroughly.

Place the broccoli in a large pot of boiling water just to cover. Add the salt and cover pot. Remove the lid when steam starts to escape. Blanch for $1\frac{1}{2}$ minutes, uncovered, until barely tender. Drain in a colander under a spray of cool water to stop the cooking; then transfer to a clean kitchen towel and pat dry. This can be cooked to this point a day ahead and refrigerated in a suitable container.

When ready to serve, warm the olive oil in a nonstick skillet over medium heat. Add the garlic and red pepper flakes and sauté for 30 to 40 seconds. Add the broccoli and sauté for $1\frac{1}{2}$ to 2 minutes to finish the cooking and to heat through. Season with salt and freshly ground pepper to taste, toss to mix, and serve warm or at room temperature.

NOTE: Purple sprouting broccoli is a northern European heirloom variety. It is planted in late summer and kept in the ground for 180 days for the spring crop.

POTATO TART WITH SORREL

AS I FLIPPED THROUGH THE MANY HUNDREDS OF RECIPES IN MY FILES I WAS DELIGHTED TO stumble upon a recipe for a potato tart sandwiched with sorrel. I have a passion for potatoes in any form and love the acidity of sorrel. Both of these ingredients grow very well on the East End.

YIELD: 4 TO 6 SERVINGS

FOR THE SORREL

$^1/_3$ to $^1/_2$ pound sorrel

2 tablespoons unsalted butter

2 shallots, finely chopped (about 2 tablespoons)

Kosher salt and freshly ground black pepper

2 tablespoons dry white wine

$^1/_4$ cup half-and-half

FOR THE POTATOES

$1^1/_2$ tablespoons unsalted butter, divided

$2^1/_2$ pounds all-purpose potatoes, peeled and sliced into very thin rounds

Kosher salt and freshly ground black pepper

For the sorrel, pull the sorrel leaves from the stems and discard the stems. Rinse the leaves in the basket of a salad spinner and soak to refresh them for 10 to 15 minutes. Drain and spin dry.

Heat the butter in a large, heavy nonstick skillet over medium heat. When the foam subsides, add the shallots. Sauté, stirring occasionally, for 2 minutes. Add the sorrel and season with salt and pepper to taste. Cook the sorrel leaves until they begin to wilt, about 2 minutes. Add the wine, stir, and cook at a brisk simmer to reduce the liquid in the pan, 1 to 2 minutes. Remove from the heat, add the half-and-half, and cook at a brisk simmer for 1 to 2 minutes to incorporate into the sorrel. This can be prepared a day or two ahead. Refrigerate in a suitable container.

Preheat the oven to 425°F.

For the potatoes, heat 1 tablespoon of the butter in a large ovenproof nonstick skillet over medium-high heat, and when the butter foam subsides, place 1 potato slice in the center of the pan. Then arrange the potato slices in a single layer to the edges of the skillet, overlapping them. Spread the cooked sorrel over the potatoes and cover with another layer of potatoes. Sprinkle with salt and pepper, dot with the remaining $^1/_2$ tablespoon butter, and press on the potatoes with a flat spatula to compress. Cook until the potatoes brown and crisp on the bottom, 10 to 12 minutes. Watch carefully and do not to allow the bottom layer to burn. Cover the skillet with parchment paper and transfer to the oven. Bake for 10 minutes, remove the foil, and bake for 15 minutes longer. Turn off the oven and leave the tart to crisp around the edges.

Carefully run a thin spatula around the edge of the skillet to loosen the tart. With pot holders in both hands, place a serving plate on top of the skillet and carefully invert the tart onto the plate. If any potato slices stick to the pan, simply loosen with the spatula and replace them. Blot the top of the tart with a paper towel. Season with salt and pepper to taste and cut into wedges for serving. The tart may be reheated in a 350°F preheated oven for 10 minutes, if preparing ahead.

Wine suggestion : Shinn Estate Vineyard Chardonnay

THE STONE CREEK INN
East Quogue

In 2007 THE STONE CREEK INN WENT THROUGH A RENOVATION, BUT THE original, fifteen-foot handsome dark mahogany bar was left untouched. The original large white country inn was built in the 1930s. It housed a restaurant with a checkered past and is said to have been a speakeasy and possibly a bordello. Christian Mir and his wife, Elaine DiGiacomo, purchased the restaurant in 1995 and opened in 1996.

When you enter the inn you have to walk past the wine "cellar" and down a long, narrow bar room to get to the lovely and spacious restaurant, which opens into two large dining rooms. Light pours through the attractive high-arched windows in the front room off to the right of the entry and updated lighting lends a soft glow in the evening. The newly appointed large back room was revisited with acoustical panels and plantation shutters, creating a casual but elegant look.

Christian and Elaine established a foothold in the Hamptons with the opening of Stone Creek Inn, a 150-seat restaurant on Old Montauk Highway in East Quogue. Christian was born in Toulouse, France. Along with his regular school curriculum, he chose to take a program in the culinary arts. Thus, his formal training began at age fourteen. Christian sought inspiration in Spain and Provence before coming to the United States to work at Tavern on the Green.

Elaine DiGiacomo, who has a degree in English literature, dreamed of having her own restaurant, although she never had any intention of becoming a chef. She graduated from the French Culinary Institute (FCI) and worked in the industries of restaurant marketing and public relations. One of the principals at the FCI suggested she take a job at Tavern on the Green. Elaine and Christian met at the restaurant, falling in love over a steam table.

Their dream was realized when they came out to Quogue to look at the Ambassador Inn. They were instantly attracted to this stately, abandoned Victorian building. With early renovations they created a lovely country inn with lots of ambience. The food selections on the menu focus on French and Mediterranean cuisine, carefully planned by Elaine and Christian, who have adapted to using the best products this area has to offer.

STONE CREEK INN'S ASPARAGUS FLAN WITH MUSHROOM RAGOÛT

I SUGGEST THAT YOU START THIS SPECIAL COMPANY RECIPE THE DAY BEFORE COOKING BECAUSE the puréed asparagus and spinach must be thoroughly dry before incorporating the remaining flan ingredients. The mushroom ragoût can be prepared up to several hours ahead and reheated before serving. It may be necessary to add a little more cream, or broth if you like, to the mushroom mixture when reheating.

YIELD: 8 SERVINGS

FOR THE MUSHROOM RAGOÛT

- $1/2$ pound shiitake mushrooms
- $1/2$ pound oyster mushrooms
- 3 tablespoons extra-virgin olive oil
- $1/2$ cup heavy cream
- Kosher salt and freshly ground white pepper
- 2 tablespoons port
- 1 tablespoon chopped flat-leaf Italian parsley
- 1 tablespoon minced fresh chives, plus extra stems, for garnish

FOR THE FLAN

- 1 pound spinach, heavy stems trimmed
- 2 pounds asparagus
- 1 cup heavy cream
- 2 large eggs
- $1/2$ teaspoon grated nutmeg
- Kosher salt and freshly ground white pepper

For the mushroom ragoût, remove and discard the stems from the shiitake mushrooms. Place the caps in a colander and quickly rinse under cold running water. Dry well with paper towels. Cut into $1/2$-inch-thick slices. Remove and discard the stems from the oyster mushrooms and pull the caps apart into "little fans."

Warm the olive oil in a 12-inch sauté pan over medium to medium-low heat. Add the shiitake mushrooms and stir occasionally for about 1 minute. Then add the oyster mushrooms and cook for about 4 minutes longer. Add the cream and port to the mushrooms and season with salt and white pepper to taste. Bring the liquid to the edge of a boil, reduce the heat to medium low, and cook until the sauce is creamy, about 4 minutes. Remove from the heat and stir in the parsley and chives. The mushroom ragoût can be prepared up to a day ahead, refrigerated in a suitable container as necessary.

For the flan, soak the spinach in several changes of lukewarm water to get rid of any sand and then rinse in cold water. Put the spinach in a large saucepan with just enough water to cover and bring to a boil. Reduce the heat to a brisk simmer and cook the spinach for 2 to 3 minutes, until tender. Drain and squeeze very dry in a clean kitchen towel.

Break the asparagus spears where they naturally bend and discard the tough ends. Peel away the tough points along the ends of the spears, leaving the tender points at the top; rinse the asparagus well. Cook the asparagus in a large pot of boiling salted water until tender, about 5 minutes, and then squeeze dry in a clean kitchen towel.

Place the asparagus and spinach in a food processor fitted with the steel blade and process until smooth. Transfer the purée to a colander lined with cheesecloth set over a bowl. Gather the sides of the cloth over the purée to form a bundle and press gently to remove the excess liquid. Place the purée, wrapped in the cheesecloth, over a bowl and refrigerate for several hours to remove as much liquid from the purée as possible; the purée should be very dry.

Preheat the oven to 250°F. Butter the bottom and sides of eight 4-ounce ramekins very well.

In a large bowl, whisk together the cream, eggs, nutmeg, and salt and white pepper to taste. Add the drained purée and mix until the ingredients are thoroughly incorporated. Fill the ramekins evenly with the flan mixture (they should be about three-quarters full) and place in a roasting pan. Add enough water to the roasting pan to come halfway up the sides of the ramekins. Bake for about 1 hour, until a knife inserted into the center of the flan comes out clean. Keep the flans in the water bath to stay warm.

To serve, reheat the mushroom ragoût over low heat, stirring occasionally, until warm. Unmold the flans by running a knife around the inside of each ramekin and inverting it onto a warm salad plate. Divide the mushrooms and sauce among each plate and spoon around each flan. Garnish with chive stems.

IN THE MONTH OF MAY, asparagus from our local farms are peeking out of the ground. Christian Mir of the Stone Creek Inn, in East Quogue, is one of the restaurateurs on the East End who value using local ingredients in their dishes.

DALE & BETTE'S ORGANIC PRODUCE
Sag Harbor

WHEN BETTE LACINA ASKED ME TO TASTE THE BAMBOO SHOOTS PILED HIGH at Dale & Bette's canopied stand in Sag Harbor's farmers' market, I was incredulous. Bamboo shoots are trees that grow quickly and can take over the yard before long. But eat them? Bette convinced me to take the eight-inch-long shoots to try them at home. I purchased a pound of tat soi, an Asian green, thinking I would do a stir fry with the bamboo shoots. Indeed, that day I discovered a very pleasing new dish.

Bette worked as a chef at Provisions, a health food store in Sag Harbor, which was the catalyst that brought her and Dale Haubrich together. Dale was born into a farming family in Iowa and since the 1970s was an early pioneer in organic farming. He was introduced to the East End of Long Island by a friend in the early nineties and was smitten. Dale started an organic farm in Sag Harbor on a small scale and began to sell his produce to Provisions. Bette connected with Dale through their love of wholesome food, and she eventually left Provisions to become Dale's business partner. But she had no idea what she was getting herself into: running a farm from seed to harvest, to mounting crops and marketing. Frustration set in for Dale at first because Bette had trouble planting straight rows. As a linear thinker, she would start that way but then begin to wander off. Dale relented and started to plant his crops by broadcasting seeds in patches, abandoning rows altogether.

When the Sag Harbor farmers' market opened in 2004—the first on the East End—Bette and Dale, a mom-and-pop business, plunged into the scene. Dale's reputation for growing a huge amount of produce on a small amount of land is well known. They grow and sell an amazing eighty different varieties through the seasons beginning in April and ending around Thanksgiving. Their little farm is a beautiful patchwork quilt of texture and varying shades of color.

BAMBOO SHOOT AND TAT SOI STIR-FRY

WHEN I CAME UPON BAMBOO SHOOTS AT DALE & BETTE'S ORGANIC PRODUCE STAND AT the Sag Harbor farmers' market, I didn't have a clue as to what I would do with them. Having also purchased a bag of tat soi greens, I decided to stir-fry the greens with blanched bamboo shoots. It turned out fabulous. Who knew?

YIELD: 4 SERVINGS

FOR THE SAUCE

1 large garlic clove, finely chopped, about 1 teaspoon

1 tablespoon finely chopped fresh gingerroot

1 tablespoon light soy sauce

1 tablespoon lemon juice

2 teaspoons sesame oil

FOR THE STIR-FRY

3 bamboo shoots*, about $^1/_2$ pound

1 tablespoon kosher salt

1 tablespoon peanut or canola oil

1 pound tat soi greens, washed and spun dry

Freshly ground pepper

For the sauce, combine all the ingredients in a mixing bowl and stir to mix. It makes about 3 tablespoons of sauce.

For the stir-fry, peel away the outer layers of the bamboo shoots until you reach a firm, ladder-like center. Cut the shoot into one-inch pieces. Bring a saucepan with enough water to cover vegetables to a boil. Add the salt and bamboo shoots. Return the water to a boil and simmer the bamboo shoots for 7 to 8 minutes, or until barely tender. Drain and dry on paper towels.

In a medium wok or large sauté pan over medium heat, add the oil and swirl the pan to coat it. Add the bamboo shoots and toss the pieces regularly, cooking for 2 to 3 minutes. Add 2 tablespoons of the sauce and toss to mix. Add the greens and toss to mix, cooking just enough to wilt the greens. Add drops of additional sauce to coat the mixture if necessary. Season with freshly ground pepper to taste; toss to mix and serve warm.

* NOTE: Bamboo shoots are available in early spring. If the short window of time has passed, perhaps a friend is growing bamboo trees in her yard. Pick them at eight inches to use for the recipe.

SAUTÉED BEET GREENS WITH GARLIC SCAPES

WHENEVER I PICK UP A BUNDLE OF BEETS AT MY LOCAL FARM STAND, I LOOK AT THE BEETS as well as the attached greens. I always try to find good tops. The greens make a superb side vegetable with the addition of the newly popular garlic scapes.

YIELD: 2 TO 3 SERVINGS

Greens from 1 large
  bunch beets

Kosher salt

1 tablespoon extra-virgin
  olive oil

2 to 3 garlic scapes, rinsed,
  dried, and sliced thin

Freshly ground pepper

Zest of $1/2$ lemon

2 teaspoons lemon juice

Pull the beet green leaves from the stems and discard stems. Rinse the greens and then soak in a bowl of water for 15 minutes to refresh them if necessary. Drain.

Meanwhile, bring enough salted water to a boil to cover the greens. When the water is at a rolling boil, add the greens and cook at a brisk simmer for 2 to 3 minutes. Drain in a colander under cool water to stop the cooking and squeeze dry. The greens may be prepared a day ahead and refrigerated in a suitable container until ready to use.

Warm the oil in a nonstick skillet over medium heat and sauté the garlic scapes, stirring occasionally, for 2 minutes. Add the greens and salt and pepper to taste and toss to coat. Cook 1 or 2 minutes longer to heat through. Add the lemon zest and lemon juice, stir to mix, and serve.

NOTE: Garlic scapes are the edible flower stems that garlic plants produce before the bulbs mature.

BOW-TIE PASTA WITH ASPARAGUS AND LEMON

AS FARM STANDS OPEN IN MID-SPRING, THEY ARE ABLAZE WITH THE COLOR GREEN.
Local asparagus is cooked in a lemon-flavored sauce making the bow-tie pasta the perfect choice to "catch" the asparagus pieces.

YIELD: 4 TO 5 SERVINGS

1 pound thick asparagus

1 pound bow-tie pasta

Kosher salt

2 tablespoons unsalted butter

1 cup heavy cream or half-and-half

Zest and juice of 1 large lemon (about 4 tablespoons juice)

Freshly ground black pepper

1/3 cup chopped flat-leaf Italian parsley

Freshly grated Parmigiano-Reggiano (optional)

Snap off the woody ends of the asparagus where the stalks naturally bend and discard. With the tip of a paring knife, peel away the bottoms of the stalks, leaving the tender buds at the top. Rinse well, pat dry with paper towels, and cut on the diagonal into 1/2-inch pieces.

Bring 5 to 6 quarts of water to a boil and add salt to taste. Add the pasta, stirring to keep it from sticking together. Cook in rapidly boiling water for 9 to 11 minutes, until al dente. Drain the pasta, reserving about 1/4 cup of the cooking water.

Meanwhile, combine the butter and cream in a 12-inch skillet over medium-low heat. Stir in the lemon zest, lemon juice, and salt and pepper to taste. Add the asparagus pieces to the sauce and cook for 5 to 6 minutes. Add the parsley, stir to mix, and taste for seasoning. Keep warm over very low heat as necessary.

Add the pasta to the sauce. Stir in the reserved pasta water spoonfuls at a time until a little creamy. Serve at once with Parmigiano-Reggiano, if desired.

FETTUCCINE WITH WILD MUSHROOMS

THE RICH MUSHROOM FLAVOR IS HEIGHTENED WITH OPEN MINDED ORGANICS' LOCALLY grown and cultivated "wild" mushrooms and then sweetened with shallots and cream.

YIELD: 4 TO 5 SERVINGS

2 tablespoons extra-virgin olive oil

2 tablespoons unsalted butter

2 to 3 shallots, finely chopped

$1/2$ pound shiitake mushrooms, stems removed, rinsed clean, and thinly sliced

$1/3$ pound oyster mushrooms, stems removed, rinsed clean, and thinly sliced

1 cup heavy cream

Kosher salt and freshly ground black pepper

$1/3$ cup finely chopped flat-leaf Italian parsley, plus extra, for garnish

1 pound homemade fettuccine (see page 334) or fresh store-bought fettuccine

In a skillet, heat the oil and butter over medium heat. When the foam from the butter subsides, add the shallots. Sauté for $1/2$ to 2 minutes, until opaque. Add the mushrooms, toss to coat, and sauté for about 3 minutes longer, tossing occasionally. Add the cream and cook until reduced by one-third and slightly thickened. Season the mushrooms to taste with salt and several grinds of fresh pepper. Add the parsley and stir to mix. Adjust the seasonings to taste. Keep warm over very low heat.

Meanwhile, bring $4^{1}/_{2}$ quarts of salted water to a boil in a 5 to 6-quart pot. Add the pasta and stir with a large wooden spoon or pasta fork to separate the strands. Cover and return to a boil and then remove the cover. If the pasta is very fresh, it will cook in about 30 seconds. If it is dry (even homemade pasta that has been stored for more than a few weeks), it will take 3 to 5 minutes to cook. Stir a few tablespoonfuls of the pasta water into the sauce, then drain the pasta in a colander.

Place several spoonfuls of the warm sauce onto a heated serving platter. Transfer the pasta to the warm serving platter. Pour the mushroom sauce over the pasta and toss gently to mix. Sprinkle with additional parsley and serve.

ORECCHIETTE WITH SPRING PEAS

ORECCHIETTE, MEANING "LITTLE EARS," ARE SMALL ROUNDED PASTA PIECES WITH A THUMB shape. Neapolitan in origin, this recipe is adapted from my dear friend Inez Villa Sussman. The light and tasty sauce can be prepared ahead and then simmered later while cooking the pasta.

YIELD: 6 TO 8 SERVINGS

3 to 4 tablespoons extra-virgin olive oil

2 large onions, diced

3 to 4 garlic cloves, finely chopped

1 small dried hot chile, minced

Freshly ground black pepper

1 (12 to 16-ounce) can whole plum tomatoes, drained

Kosher salt

1¹/₂ pounds pod peas, shelled, or 1 (10-ounce) package frozen peas

5 to 6 fresh basil leaves

1 pound orecchiette

In a saucepan, heat the oil over medium heat and sauté the onions, garlic, and hot chile until the onions are almost golden, about 5 minutes. Season with salt to taste and 3 or 4 grinds of pepper and sauté for another 3 to 4 minutes, until the onions are golden brown. Add the tomatoes, breaking them up with a wooden spoon or spatula. Add salt to taste and then simmer, partially covered, for 15 minutes. If there is a lot of liquid in the pan, remove the cover to allow the liquid to evaporate.

Add the fresh peas to the sauce. Stir to mix and simmer for 8 to 10 minutes. If using frozen peas, cook for 1 minute. (The sauce can be made ahead up to this point.) Place the basil leaves on top of the sauce but do not stir. Cover the saucepan and remove from the heat.

In the meantime, bring 4¹/₂ quarts of salted water to a boil in a 5 to 6-quart pot. Cook the pasta for 8 to 10 minutes, until al dente; drain.

While the pasta cooks, return the pan with the pea mixture to medium heat and simmer the sauce to warm and cook the peas. Warm the pasta plates and a serving platter in a 180°F oven. Transfer the pasta to the serving platter and pour the sauce over the pasta. Toss gently to mix and serve hot in the warm pasta bowls.

NOTE: I purchase whole dried peppers for cooking so that I can snap them in half to remove and discard the seeds, which I find too hot for my taste. By all means add the seeds if you like it hot!

SPAGHETTINI WITH CHERRY TOMATOES AND PEAS

CHERRY TOMATOES AND SWEET PEAS ADD TEXTURE AND FLAVOR TO THIS SWEET AND toothsome pasta dish.

YIELD: 4 TO 5 SERVINGS

1 pound cherry or grape tomatoes

1 pound spaghettini

6 tablespoons extra-virgin olive oil

3 garlic cloves, thinly sliced

$^3/_4$ cup fresh or frozen baby peas

$^1/_8$ to $^1/_4$ teaspoon red pepper flakes

Kosher salt

1 cup fresh basil chiffonade

$^1/_4$ cup coarsely chopped flat-leaf Italian parsley, for garnish

Preheat the oven to 375°F.

Rinse the tomatoes and pat dry with paper towels. Place in a baking dish and bake for 6 to 7 minutes. Remove from the oven and let cool for about 10 minutes; cut in half.

Bring $4^1/_2$ quarts salted water to a boil in a 5 to 6-quart pot. Add the pasta and stir to separate the strands; cover the pot. Return to a boil, uncover, and maintain a boil while the pasta is cooking. Cook for 9 to 12 minutes or until al dente. Drain, reserving $^1/_4$ cup of the cooking water. Return the pasta to the saucepan.

Meanwhile, heat the oil in a 10 to 12-inch nonstick skillet over medium-high heat. Add the garlic and sauté until just tender. Add the tomatoes and peas and sauté for 5 minutes longer and then add the reserved pasta water a tablespoon at a time until a little creamy. The tomatoes will soften but not dissolve completely. Season the sauce with the red pepper flakes and salt to taste and simmer for 2 to 3 minutes longer. Stir in the basil and remove from the heat.

Ladle three-fourths of the sauce into the pasta and stir gently to mix. Divide equally on four or five warm plates. Spoon the remaining sauce over the pasta on each plate and garnish with chopped parsley. Serve at once.

RISOTTO WITH ASPARAGUS, GREEN BEANS, AND MUSHROOMS

RISOTTO IS A UNIQUELY ITALIAN TECHNIQUE FOR COOKING RICE. THE BEST OF THE RICE VARIETIES are Carnaroli, Arborio and Vialone Nano, which is cultivated only in the Po Valley in northern Italy. The grains are oval and pearly in color and are cooked slowly and stirred continuously until creamy, with a slight resistance to the bite.

YIELD: 6 TO 8 SERVINGS

$^1/_3$ pound asparagus, rinsed and trimmed

$^1/_3$ pound green beans, rinsed and trimmed

$^1/_3$ pound shiitake mushrooms, rinsed and trimmed

$5^1/_2$ cups chicken stock (see page 335) or low-sodium canned

3 tablespoons extra-virgin olive oil

2 tablespoons unsalted butter

1 small red onion, finely chopped

2 cups Italian Carnaroli Arborio or Vialone rice

Kosher salt and freshly ground black pepper

$^1/_3$ pound fresh sweet peas, shelled or $^1/_2$ (10-ounce) package frozen peas

2 ripe tomatoes, peeled (see note below), seeded, and diced

7 to 8 sprigs flat-leaf Italian parsley, chopped

$^1/_3$ to $^1/_2$ cup grated imported Parmigiano-Reggiano cheese, plus more for serving (optional)

Cut the asparagus and green beans on the diagonal into 1-inch pieces. Thinly slice the mushrooms.

In a saucepan, bring the chicken stock to a boil. Reduce the heat to a low simmer and keep warm.

Place the oil and butter in a flameproof casserole over moderate heat. When the butter melts, add the onion and sauté for 1 to 2 minutes. Add the green beans and asparagus and sauté for 3 minutes, stirring with a wooden spoon until lightly caramelized. Add the rice and sauté for 1 to 2 minutes, stirring constantly until it is well coated and has absorbed some of the oil. Season with salt and pepper to taste.

Ladle in $^1/_2$ cup of the hot chicken stock and stir constantly until the rice has absorbed the liquid. Add the remaining chicken stock, $^1/_2$ cup at a time, and stir, allowing each addition to be absorbed by the rice before adding more liquid. Add the peas and mushrooms about halfway through and continue adding the stock until the rice is tender, creamy, and slightly resistant to the bite. Add the tomatoes, parsley, and cheese and stir to mix.

Taste for salt and pepper and adjust the seasonings as necessary. The total cooking time should be about 25 minutes. Serve immediately on warm plates with additional cheese, if desired.

NOTE: To peel the tomatoes, make an X in the rounded end and plunge into boiling water for 30 seconds. Immediately transfer to a bowl of ice water. When cool enough to handle, peel, seed, and coarsely chop the tomatoes.

BLACKFISH WITH GINGER AND VERJUS

BLACKFISH, ALSO KNOWN AS TAUTOG, IS A STURDY FISH WITH FIRM WHITE MEAT THAT CAN stand up to strong flavors. The ginger and verjus, fermented grape juice vinegar, season the fish perfectly with a bit of a sharp edge and acidity.

YIELD: 4 SERVINGS

2 thick skinless blackfish fillets (about $^3/_4$ pound each)

All-purpose flour for coating

Kosher salt and freshly ground pepper to taste

$^1/_2$ teaspoon paprika

3 tablespoons canola oil, divided

2 shallots, finely chopped

2 teaspoons freshly grated ginger

2 tablespoons vermouth

$^1/_4$ cup verjus

2 to 3 tablespoons chopped flat-leaf Italian parsley or chives

Remove the thin line of bones from the center of the fillets and then rinse and pat dry with paper towels. Lightly coat the fillets with flour and season with salt, pepper, and paprika.

Heat 2 tablespoons of the oil in a large oven-proof skillet over medium-high heat. When hot but not smoking, add the fillets and brown lightly, about 3 minutes on each side. Remove from the heat.

Preheat the oven to 400°F

Heat the remaining oil in a medium skillet over medium-low heat and sauté the shallots for 3 to 4 minutes, stirring occasionally. Add the ginger and sauté for 2 to 3 minutes longer. Add the vermouth, bring to a boil, and cook vigorously until reduced by half. Add the verjus and salt and pepper to taste and stir to mix. Keep warm.

Place the fillets in the oven and bake for 3 to 5 minutes, depending on the thickness of the fish. When done, remove from the oven and cut each fillet in half. Divide among four plates and spoon the sauce equally over each serving. Garnish with the parsley or chives.

LIEB CELLARS
Cutchogue

LIEB CELLARS IN CUTCHOGUE HAS A WINEMAKING PHILOSOPHY THAT CENTERS on vineyard management. Mark Lieb bought parcels of Cutchogue farmland in 1992. He brought in Gary Madden as "Engineering Manager" in 2000. Madden began expanding production of the wines and focused on building the brand in creative ways. Madden came to Long Island having worked at Apple Computers in California. Frequent trips to the Napa Valley had piqued his interest in wine, first as a hobby and then as a career that would combine science with nature.

Lieb Cellars has found a niche in producing Pinot Blanc as both still and sparkling wines. Madden reveals that "we made the wine for Kathy Lieb, Mark's wife. She loves sparkling wines, and it had to be bone dry. Now it's our flagship wine."

Building a strong altruistic mission at Lieb, Madden also has developed several wines to raise money for charities. Most recently, he introduced a white Merlot, made from free-run Merlot juice that has had zero skin contact, for the Carol M. Baldwin Breast Cancer Research Fund. He also made a wine called "Syrah" in honor of his beloved Belgian Shepherd of the same name who died of kidney disease. Money from that wine goes towards the Animal Medical Center in New York City. The entire wine for charity project began after the terrorist attacks in 2001, leading Madden to create a wine called "September Mission Merlot" to raise funds for the September's Mission Foundation.

Madden describes the model at Lieb Cellars as "keeping the family genetics throughout. The vineyard comes first, and we have good terroir, minerality, and acidity that are consistent throughout our wines. We don't over-extract the fruit or over-oak the wines. The reserve wines are more complex, and serious and are intended to age well since they are made from the first pressing of the fruit. The Bridge Lane wines (their popular priced line) are more fruit forward, bold, and in your face with a lower price point."

The wines at Lieb Cellars are made by the Premium Wine Group (PWG), a custom crush facility that is partly owned by Mark Lieb. As Madden explains, "because of our relationship with PWG, there is not a lot of variation in our wines. We don't have a winemaker trying to make an earth-shatteringly different wine to make his mark, so we can be really consistent from year to year. We've had the same four guys working in the fields since I started here, so we have great loyalty and consistency there as well."

While consistency is the goal in the cellar, there is an effort to have "cool and distinctive packaging and marketing." Madden has put a couple of cases of the white Merlot aside to turn it into a Blanc de Noir sparkling wine as an experiment. If the project works, "then we'll really upset the French. It would be an illegitimate wine, made from the wrong grape" since Blanc de Noir is typically made from Pinot Noir. As Madden says, "I like to be a little out there, and always have to have something new and fun."

Madden approaches the wines "with an idea and a vision of how the label should look and how the wines should taste. I can taste through the wine and tweak it and make each vintage better, depending on what fruit came in." Because of the small size of the vineyard, Madden can afford a nimble approach with the wines. He can experiment on a minor scale, as in the white Merlot, or in using less ripe red fruit harvested in 2009 towards a rosé "which will be a really nice wine, and a fun blend of Cabernet Sauvignon and Petite Verdot."

The cellaring practices at Lieb Cellars ensure that customers who open their bottles within twenty-four hours of purchase will not be opening the wine before its time. As Madden says, "we don't release the wines prematurely, and the wines are built to last. . . . We just released the 2005 sparkling Pinot Blanc, which spent three to four years aging before we could even think of selling it. There is an incredible amount of time and labor in handling sparkling wine, from the special riddling racks to the eight separate components needed to bottle the wine, compared to only three pieces needed for a still wine."

Madden sees Long Island's "proximity to the biggest, most sophisticated wine market in the world as our greatest advantage. Sommeliers and wine enthusiasts can just come right through here and taste the wines at the source. There is a terrific confluence of people from around the world here, sharing their knowledge. We really benefit from the sheer number of winemakers and interns from other regions coming through."

SEA SCALLOPS IN VINEGAR SAUCE

SCALLOPS ARE ONE OF THE MOST POPULAR SHELLFISH COMING OUT OF OUR ATLANTIC waters, and for good reason: the meat inside the handsome scallop shell is sweet, plump, and nutty. When ready to sauté, be sure the scallops are very dry and the pan is very hot—they should sizzle and brown as soon as they hit the pan.

YIELD: 6 SERVINGS

18 large sea scallops, side muscle removed

Kosher salt and freshly ground black pepper

2 to 3 shallots, finely chopped

3/4 cup dry white wine

3 tablespoons tarragon or white wine vinegar

2 tablespoons unsalted butter

4 tablespoons extra-virgin olive oil, divided

3 to 4 tablespoons coarsely chopped flat-leaf Italian parsley, chives, and tarragon

Rinse the scallops and pat dry with a paper towel. Season lightly with salt and pepper to taste.

In a saucepan combine the shallots, wine, and vinegar over medium-high heat. Bring to a boil and cook until reduced by half. Slowly whisk in the butter and 2 tablespoons of the oil until creamy. Season with more salt and pepper and add the fresh herbs; stir to mix. The sauce can be prepared ahead to this point. Warm over low heat for 1 to 2 minutes just before serving.

When ready to serve, heat the remaining 2 tablespoons olive oil over medium heat in a cast-iron or other heavy skillet for 1 to 2 minutes. Add the scallops and sauté until lightly caramelized and golden brown, about 1 to 1 1/2 minutes on each side, being careful not to overcook. Place 3 scallops on each plate and serve with a ring of sauce poured around them.

NOTE: Scallops are a delicate mollusk that should be quickly but carefully cooked.

Wine suggestion: Lieb Cellars Pinot Blanc

THE BAYKEEPER

THE PHRASE "SLOW FOOD," WHICH GAVE BIRTH TO AN ORGANIZATION AND movement, has a quiet and certain patina in the food world, one that has always been more about farmers and artisans than delayed cooks. I first met Kevin McAllister at a slow food dinner where he lectured on saving our bays.

Kevin McAllister grew up next to Moriches Bay in a house on Bay Street. This was indeed prophetic as today Kevin McAllister is our baykeeper striving to preserve our bay heritage.

After graduating from Morrisville College in upstate New York with an undergraduate degree in natural resources conservation, Kevin continued his education in Florida, earning a degree in marine biology and in coastal zone management—taking a look at the intrinsic link between land and sea. While in Florida he heard about the newly created position of Peconic baykeeper. The catalyst for returning home was to share his love for the great outdoors—surfing, scuba diving, rowing, and kayaking—with his wife and son. Kevin was unanimously selected by a panel of committee members for the position as baykeeper in 1998. At the time, Robert Kennedy Jr. was president of the Waterkeeper Alliance when only nineteen waterkeepers existed. Today, there is an international movement of nearly two hundred waterkeepers throughout the world to save the waters.

Kevin's work is locally focused and yet part of a much bigger picture. "Estuaries are woven into the fiber of our communities. They need close attention and nurturing from the people. Consciousness about how the bounty of shellfish and fin fish is affected; the priority is its protection and sustainability, perpetuating what the seas give us. We can't take and not give back, and we cannot allow water quality to deteriorate and important habitats to be lost—such as tidal wetlands (the kidneys of the bay) to cleanse the water that comes into the bays," says Kevin.

His favorite delicacy is blue crab, and how he catches them is different from the norm. He puts on a mask and snorkel and heavy work gloves. From July through September, as the crabs grow to five to six inches across the top shell or carapace, he literally crawls around the eel grass beds, which can grow to two feet in shallow water areas. When crabs see a fisherman, they hide in the grass for protection. Kevin tricks them by wiggling a couple of fingers in his left hand then crouching to grab them with his right hand. He admits it's a sneaky thing to do. Once when he was carrying a bushel full of crabs, covered with a wet towel, close to his bare chest, a large bay crab came up and locked down into his chest. In extreme pain, he lowered himself into the water to release the crab, and the pain. The crab swam away.

There's a lot of work that goes into cracking and picking fresh crabs. Kevin steams them for ten to fifteen minutes or just until the shells turn red. Families and friends spread newspapers over a large table and sit for an hour or two, picking at the crabs in messy splendor and enjoying their sweet flavor with ice-cold beer.

As crabs experience a growth spurt, they shed their shells. A new one develops from the soft tissue. Soft-shell crabs are the ones that are caught before the new shell develops. Crabs molt at different times, and there is only a small window of opportunity to catch the soft-shell crabs.

When clamming, Kevin likes to use the old method of treading. He wades into waist high water, buries his feet a couple of inches in the sand, and, with a twisting motion, he rotates his feet into the sand like he is crushing grapes in a wine vat. He covers quite a bit of the bay bottom, sometimes using his bare feet and sometimes using sweat socks for protection. To collect the clams, Kevin uses a bushel basket tucked inside an inner tube that is tethered to his waist. When he finds a clam with his feet, he bends over to pick it out with his hands, becoming completely submerged. Most clammers use the more modern method that involves a rake, but Kevin likes "the old-school style." Occasionally he'll see a bay scallop swimming by, and if he is lucky enough to catch it, he will pry open its shell and eat it on the spot. He claims it's "the sweetest flavor of the bay."

SOFT-SHELL CRABS WITH MESCLUN AND HERB VINAIGRETTE

SEASON THE CRABS WITH A BIT OF CAYENNE FOR A SPICY COUNTERPOINT TO THEIR sweetness and serve over a bed of mixed greens for contrasting color.

YIELD: 4 TO 6 SERVINGS

FOR THE VINAIGRETTE

1 garlic clove, minced

2 teaspoons coarse-ground Dijon mustard

1 tablespoon sherry vinegar

Kosher salt and freshly ground black pepper

2 tablespoons extra-virgin olive oil

1 tablespoon canola oil

1 tablespoon chopped fresh chives

1 tablespoon chopped fresh tarragon

1 tablespoon chopped fresh chervil

FOR THE SALAD

$^{1}/_{2}$ pound mesclun, washed and spun dry

2 to 3 tablespoons flour

$^{1}/_{8}$ teaspoon cayenne pepper

Kosher salt and freshly ground black pepper

4 to 6 (equal in size) soft-shell crabs, cleaned

2 tablespoons canola oil

Fresh herbs, for garnish (optional)

For the vinaigrette, in a mixing bowl whisk together the garlic, mustard, vinegar, and salt and pepper to taste. Combine the oils and slowly whisk into the mixture until emulsified. Add the herbs and stir to mix; set aside.

For the salad, wrap the mesclun in paper towels to absorb any excess moisture. Transfer to a large mixing bowl and set aside.

Combine the flour, cayenne, and salt and pepper to taste in a bowl. Lightly coat the crabs with the seasoned flour, shaking off any excess. In a nonstick skillet large enough to hold the crabs in one layer, heat the oil over medium-high heat until hot but not smoking. Sauté the crabs in two batches if necessary and cook for 3 to 4 minutes belly side up, turn and sauté for about 3 minutes longer.

Toss the greens with the vinaigrette and divide evenly onto four to six plates. Center the soft-shell crabs on the greens and garnish with fresh herbs, if desired.

NOTE: Select very fresh soft-shell crabs and cook within 24 hours of purchase.

SALMON SCALLOPS IN SORREL SAUCE

SORREL, ALSO KNOWN AS SOUR GRASS, IS A LEAFY GREEN AND MAY BE CONSIDERED MORE an herb than a vegetable. Sorrel cooks down to a delectable sauce and lends its rich acidity to enhance this classic French salmon dish.

YIELD: 6 SERVINGS

FOR THE SALMON SCALLOPS

2$^1/_4$ pounds center-cut
   skinless salmon fillets

Kosher salt and freshly
   ground black pepper

2 tablespoons finely chopped
   shallots or scallions

FOR THE SORREL SAUCE

$^1/_2$ pound fresh sorrel

2 tablespoons unsalted butter

2 shallots, finely chopped

1 cup fish stock
   (see page 336)

$^1/_2$ cup dry white wine

$^1/_2$ cup heavy cream or
   crème fraîche

Kosher salt and freshly
   ground black pepper

Sea salt, for garnish

Whole chives, for garnish

Preheat the oven to 375°F.

For the salmon scallops, cut the fillets in half lengthwise and cut each piece into 6 medallions weighing about 6 ounces each. Place each piece of salmon between two pieces of wax paper and lightly pound with a mallet to flatten slightly. Season the salmon scallops with salt and pepper to taste and place in a buttered nonreactive (glass or ceramic) baking dish. Sprinkle with the shallots and cover with a tent of buttered parchment paper and set aside.

For the sorrel sauce, remove and discard the coarse stems of the sorrel and rinse leaves clean. Pat dry with a paper towel. Tear the leaves into bite-size pieces.

Melt the butter in a skillet over medium-high heat. Add the shallots and sauté for about 2 minutes, or until opaque. Add the fish stock and wine and cook until reduced by half. Add the cream and bring to a boil and cook until the cream is thickened slightly. Add the sorrel and stir into the sauce for 1 to 2 minutes, until puréed. Season with salt and pepper to taste and keep warm.

Bake the salmon scallops for 3 to 4 minutes, until tender and lightly pink within. Spoon the sorrel sauce equally among six warm plates. Place the salmon scallops on the sauce and sprinkle lightly with sea salt. Crisscross whole chives over the salmon and serve.

NOTE: Reserve the salmon trimmings for a simple and quick fish stock (see page 336).

Wine suggestion: Bedell Cellars Chardonnay

ALMOND RESTAURANT
Bridgehampton

EXECUTIVE CHEF JASON WEINER AND PARTNER, ERIC LEMONIDES, CO-OWNERS of Almond Restaurant in Bridgehampton, have known each other since childhood. A Park Slope kid, as Jason likes to think of himself, he loved to cook with his older brothers and even fudged his résumé to work at Regine's, "an old school French restaurant" in New York City. He went off to San Francisco, where the importance of local and sustainable food was gaining momentum, and saved his pennies to dine at the now-famous Chez Panisse in Berkeley. From his California experiences he understood that good food was all about the product: "One can learn all the best techniques," he said, "but the role of the chef is to know when to let the ingredients speak for themselves."

Jason's strong culinary background was attained on the West Coast. He was involved in the opening of Acqua at the famed Bellagio Hotel in Las Vegas, eventually becoming executive sous chef at the restaurant. He was also the opening chef of Charles Nob Hill in San Francisco when the *San Francisco Chronicle* gave the restaurant three stars.

He came to the East End initially to fish, but then became sous chef at Nick & Toni's in the summer of 1997. Jason and his partner, Eric, who also did a few stints in the culinary world, opened Almond in 2001. The restaurant quickly garnered rave reviews from *The New York Times* saying, "The boldly flavored food here represents honest, unpretentious French bistro fare at its best." The restaurant has become one of the most popular year-round spots in the Hamptons.

STEAMED BLACK MUSSELS WITH WHITE WINE

JASON WEINER, EXECUTIVE CHEF AND CO-OWNER OF ALMOND RESTAURANT IN BRIDGEHAMPTON, serves a delectable buttery mussel appetizer for mussel enthusiasts.

YIELD: 4 SERVINGS

3 pounds local in-season mussels

1 cup dry white wine

2 tablespoons finely chopped garlic (about 2 large cloves)

1/2 cup sliced shallots (about 2 large)

1 teaspoon kosher salt

6 tablespoons unsalted butter, cut into pieces

2 tablespoons chopped flat-leaf Italian parsley

Freshly ground black pepper

Toasted or grilled thin bread slices, for serving

Scrub the mussels clean with a vegetable brush in a bowl of cold water and remove the beards.

Place a wide, sturdy Dutch oven over high heat for 2 to 3 minutes until hot. Add the wine, garlic, shallots, and salt and bring to a boil. Reduce the heat to medium high, add the mussels, and cover the pan tightly to capture the steam. Cook for 3 to 4 minutes, until the mussels open. Remove the lid and toss the mussels. Most of the mussels should be open by now. Add the butter, parsley, and lots freshly ground pepper. Cover and cook for another 30 seconds.

Divide the mussels into warm soup bowls, discarding any mussels that do not open. Pour some of the buttery broth over each serving and serve with toasted or grilled thin crusty bread slices.

NOTE: Be sure to purchase mussels with unbroken shells. Keep them refrigerated in a bowl covered with damp paper towels and use within 24 hours. Fresh mussels should be tightly closed. Discard any mussels that do not close while working with them. Some mussels may close if massaged gently.

Wine suggestion: Channing Daughters Meditazione

THE BEACON
Sag Harbor

SAM MCCLELAND, A GRADUATE OF JOHNSON & WALES UNIVERSITY IN RHODE Island, is from Illinois, where he grew up in the country surrounded by miles and miles of cornfields. His culinary inspiration comes from both the heartland where he was raised and the Caribbean where he worked on yachts. His mother and grandmother, of English and Irish ancestry, inspired him to put the kind of food on the table that was appealing to eat.

Sam was briefly sous chef at the Beacon, a restaurant in Sag Harbor, for two years prior to taking the reins as executive chef and partner in 2001. He formerly worked with restaurateur David Loewenberg at 95 School Street (no longer in business) and Nick & Toni's in East Hampton, where they enjoyed a great relationship for a number of years. David and Sam were friends before they were partners, and Sam was also best man at David's wedding.

The Beacon is primarily a seafood restaurant, situated on the Sag Harbor waterfront overlooking a marina. One happy, sunny Sunday in May, I enjoyed one of the most delicious lobster rolls served with homemade potato chips. While savoring my lobster roll, chock-full of lobster in a luscious tomato emulsion sauce, and those homemade chips, looking out over the bay crowded with boats, as a local, I felt like I was on vacation.

THE BEACON LOBSTER ROLL

EXECUTIVE CHEF SAM MCCLELAND OF THE BEACON RESTAURANT IN SAG HARBOR GIVES US this outstanding lobster roll. Sam serves the roll with the crispiest homemade potato chips. Select female lobsters, if possible, to enjoy the delicious roe.

YIELD: 4 SERVINGS

4 (1¼-pound) live lobsters

FOR THE TOMATO EMULSION SAUCE

1 large ripe plum tomato, peeled (see note on page 57), seeded, and diced

1 teaspoon Dijon mustard

¼ cup extra-virgin olive oil

⅔ cup light mayonnaise

⅓ cup sour cream

¼ cup julienned fresh basil leaves

2 tablespoons coarsely chopped fresh tarragon leaves

Grated zest and juice of ½ lemon (about 2 tablespoons juice)

Kosher salt and freshly ground black pepper

4 hot dog buns

Thinly sliced chives, for garnish

Bring 6 to 8 cups water to a boil in a stockpot large enough to hold the lobsters. Plunge the lobsters into the water and cook, covered tightly, for 8 minutes. Carefully remove the lobsters from the pot using tongs and place them on their backs on a large baking sheet or platter. When cool enough to handle, insert a sharp knife into the soft shell between the claws. Apply pressure and cut all the way down to split each lobster vertically from head to tail. Then, with a lobster cracker or mallet, crack the claws. Be careful of the hot liquid inside the lobster shells. Pour off the liquid and reserve if desired. When the lobster meat is completely cool, carefully extract as much meat as possible and coarsely dice; set aside.

Prepare the sauce. Put the tomato and mustard in a food processor and purée. With the machine still running, pour the oil in a slow steady stream. Process until smooth. Scrape the mixture into a bowl using a rubber spatula; set aside 2 to 3 tablespoons of the emulsion for garnish. Add the mayonnaise, sour cream, basil, tarragon, lemon zest, lemon juice, and salt and pepper to taste to the emulsion in the bowl and stir to mix. Adjust the seasonings to taste.

Place the lobster in a bowl and mix with enough sauce to generously coat the pieces of lobster. You will have sauce left over, which can be used for crabmeat or monkfish salad. The lobster salad may be refrigerated for several hours or overnight in a suitable container.

To serve, toast the hot dog buns. Divide the lobster meat and spoon generously into the rolls. Drizzle a small amount of the reserved sauce over each roll and sprinkle with chives. Serve with quality local farm potato chips, if desired.

NORTH FORK POTATO CHIP COMPANY
Mattituck

SEVERAL YEARS AGO WHEN SHOPPING AT A FARMERS' MARKET IN SAG HARBOR I was elated to see that a local potato chip was being marketed. The shiny, well-designed bag read, "North Fork Potato of Long Island—Kettle Cooked." As a potato lover, I was hooked!

Martin Sidor, a third generation potato farmer, lives with his wife, Carol, in the same house his grandparents bought on Oregon Road in Mattituck. They plant potatoes, cauliflower, and cabbage, the "cold crops," in fall. But something was nagging at Martin, and he thought about diversifying.

In 2004, Martin and Carol knew someone who was closing his small potato chip business called Long Island Potato Chip. Another acquaintance mentioned to the Sidors that he had a product line of "chip" equipment that would be suitable for their new endeavor. The Sidors have the advantage of using their potatoes to produce their own product. The Sidors are committed to making the best potato chip they can make using only safflower oil. The chip-making process begins with unpeeled and unwashed potatoes in a de-stoner machine that both washes and de-stones. The chips go through several processes before going into the kettle fryer. The kettle holds four fifty-gallon drums of safflower oil. The slices are cooked until they reach a pre-set temperature.

The most popular potato chip that the chip plant turns out is regular lightly salted, which is also my personal favorite because the true flavor of the potato comes through. Other distinctive varieties include sweet potato, sour cream and onion, cheddar onion, and barbecue. North Fork Potato Chip Company is a growing business with distribution throughout the tri-state area. There is excellent local support on the twin Forks at wineries and farm stands, and in 2009, the chip was represented at the U.S. Open in Bethpage, Long Island. Happily for us, Carol and Martin Sidor chose to do what they know—potatoes!

PAUMANOK VINEYARD

Aquebogue

IN 1968, WHEN URSULA MASSOUD OF PAUMANOK VINEYARD IN AQUEBOGUE was doing her undergraduate work and studying American Poetry as an elective, her professor introduced her to Walt Whitman. That's when she read the name Paumanok, "a word that Walt Whitman used for Long Island," as Ursula recounts.

In the same year, Ursula and Charles met in Philadelphia. She was an undergraduate at Chestnut Hill College majoring in social science and anthropology while Charles was studying for his MBA at Wharton. They discovered they had much in common—there was always wine on the dinner table at both their homes growing up. Ursula came from a wine growing family in the *Pfalz* in Germany. Charles' family owned a hotel in Beirut and imported French wines. They married in a wine barrel–shaped restaurant in the *Bad Durkheim*, Germany.

They ended up settling down in Connecticut. One fateful day in 1980, Charles read an article in *The New York Times* about Alex and Louisa Hargrave, who were growing vinifera grapes on the North Fork of Long Island. Charles drove out to the North Fork to meet Alex and Louisa—and that was it! They started the winery in 1990, and when they had their first crush of grapes, they chose the name Paumanok. They opened their doors to the public in 1991.

Reflecting the Bordeaux classics from the Loire, they make a Sauvignon Blanc and Cabernet Franc. And most important, "we are the only producers of Chenin Blanc on the East Coast," Ursula proudly exclaims. These varieties go well with all the local seafood and oysters.

When Charles was asked about what made Paumanok wines distinctive, he replied how passion played a role and that "perfection is an affliction, which some people consider to be a flaw rather than a quality. You get to the point where improvements don't come easy. We try to learn from each other and apply what we have learned to try to improve the quality. We pursue improvements from all angles, in the vineyards, in the winery, in the marketing," said Charles. "For instance, we have started pulling the leaf more aggressively. By removing the leaves early and exposing the fruit to the sunlight you are creating a microclimate where the fruit can grow more cleanly and with more complex flavors. We are always trying to come up with a better way of how to do what we do."

BUTTERFLIED PRESSED CHICKEN WITH HERBS

I LOVE ROAST CHICKEN AT ANY TIME OF THE YEAR. AS THE WEATHER WARMS I PREFER TO PAN roast chicken so I don't have to turn on the oven. Traditionally a butterflied chicken is cooked between two pieces of heated terra cotta. To simulate this process, heat a heavy nonstick skillet and then weigh down the chicken with foil-covered, heated, unglazed ceramic tiles or a foil-wrapped brick.

YIELD: 4 TO 6 SERVINGS

1 (3 to 3½-pound) chicken

2 to 3 garlic cloves, finely chopped

¼ cup finely chopped flat-leaf Italian parsley

1 tablespoon chopped fresh rosemary leaves

Kosher salt and freshly ground black pepper

5 to 6 tablespoons extra-virgin olive oil, divided

1 tablespoon unsalted butter

2 to 3 tablespoons freshly squeezed lemon juice

1 bunch watercress, washed and spun dry

¼ cup dry white wine

Clean the chicken, removing the pin feathers and excess fat from the cavity. With a sharp knife or kitchen shears, cut along both sides of the backbone and remove. Remove the giblets. (Reserve and freeze the backbone and any giblets for stock.) Open the chicken on a work surface and press to flatten, breaking the wing bones. Rinse the chicken thoroughly and pat dry with paper towels.

Mix the garlic, parsley, rosemary, and salt and pepper to taste in a bowl. Add 1 to 2 tablespoons of the olive oil and stir to mix. Gently loosen the skin around the chicken, being careful not to tear it. Spread the mixture evenly under the skin. Rub 2 tablespoons of the olive oil over the chicken. Cover and let marinate for several hours in the refrigerator or at room temperature for about 1 hour.

When ready to cook, heat the remaining 2 tablespoons olive oil and the butter over medium heat in a large, heavy, nonstick skillet. When the butter melts, sprinkle the pan with a large pinch of kosher salt. Put the chicken in the skillet, skin side down, and season with salt and pepper. Cover the chicken with a tent of foil, shiny side up. Place foil-wrapped ceramic tiles or brick on top and then add a heavy weight, such as a cast-iron skillet. Cook for 20 minutes.

Remove the weight, tiles, and foil. With two spatulas, carefully turn the chicken over and season lightly with salt and pepper. Replace the foil, tiles, and weight and cook for an additional 18 minutes, or until an instant thermometer inserted into the thickest part of the thigh registers 165° to 170° F. Sprinkle the lemon juice over the chicken and transfer to a cutting board.

Pour off the accumulated fat from the pan and discard. Add the wine to the drippings in the bottom of the pan. Bring to a boil and deglaze the pan using a wooden spoon.

To serve, cut through the joints of the chicken. Line a platter with the watercress and arrange the chicken on the platter. Pour the warm sauce over the chicken and serve warm or at room temperature.

Wine Pairing: Paumonok's Chenin Blanc

IACONO CHICKEN FARM

East Hampton

THE BLACK WALL PHONE AT THE END OF THE LONG STAINLESS STEEL WORK counter rings off the wall at Iacono's, a legendary poultry farm in East Hampton. Mrs. Iacono, the widowed wife of founder Salvatore Iacono, amiably answers in her friendly but high-pitched voice as she calls out to her son Anthony, who can be seen eviscerating chickens through an opening in the next room, "Do you have a six or seven-pound hen? Mrs. Davis would like to pick one up this afternoon," or another request could be for baby chicks or Cornish game hens or freshly laid eggs. No matter how often the phone rings, Mrs. Iacono, ever cheerful, is there to accommodate requests whether on the phone or with the steady flow of customers in the store.

Anthony Iacono, a soft-spoken, tall, good-looking fellow, worked with his dad, Salvatore, for more than thirty-five years, ever since he was fourteen. Anthony is serious about the chicken business and about the purity of the product. He is quick to point out that their poultry is carefully and thoroughly cleaned after processing; if not, any leftover debris could cause harmful bacteria. Seedlings, as big as a minute and a day old, come into the farm from different hatcheries in Pennsylvania. If you're at the East Hampton post office you might even catch the chirping chicks arriving.

Once hatched, the Cornish Cross variety of chickens go into a brooder (heated) pen with immaculately clean sawdust, where they run free range from then on. Their feed is free of chemicals, hormones, and antibiotics and consists of a mixture of soybeans and corn with an emphasis on the corn. The chickens range in weight anywhere from one and a half pounds to up to ten pounds at the holidays.

Iacono brings Muscovy ducks into the farm in May and June and processes them five months later, just in time for Thanksgiving and the winter holidays. Freshly laid eggs are an important product at Iacono Farm and include white eggs from the white leghorns or brown eggs from the Black Sex-links stacked in boxes signifying their size.

Customers enjoy the idea of going to the farm and retail store where a large carved wooden chicken sign hangs at the entrance. Local restaurants make a point of noting on their menu that they serve Iacono chickens, and their patrons are willing to pay a little more for them.

BRAISED CHICKEN WITH SHIITAKE MUSHROOMS AND GARLIC PURÉE

THE GARLIC PURÉE ADDS A SUBTLE AND SWEET EDGE TO THE CHICKEN.

YIELD: 4 TO 6 SERVINGS

1 chicken (3 to 3$^{1}/_{2}$ pounds), cut into eight pieces

Kosher salt and freshly ground black pepper

$^{1}/_{2}$ teaspoon paprika

3 tablespoons extra-virgin olive oil

10 to 12 large garlic cloves, unpeeled

2 shallots, finely chopped

$^{1}/_{3}$ pound shiitake mushrooms, cleaned and sliced

$^{1}/_{2}$ cup dry white wine

$^{1}/_{2}$ cup chicken stock (see page 335) or low-sodium canned

3 to 4 plum tomatoes, peeled (see note on page 57), seeded, and diced

1 teaspoon fresh thyme leaves

2 to 3 tablespoons finely chopped flat-leaf Italian parsley

Trim and clean the chicken pieces of excess fat and bone. Rinse the chicken and pat dry with paper towels. Season with salt and pepper to taste and the paprika.

Warm the oil in a large heavy skillet over medium-high heat and when hot, add the chicken, skin side down, without crowding the pan. This may have to be done in batches. Sauté as many chicken pieces as will fit without crowding, turning occasionally, until golden brown on both sides, 2 to 3 minutes per side. Transfer the browned pieces to a dish and cook the remaining pieces, if necessary.

Drain the drippings from the skillet, reserving 2 tablespoons in the pan. Return the chicken to the skillet and add the garlic, shallots, and mushrooms and cook over medium-high heat for about 3 minutes, stirring occasionally. Add the wine and chicken stock and bring to a boil, stirring to deglaze the pan. Add the tomatoes and thyme and stir to mix. Taste to adjust the seasonings; then cover and simmer for 20 minutes.

With a slotted spoon, remove the garlic cloves. When cool enough to handle, squeeze out the pulp and mash with a fork. Stir the puréed garlic into the mixture and bring to a simmer for 1 to 2 minutes. Garnish with the parsley and serve hot.

Wine suggestion: Pellegrini Vineyards Vintners Pride Chardonnay

PELLEGRINI VINEYARDS
Cutchogue

A VISIT TO LONG ISLAND WINE COUNTRY IN 1981 WAS APPEALING ENOUGH TO make Bob Pellegrini and his wife, Joyce, want to get more involved. The plan was "to buy a few acres and have some fun. I had no idea that it would turn into what the vineyard has become. This started as a hobby, and then reality set in. There is an economy of scale, and once you buy a thirty-thousand-dollar tractor, you have to make use of it. You have to be a certain size in order to survive." In 1982, the Pellegrinis purchased farmland in Cutchogue. Their first commercial vintage was in 1991, with wines made by Russell Hearn.

The wines at Pellegrini are made in "an intentionally forward fruit style. Our winemaker, Russell Hearn, has brought some innovative winemaking ideas with him from his training in Australia," said Joyce. The cellar at Pellegrini includes a mechanized punch-down station, which allows red grape skins to be fully immersed in the juice during fermentation. This gentle process leads to softer tannins and deeper color in the red wines. Bob Pellegrini describes the end result as "wines that are drinkable from an early age, but that also will age for a long time. . . . Russell's talent is to make wines that drink well both when the wines are released and after years in the cellar. But 90 percent or more of wines purchased at a wine shop or our retail store are drunk that very day. . . . So we try to make wines that are palatable on release, but that still have aging capacity."

Pellegrini describes the house winemaking style as using "as little intervention as possible. We use the same type of oak and the same size of barrel each year. We don't say 'I want the wine to taste a certain way,' and then try to make the wine meet that goal. The idea is to encourage a natural expression of what the fruit brings in."

Pellegrini considers that the East End of Long Island has "the best of both worlds. We are the only place east of the Mississippi that can consistently ripen fruit, and we are close to New York City. We are the closest local wine region, and now there is increased focus on buying local. It's greener, with less transportation required to bring in the wines, and very high quality."

LAMB STEW WITH POTATO BAKER'S STYLE

MY DEAR PARISIAN FRIEND, GRACIEUSE RIVE-GEORGES, GAVE ME THIS TIMELY SPRING LAMB RECIPE. With local vegetables and herbs to cook with, it becomes a spring Hampton classic.

YIELD: 6 SERVINGS

3 to 4 tablespoons extra-virgin olive oil, divided

1 bunch carrots, peeled and thinly sliced

2 to 3 leeks, washed and thinly sliced

2 to 3 garlic cloves, finely chopped

1 teaspoon fresh thyme or $1/4$ teaspoon dried

Kosher salt and freshly ground black pepper

$2^1/2$ to 3 pounds lamb shoulder or leg of lamb, trimmed of all excess fat and cut into $1^1/2$-inch cubes

Flour, for dusting

$1/2$ cup dry white wine

2 large russet potatoes, peeled and thinly sliced

1 cup chicken stock (see page 335) or low-sodium canned

2 to 3 fresh rosemary sprigs

1 tablespoon red wine vinegar

Heat 2 tablespoons of the oil in a 5-quart Dutch oven or enamel-over-iron casserole (such as Le Creuset) over medium heat. Add the carrots and leeks. Sauté the vegetables, stirring occasionally, for 1 to 2 minutes. Add the garlic and sauté for 30 seconds longer. Season the mixture with the thyme and salt and pepper to taste. Cover the vegetables with a piece of wax paper and then cover the pot and sweat the vegetables for 7 to 8 minutes. Remove from the pot and set aside.

Add the remaining oil to a heavy skillet. Dust the lamb cubes with flour and sauté several pieces at a time until browned on all sides. Do not crowd the pan. Transfer the lamb to a plate as they are done and continue to sauté the remaining pieces. When all of the lamb has been sautéed, pour in the wine to deglaze the pan drippings, and cook until reduced by half. Add stock and bring to the edge of a boil. Remove from the heat and pour over the lamb. Taste and adjust the seasoning with salt and pepper as necessary.

Preheat the oven to 350°F.

Return the vegetables to the pot and spread in an even layer. Arrange the potato slices over the vegetables and season with salt and pepper to taste. Spoon the meat over the vegetables, pour the sauce over the meat and vegetables, and add the rosemary sprigs. The meat and vegetables may be left at room temperature up to 1 hour before baking. Drizzle with the vinegar just before baking and bake for $1^1/2$ hours. Taste to adjust seasonings if necessary and serve hot.

Wine suggestion For cooking: Peconic Bay Steel Fermented Chardonnay. For drinking: Bedell Cellars Reserve Merlot

BEDELL CELLARS
Cutchogue

"THE ONLY RULE ABOUT DRINKING WINE IS TO DRINK WHAT YOU LIKE," SAYS Kim Folks Mackinnon. Kim is the special events and product manager at Bedell Cellars Winery in Cutchogue, New York. Right out of college, Kim began her career as a tour guide at Pindar Vineyard. "I was lured," said Kim, "by the romance of the industry, an appreciation for wine, what the industry is doing to maintain the open vistas, and, of course, the flavor of the terroir."

Winemaker Richard Olsen-Harbich has been making wine on Long Island since 1981. Olsen-Harbich went to Cornell University intending to study tropical agriculture, but was soon intrigued by the university's nascent viticulture program. "It seemed romantic and exciting, and winemaking appealed to me since it is really half science and half creativity." In those twenty-nine years, Olsen-Harbich has worked both in the fields and in the cellar, and has real devotion to the region. "I had an introduction from the ground up, and never expected I would end up making wine on Long Island, but I really love the North Fork, and this is where I want to be."

"We are truly beginning to identify, after forty-plus years of growing grapes on Long Island, to really see what grows well and what blends well; these are really important milestones in the industry," said Kim. "And we're still learning," she continued, "because, for example, we're finding Cabernet Franc is making a wonderful varietal. . . . It's almost becoming a sort of Cabernet Sauvignon.

"What makes a wine distinctive begins in the vineyard. It is all the growing elements: the soil, the weather, the quality of the vines, the varieties you choose to grow, and how they are tended. There are some differences in being near the sound or near the ocean, yet they have the same coastal pros and cons. And many more pros than there are cons," continued Kim. There are many benefits to making wine in the Hamptons. "We're finding out that we can really grow most varieties," said Kim. "There is a lot to say about the soil," she continued. "The sandy content of the soil allows for excellent drainage."

There are also some obstacles to being in the wine business on Long Island. "One challenge is that there are assumptions still being made about the quality of the wines," said Kim. "Vineyards are still being challenged by the perceived youth of the industry." It's a boutique industry, and vintners on Long Island are people who are true pioneers. "You ultimately do it on a boutique level, as most vintners are in it for the passion and the quality of life and not necessarily for financial gain. Most of the vineyards are nevertheless doing well."

SLOW ROASTED LEG OF LAMB
WITH CHUNKY SEA SALT

SOUTHAMPTON RESIDENT GLORIA MAVRIKIS REILLY'S DELECTABLE SLOW ROASTED LEG of lamb is seasoned with imported Greek oregano and chunky coarse sea salt from the coves around the Island of Icaria, where the Reillys spend their summers.

YIELD: 8 TO 10 SERVINGS

1 (7 to 8-pound) leg of lamb

3 to 4 large garlic cloves, sliced into slivers

1½ tablespoons good quality dried Greek oregano

⅓ cup fresh lemon juice

2 to 3 teaspoons coarse sea salt

Freshly ground black pepper

1 cup red wine for a natural jus (optional)

1 cup water for a natural jus (optional)

Preheat the oven to 300°F.

Remove the fell, the thin skin over the top of the lamb, along with the excess fat. Make slits with a sharp knife and insert the slivers of garlic into the lamb. Rub the meat all over with the oregano and place on a rack in a roasting pan. (The roast can be seasoned several hours before cooking and refrigerated, covered with a tent of plastic wrap. If refrigerated, bring to room temperature about 1 hour before placing in the oven.) Pour the lemon juice over the lamb and baste by spooning the juice that has run off back over the meat while waiting for the oven to pre-heat.

Rub the salt and pepper to taste into the meat. Place in the oven and roast for 1 hour. Remove the roasting pan from the oven and add about 1 cup of water to the roasting pan and deglaze by scraping any browned bits stuck to the bottom of the pan. Baste the lamb with the resulting pan juices. Reduce the oven temperature to 225°F. Return the lamb to the oven and cook for about 5 hours, or until an instant thermometer reaches an internal temperature of 150°F.

Transfer the roast to a carving board and let rest for 15 minutes before carving. For a natural jus, if desired, add the red wine and water to the juices in the roasting pan. Bring to a simmer over medium-high heat, deglazing the pan juices. Adjust the seasonings if necessary. Serve over the carved slices of lamb.

Wine suggestion : Raphael Vineyards Petit Verdot

RAPHAEL VINEYARDS
Peconic

RAPHAEL VINEYARDS WAS STARTED BY THE PETROCELLI FAMILY IN 1996 WITH the goal of creating premium wines on eastern Long Island, and with a focus on merlot as Long Island's great red wine varietal. The family built a grand statement winery and tasting room in the Italianate manner to make a visual link to the family's Italian-American heritage.

In keeping with the goal of making premium wines, Paul Pontallier of Chateau Margaux, a major player from the Bordeaux wine industry, was brought in to consult on Raphael wines. "There are so many comparisons in terms of climate and varieties the winery grows; these are the elements that are key to Raphael's signature Bordeaux grape varieties of Merlot and Sauvignon Blanc." In addition Raphael produces Petit Verdot, a rich, bold wine with a smooth finish, along with Cabernet Franc, Malbec, Reisling and Semillon.

LUCE & HAWKINS

Jamesport

GROWING UP ON A FAMILY FARM ON THE NORTH FORK OF LONG ISLAND, where the raw products and homemade dishes were remarkable, left young Keith Luce's taste buds yearning for more. At age nineteen Keith found work in some of Manhattan's finest restaurants, such as the Rainbow Room, La Côte Basque, and Le Cirque when Daniel of Daniel's was at the helm. "There isn't a school," said Keith, "who could have given me a better start in the culinary arts." To experience volume he worked at the Greenbrier, a historic landmark and luxury resort hotel in White Sulphur Springs, West Virginia, with executive chef Walter Sheib.

This enterprising young man understood the need to diversify and spent time in France and Italy, where he worked in Michelin three-star restaurants. When he returned, Walter Sheib of the Greenbrier was chef at the White House and tapped Keith to be his sous chef during the first Clinton administration. Keith connected with Dan Sachs, a protégé of restaurateur Danny Meyer, to open the fabled Spruce in Chicago in 1996. In their first year of operation, they were named "best new restaurant" in the country by John Mariani of Esquire magazine, and were also recognized by the James Beard Foundation as "best new restaurant" of 1996. In 1997, *Food & Wine* magazine chose Keith as one of America's "Top Ten Chefs." A year later the James Beard Foundation named him "Rising Star Chef of the Year."

Keith went on to become the executive chef at The Herb Farm, a culturally rich restaurant in Seattle, Washington. During his tenure, he started to churn butter, make cheese, and raise pigs for house-made charcuterie, chickens for their eggs, and quail and duck. It was after he was married and with a small child that he thought seriously of returning to his roots, to his family—one of the early founding farm families on the North Fork of Long Island. Kismet found him speaking with the proprietor of the historic Jedediah Hawkins Inn in Jamesport. The stars aligned, and now Keith Luce is the chef and proprietor of what is now called the Luce & Hawkins restaurant, and he brings a celebration of local food and wine to the table.

CRISP DUCKLING WITH RHUBARB CHUTNEY

KEITH LUCE, EXECUTIVE CHEF OF LUCE & HAWKINS RESTAURANT IN JAMESPORT, NEW YORK, offers this superb preparation of sliced duck breast served rare with crispy duck leg and rhubarb chutney.

YIELD: 4 SERVINGS

FOR THE RHUBARB CHUTNEY

1 pound fresh rhubarb, chopped

1 shallot, finely chopped

3/4 cup packed light brown sugar

1/2 cup cider vinegar

1 teaspoon ground cinnamon

1-inch piece fresh ginger, peeled and finely chopped

1/8 teaspoon ground cloves

1/2 teaspoon kosher salt

FOR THE DUCK BREASTS

2 whole fresh, not frozen, duck breasts, halved

Kosher salt and freshly ground black pepper

4 confited duck legs (optional)

2 to 3 scallions, thinly sliced for garnish

For the chutney, place the rhubarb, shallot, brown sugar, vinegar, cinnamon, ginger, cloves, and salt in a large heavy saucepan over medium heat. Bring up to a simmer and cook, stirring frequently, until thickened slightly, about 20 minutes. Let cool; then refrigerate in a suitable container for up to one week.

For the duck breast, with a sharp knife score the duck skin in a cross-hatch pattern, taking care not to cut into the flesh. Liberally season with salt and pepper, rubbing the seasoning well into the skin. Place on a rack on a dish. Refrigerate, uncovered, for 1 to 2 hours—but no longer than 2 hours—for the skin to dry out. This step will help the skin to render when it cooks.

When ready to cook the duck breasts, remove them from the refrigerator and wipe dry with a clean kitchen towel. Again, season liberally with salt and pepper. Preheat a 12-inch cast-iron skillet or heavy-bottomed sauté pan over medium-low heat and add the duck breasts skin side down. Render the fat for about 10 minutes, removing excess fat frequently by carefully pouring the fat into a clean container. (Reserve the rendered fat for confit.) When the skin has rendered to the point that it has begun to turn golden brown and there is about 1/8 inch of skin remaining over the breast meat, increase the heat to medium high and cook the duck until crisp and golden brown, about 2 minutes. Flip the breasts over and cook for 2 to 3 minutes longer.

Remove the breasts from the pan and allow to rest at room temperature on a rack on a plate for 10 to 15 minutes. Reduce the temperature to medium low and add the duck legs, if using. Cook until crisp, about 10 minutes.

To serve, slice each duck breast across the grain and divide among four plates, arranging the slices so they are slightly overlapping. Add a duck leg and a couple spoonfuls of rhubarb chutney to each plate. Garnish with scallions.

NOTE: Another great accompaniment to the dish are thinly sliced Long Island Yukon Gold potatoes roasted in the rendered duck fat.

STRAWBERRY SHORTCAKES

THE LOCAL STRAWBERRY SEASON ON THE SOUTH FORK IS IN FULL BLOOM IN THE MONTH of June at various farms. The North Fork boasts the Oyster Pond Berry Farm in Orient with all varieties of berries growing through the summer and into the fall. This is the time of year to prepare crispy, crumbly delectable little shortcakes made for sandwiching strawberries 'n' cream.

YIELD: 6 TO 8 SERVINGS

FOR THE SHORTCAKES

$1^3/_4$ cups all-purpose flour

$1/_4$ cup sugar

1 tablespoon baking powder

$1/_2$ teaspoon salt

$1/_4$ pound (1 stick) cold unsalted butter, cut into small pieces

7 tablespoons heavy cream, divided

FOR THE STRAWBERRIES 'N' CREAM

1 pint strawberries, rinsed and hulled

$3/_4$ cup heavy cream

2 to 3 tablespoons confectioners' sugar

For the shortcakes, in the bowl of an electric mixer with the paddle attachment, combine the flour, sugar, baking powder, and salt on low speed for about 10 seconds to mix. Add the butter and mix until the mixture resembles small crumbs. Continue to mix slowly, adding 6 tablespoons of the cream until the dough is moist enough to come together. Preheat the oven to 375°F.

Turn the dough onto a lightly floured work surface and gather into a ball. Flatten the dough into a round or rectangle, wrap in wax paper and refrigerate for an hour or more. Flour a rolling pin and roll out the chilled dough on a lightly floured surface to about $1/_4$ inch thick. With a $2^1/_2$-inch round cookie cutter, cut the dough into 7 circles. You should be able to cut one more circle of dough from the leftover trimmings. Transfer the rounds to a parchment paper or Silpat-lined baking sheet. Brush the tops of the shortcakes with the remaining 1 tablespoon cream. Bake the shortcakes for 25 minutes, until golden brown and crisp. Transfer to a rack to cool. Store the shortcakes in a wax paper–lined container and use within 24 hours.

For the strawberries 'n' cream, slice the strawberries, reserving a few whole berries for garnish; set aside. Whip the cream in a cold bowl with cold beaters and gradually add 1 tablespoon of the confectioners' sugar at a time until soft peaks form. Fold in the sliced berries.

To serve, sandwich the shortcakes with three-quarters of the whipped cream and sliced berries. Dust the top of each sandwich with remaining confectioners' sugar, a dollop of whipped cream, and a whole berry.

STRAWBERRY RHUBARB COMPOTE WITH VANILLA PARFAIT

PREPARE THIS PERKY PUNGENT COMPOTE AHEAD AND TOP WITH YOUR FAVORITE ICE CREAM in a parfait or glass dessert dish topped with praline when ready to serve.

YIELD: 6 TO 8 SERVINGS

FOR THE PRALINE

1/2 cup sugar

2 to 3 tablespoons blanched almonds

FOR THE PARFAIT

1 1/2 pounds rhubarb

1 cup sugar

1/2 cup water, plus more as needed

Zest of 1 orange

1 pint strawberries, hulled, washed, and halved or quartered

1 tablespoon Grand Marnier or Triple Sec

Vanilla ice cream

For the praline, grease a baking sheet and set aside. Place the sugar in a small heavy saucepan over medium heat. The sugar will begin to liquefy and then turn a light amber color. If crystals form, brush down the sides of the pan with a wet pastry brush. When the color deepens to caramel color, add the nuts all at once; stir to mix. Quickly but carefully, pour the caramel onto the prepared baking sheet. When completely cool and brittle, break into pieces and chop coarsely in a food processor. Praline may be stored in an airtight container in the refrigerator until ready to use.

For the parfait, trim the leaves from the rhubarb and discard. If the rhubarb stalks are slim, do not peel, only wash. If the stalks are thick, peel off the tough strings.

Cut the rhubarb into 1-inch-long pieces and place in a heavy nonreactive saucepan. Add the sugar and water and stir to mix. Cover the pan tightly and bring to a simmer over medium heat, 4 to 5 minutes. Add the orange zest and cook, covered, for about 8 minutes after it has begun to simmer. Stir the rhubarb gently with a wooden spoon once during the cooking. If the mixture seems dry, add more water a teaspoon at a time until it is a spreadable texture. Remove from the heat. Taste and adjust the sugar if necessary. Add the strawberries and stir just to mix. Cover the pan so the berries soften slightly.

When the compote is lukewarm, stir in the Grand Marnier. The compote can be prepared several days ahead. Refrigerate, covered, in a suitable container.

When ready to serve, layer the compote with vanilla ice cream in a parfait glass and sprinkle praline over the top.

STRAWBERRY RHUBARB COBBLER SCENTED WITH ROSEWATER

CLAUDIA FLEMING, PASTRY CHEF AND OWNER OF THE NORTH FORK TABLE & INN, GIVES US THIS classic with a twist. The fruit filling has the scent of rosewater, and the crème fraîche is sweetened with rose preserves.

YIELD: 8 TO 10 SERVINGS

FOR THE DOUGH

1^2/$_3$ cups all-purpose flour

3^1/$_2$ tablespoons granulated sugar

1^1/$_2$ tablespoons baking powder

^{1}/$_8$ teaspoon salt

2 eggs, hard-boiled and separated

6 tablespoons cold unsalted butter, cut into ^{1}/$_2$-inch pieces

^{2}/$_3$ cup very cold heavy cream

FOR THE FRUIT FILLING

1-inch piece vanilla bean, split lengthwise

^{3}/$_4$ cup granulated sugar

^{1}/$_2$ pound strawberries, hulled and halved or quartered

1^1/$_2$ pounds rhubarb, trimmed and cut into 1-inch pieces

^{1}/$_2$ tablespoon cornstarch

1 teaspoon rosewater

2 tablespoons heavy cream

2 teaspoons turbinado sugar

For the dough, in the bowl of a food processor with steel blade attachment, combine the flour, granulated sugar, baking powder, salt, and hard-boiled egg yolks (enjoy the whites on toast). Pulse the mixture for a few seconds until the yolks are broken down. Add the cold butter and mix until the dough resembles fine meal. Add the cream and pulse until the dough just comes together.

Turn out the dough onto a lightly floured board. With lightly floured hands, gently gather the dough into a ball (the dough does not need to be smooth). Using a large spoon dipped in flour, shape the dough into eight to ten 2-inch balls. With floured hands, flatten the balls to about ^{1}/$_2$ inch thick. Chill for 30 minutes or up to 8 hours.

Preheat the oven to 350°F.

For the fruit filling, scrape the seeds from the vanilla bean into a small bowl. Add the sugar and mix until the vanilla bean is evenly dispersed in the sugar. In a large bowl, gently toss the strawberries, rhubarb, cornstarch, rosewater, and vanilla sugar. Allow to macerate 20 minutes.

Pour the macerated fruit in a shallow 2^1/$_2$-quart baking dish in an even layer. Arrange the biscuits over the fruit to cover, leaving approximately 1 inch between each biscuit. Brush the biscuits with the cream and sprinkle with the turbinado sugar. Bake the cobbler until the fruit is bubbling and the biscuits are golden brown, 30 to 40 minutes

When ready to serve, whip the crème fraîche in the

FOR THE ROSE CRÈME FRAÎCHE GARNISH

1 cup crème fraîche

¹/₄ cup rose preserves (optional)

bowl of an electric mixer on medium-high speed to lighten. Add the preserves, if using, and whip until stiff peaks form. Spoon the cobbler into shallow dessert bowls with a dollop of rose crème fraîche.

Savoring the Hamptons in
SUMMER

With farmers' markets in their season of glory and literally at our back door, inspiration abounds when preparing summer meals of excellent quality. Summer food offers a welcome change from food that is eaten through the rest of the year. For instance, the deluge of tomato varieties in late summer is staggering. Simply slice them to serve with ribbons of fresh basil and a drizzle of olive oil or enjoy them straight up with only a dash of coarse salt to bring out their juicy sweetness. The snap of fresh green beans or local corn popped into boiling water for just a minute or two provide unforgettable tastes. The fruits of the season—the sweetest berries, peaches, cherries, plums, and melons—create a delectable finish to any meal.

You can blanch vegetables that can later be tossed into a skillet for a stir-fry. Briefly boil trimmed broccoli florets, for example, and then plunge them into ice water to set the color. When ready to cook, sauté the florets in extra-virgin olive oil with slivers of garlic and a pinch of hot pepper flakes. When I bring beets topped with their fresh leafy greens home from the farmers' market, I quickly blanch the leaves to use later in a sauté with garlic and a squeeze of lemon. Parboil new potatoes and store them, covered, in the fridge. When ready to serve, brush them with olive oil and toss them in a sauté pan or, if having a cookout, place them on the grill until the edges crisp and brown.

Cold soups are a bowl of instant revival in summer. Serve gazpacho in mugs at your next dinner party for a zesty starter. A big bowl of chilled vichyssoise, the classic potato and leek soup, puréed and spiked with French tarragon from your herb garden, is a delicious cold entrée served with slices of crusty bread on the side.

I love barbecue: sweet, smoky barbecued chicken or baby back ribs, dry-rubbed beefy steaks and grilled whole fish, grilled summer vegetables, even grilled fruit, whose natural sugars caramelize from the heat of the smoldering embers. Clearly summertime is the time when food and entertaining play all-important roles. Grills are at the ready for all manner of foods, and tables are set for the sheer pleasure of dining out of doors. It's summertime and the living should be very easy.

"FIERY" PITA TOASTS

MIDDLE EASTERN—STYLE PITA, OR "POCKET" BREAD AS IT IS ALSO CALLED, IS READILY available at supermarkets and specialty food stores. This recipe produces a wonderfully crisp and flavorful cracker that will keep very well in a crisper, so make a big batch and watch them disappear. Dried thyme and garlic powder, rather than their fresh counterparts, work best due to the evenness with which they adhere

to the pita triangles.

YIELD: 8 TO 10 SERVINGS

1 (1-pound) package
    pocket-less pita bread

Extra-virgin olive oil
    to drizzle

1^1/$_2$ to 2 teaspoons dried
    thyme

^{1}/$_2$ to 1 teaspoon garlic
    powder

^{1}/$_8$ to ^{1}/$_4$ teaspoon cayenne
    pepper

Preheat the oven to 375°F.

Stack 3 to 4 pitas on a cutting board and cut in half, then cut each half into 5 triangles about 1^1/$_4$ inches wide at the base. Each pita will yield 10 triangles.

Place the triangles bottom to top and as closely as possible on baking sheets. Lightly drizzle with olive oil and, with fingertips, evenly coat the triangles.

Sprinkle small amounts of the thyme and garlic powder over the pita triangles, distributing evenly. Place the cayenne in a fine strainer and tap the side of the strainer with your finger to spread as evenly as possible. Try not to dust too heavily in any one area so that none of the triangles ends up more "fiery" than others.

Place one baking sheet at a time on the middle rack of the oven and bake for 7 to 8 minutes, until crisp and golden brown. Enjoy within a few hours or the next day, or store in a wax paper—lined container for up to one week.

CROSTINI WITH TOMATO RUB

MAN CANNOT LIVE BY BREAD ALONE. BUT IF YOU ADD TOMATO AND SEASONINGS, you can certainly live well.

YIELD: 6 TO 8 SERVINGS

14 to 16 ($^1/_2$-inch-thick) slices crusty baguette

Several unpeeled garlic cloves, halved lengthwise

2 to 3 plum tomatoes, halved lengthwise

Kosher salt and freshly ground black pepper

2 to 3 tablespoons extra-virgin olive oil

Spanish olives, for garnish

Fresh sprigs of parsley, for garnish

Preheat the broiler.

Place the bread slices on a baking sheet and broil 3 to 4 inches from the heat source until golden, about $1^1/_2$ minutes on each side. While the slices are warm, rub with the cut sides of the garlic and then with the cut sides of the tomatoes, squeezing slightly to release some juice and pulp. Sprinkle with salt and pepper to taste and drizzle with the olive oil. Arrange on a tray garnished with Spanish olives and parsley sprigs. This can be prepared up to several hours before serving.

GUACAMOLE WITH TOMATILLOS

THIS INSPIRED GUACAMOLE IS INFUSED WITH TOMATILLOS, GARLIC, AND A BIT OF JALAPEÑO to give it lots of flavor and an extra kick!

YIELD: ABOUT 1½ CUPS

4 large or 6 to 7 medium tomatillos, husked and rinsed

4 to 6 garlic cloves, peeled

1 medium jalapeño, seeded

2 plum tomatoes, peeled, seeded, and diced

2 ripe avocados, peeled, pitted, and coarsely chopped

1½ to 2 tablespoons freshly squeezed lime juice

⅓ cup thinly sliced scallions

Kosher salt and freshly ground black pepper

4 to 5 tablespoons chopped fresh cilantro or flat-leaf Italian parsley

Tortilla chips or toasted pita wedges, for serving

Place the tomatillos in a small saucepan with the garlic cloves and jalapeño. Pour into the pan enough water to barely cover the ingredients, partially cover the pan, and bring to a boil. Reduce the heat to a simmer and cook for 8 to 10 minutes, until the tomatillos are soft. Drain thoroughly, let cool, and pat the ingredients dry with paper towels. Purée in a food processor or blender until smooth.

Combine the tomatoes, avocados, tomatillo purée, lime juice, scallions, salt and pepper to taste, and cilantro and stir to mix. Spoon into a rustic bowl and serve with tortilla chips or toasted pita wedges.

NOTE: An easy way to peel tomatoes is to cut a criss-cross in the rounded end and plunge them in boiling water for 30 seconds. The skin will slip off easily.

GREEK EGGPLANT SPREAD

THIS LIGHT AND DELICIOUS SPREAD IS TYPICAL MEZE IN GREECE. "MEZE" IS THE GREEK word for middle, as in the middle of the day or between lunch and dinner. The secret to its success is to drain the grilled eggplant pulp for several hours or overnight to extract the bitter juices.

YIELD: 1 TO 1½ CUPS

1 large eggplant
  (about 1 pound)

1 or 2 garlic cloves,
  finely chopped

2 tablespoons finely chopped
  flat-leaf Italian parsley

1 medium plum tomato,
  peeled (see note on page
  57), seeded, and diced

1 to 1¼ tablespoons red
  wine vinegar

2 to 3 tablespoons extra-
  virgin olive oil

1 to 1¼ tablespoons
  prepared mayonnaise

Kosher salt and freshly
  ground black pepper

Pita toasts or crackers,
  for serving

Preheat the broiler or grill.

Prick the skin of the eggplant with a fork. Broil or grill the eggplant 3 to 4 inches from the heat source, turning as necessary until the skin has blistered and blackened and the flesh is soft and pulpy, 12 to 15 minutes.

Transfer the eggplant to a large plate and, when cool enough to handle, strip away the skin and mash with a fork to a purée. Then, scoop the purée into a sieve and let it sit for 4 to 6 hours, allowing the bitter juices to drain.

Transfer the drained eggplant to a mixing bowl. Add the garlic, parsley, tomato, vinegar, oil, mayonnaise, and salt and pepper to taste and stir to mix well. The mixture can be prepared up to three or four days ahead. Refrigerate, covered, in a suitable container until ready to serve. Bring to room temperature and transfer to a small serving bowl. Serve with pita toasts or crackers.

CLAMS ON THE GRILL

CLAMS ON THE GRILL ARE A QUICK AND EASY APPETIZER. A MESH-TYPE GRILL ACCESSORY over the grate will stabilize the clams while cooking. It is easy to pick the clams up off the grill, by hand, to enjoy while sipping drinks. Serve with grilled crusty Italian or French bread slices to sop up their juices.

YIELD: 4 TO 8 SERVINGS

1 to 2 dozen cherrystone clams

Grilled Italian or French bread slices, drizzled with extra-virgin olive oil

Lemon quarters (optional)

Put the clams in a bowl, cover with cold water, and place in the kitchen sink. Place a second bowl with cold water next to the bowl containing the clams. Scrub the clams, rubbing them one against the other in the water, and placing them in the second bowl of cold water. Discard the sandy water from the first bowl and refill the second bowl with fresh cold water. Repeat two or three times until there are no traces of sand left in the water. The clams are ready for the grill.

Preheat a gas grill to medium high or a charcoal grill until the coals are ashen gray. Place the well-scrubbed clams on the grill and cook until they open, 2 to 3 minutes. Clams have a self-timer; they open when they are done. With tongs, carefully transfer them to a serving platter. Serve with grilled bread slices and lemon quarters, if using.

GRILLED SWEET PEPPERS
WITH BASIL AND CAPERS

I TRY TO ALWAYS HAVE A COUPLE OF SWEET PEPPERS ON HAND TO GRILL OR BROIL WHENEVER
I have the time. Just be sure never to rinse them to remove the blackened skins and seeds or you will
wash away the precious sweet pepper juices. They can be refrigerated for up to one week and ready
when you are to serve as an appetizer on crostini or add to antipasto or a salad.

YIELD: 6 TO 8 SERVINGS

3 or 4 red and yellow
   bell peppers

2 garlic cloves, finely
   chopped

2 tablespoons red wine or
   balsamic vinegar

Kosher salt and freshly
   ground black pepper

$1/4$ cup extra-virgin olive oil

1 to 2 tablespoons capers,
   drained

$1/4$ cup fresh basil
   chiffonade*

Parsley sprigs, for garnish
   (optional)

Olives, for garnish (optional)

Grill the bell peppers over a medium-hot grill to char evenly on all sides, turning the peppers only as each side blackens. You may also place on a foil-lined baking sheet and broil about 3 inches from the heat source to char evenly on all sides, 10 to 12 minutes.

Transfer the roasted peppers to a brown paper bag, close tightly, and let steam for several minutes until cool enough to handle. Place the peppers in a colander over a bowl to catch the juices as you remove the core and seeds and then julienne. Put the julienned strips into a mixing bowl.

Add the chopped garlic and vinegar to the strained pepper juices in the bowl. Season to taste with salt and pepper and then whisk in the olive oil. Add the capers and basil and stir to mix. Pour the dressing over the pepper strips and stir gently to mix. This can be prepared ahead and refrigerated, covered, for up to two days.

Spread a small amount on garlic crostini (see note for Crostini with Garlic on the next page) and arrange on a platter. Garnish the platter with parsley sprigs and olives, if desired.

* NOTE: For the basil chiffonade, stack several basil leaves and roll up tightly like a cigar. Cut crosswise into thin strips.

CROSTINI WITH GARLIC

CROSTINI ARE ITALIAN CANAPÉS OR SMALL VERSIONS OF BRUSCHETTA THAT CAN BE SERVED with a variety of toppings, while bruschetta is grilled, seasoned with garlic and olive oil, and most often eaten as a snack. Use narrow loaves of Italian bread or French baguette for the crostini and cut the bread into $^1/_4$-inch slices.

YIELD: 6 TO 8 SERVINGS

1 narrow crusty baguette

3 garlic cloves, unpeeled and halved lengthwise

Extra-virgin olive oil

Kosher salt (optional)

Preheat the oven to 375°F.

Cut the baguette on the diagonal into $^1/_4$-inch-thick slices. Arrange the bread slices on a baking sheet in a single layer. Bake for 8 to 10 minutes, until lightly golden and crisp.

While the toast is still warm but cool enough to handle, rub the garlic over the cut side of the bread and then drizzle with a bit of the oil. Sprinkle with salt, if desired. Serve the crostini warm or at room temperature.

The toast rounds may be prepared up to several days before serving. Store in a wax paper–lined container. To serve, pile the crostini into a napkin-lined basket or arrange on a platter and spoon your favorite topping over the crostini.

NOTE: For grilled garlic bruschetta, heat a gas grill to medium high. Cut a large Tuscan loaf on the diagonal. Grill the slices until toasted. Rub with the garlic halves, drizzle with olive oil, and sprinkle with salt to taste.

STEAMED MUSSELS WITH SHALLOTS AND TOMATO SAFFRON BROTH

ITALIAN-BORN PAOLO PENATI WAS A GIFTED ARTIST AS WELL AS AN IMAGINATIVE COOK. His soul-satisfying dishes, such as this delectable mussel recipe, are a contribution to the legacy he left us.

YIELD: 4 TO 6 SERVINGS

3 to 4 large shallots, peeled and thinly sliced

2 cups fish stock or clam broth

Pinch of saffron threads

1 cup chopped tomatoes

4 to 6 dozen mussels, scrubbed and debearded

12 to 15 fresh basil leaves, rinsed, dried, and torn

8 to 10 roasted garlic cloves (see page 334)

2 tablespoons unsalted butter

Crusty bread, for serving

In a large noncorrosive, heatproof casserole with a cover (such as Le Creuset), combine the shallots, fish stock, saffron, and tomatoes and stir to mix. Add the mussels, basil, and garlic. Top with the butter.

Cover the casserole and cook over medium-high heat for 6 to 8 minutes, until the mussels open and release their juices into the broth. Divide the mussels into four to six large soup bowls and ladle the broth equally over the mussels. Serve hot with lots of crusty bread to sop up the broth.

TOMATO ONION BASIL SALSA

COARSELY CHOPPED FRESH RIPE TOMATOES MIXED WITH DICED SWEET RED ONION AND basil chiffonade make a fine topping for crostini.

YIELD: 1 CUP

5 ripe tomatoes

1 small red onion, diced

15 fresh basil leaves, cut into chiffonade (see note on page 104)

2 tablespoons finely chopped flat-leaf Italian parsley

1½ tablespoons red wine vinegar

2 tablespoons extra-virgin olive oil

Kosher salt and freshly ground black pepper

Crostini, for serving (see page 105)

Italian parsley or basil leaves, for garnish (optional)

To peel the tomatoes, make an X in the rounded end and plunge into boiling water for 30 seconds. Immediately transfer to a bowl of ice water. When cool enough to handle, peel, seed, and coarsely chop the tomatoes. Put in a mixing bowl with the onion, basil, parsley, vinegar, olive oil, and salt and pepper to taste. The salsa can be made up to several days in advance. Refrigerate in a covered container and bring to room temperature when ready to use.

Spread the salsa on the crostini and arrange on a platter. Garnish with fresh parsley or basil leaves, if desired.

CHILLED BEET AND CUCUMBER SOUP

THIS TANGY BUT LIGHT VERSION OF BORSCHT IS CHOCK-FULL OF ROASTED BEETS, CUCUMBER, and dill. This delicious, make-ahead soup is sure to please in the heat of summer.

YIELD: 6 TO 8 SERVINGS

3 to 4 medium red beets (about ⅔ pound)

2 garlic cloves, finely chopped

3 cups buttermilk

¼ cup chopped fresh dill

1 tablespoon rice wine vinegar

Kosher salt and freshly ground white pepper

1 large cucumber, peeled, seeded, and diced (about 1 cup)

Low-fat sour cream or yogurt, for garnish (optional)

Fresh sprigs of dill, for garnish (optional)

Preheat the oven to 400°F.

Trim the greens from the beets and reserve for another use. Cut the stems to 1 inch from the top. (If greens are fresh and lively, remove the heavy stems, wash greens well and blanch for 2 to 3 minutes. Drain and you have a bonus green when ready to sauté with a bit of olive oil and garlic.) Scrub the beets under running water with a vegetable brush and pat dry with a paper towel. Wrap the beets securely in heavy-duty foil, place on a baking sheet, and roast for 1¼ hours or until tender when pierced with the tip of a knife. The roasted beets can be prepared up to several days ahead, left in the foil, and refrigerated until ready to use.

When cool enough to handle, peel the beets and cut into chunks. Put the beets in the work bowl of a food processor and pulse until finely minced, scraping down the sides with a rubber spatula as necessary. Add the garlic, buttermilk, dill, vinegar, and salt and white pepper to taste and process to thoroughly mix. Taste to adjust the seasonings as necessary. Transfer to a suitable bowl with a cover. Add the diced cucumbers to the soup, cover, and chill until ready to serve. The soup may be prepared up to two days ahead.

Ladle into soup bowls for serving and, if desired, swirl in a dollop of sour cream and garnish with a sprig of dill.

NOTE: When roasting beets in summer, I make it a point to roast them in the cool of early morning.

ROUND SWAMP FARM

East Hampton

CAROLYN LESTER SNYDER SPEAKS OF HAROLD SNYDER, HER LATE HUSBAND, with reverence—"a farmer of land and sea, with many years' experience." He was a farmer by trade and a fisherman by heart. In the early years Harold was a "haul seiner," fishing for striped bass in the ocean with a five-man crew. There were times that, rather than unhook his truck from the dory rig, he used his farm tractor to pull a sharpie boat down to Three-Mile Harbor to check other nets he previously set for weak and bluefish. That vision was the inspiration for Round Swamp Farm's logo "Farmers of Land and Sea" and the trademark—a boat being pulled by a tractor—a fitting tribute!

Round Swamp Farm is a farm, a country market, and a happening place all at once. So drawn to the land when Carolyn was a young girl, her adored father built her a small red stand from which she could sell some tomatoes, cucumber, and corn. A country market evolved from this small farm stand on the family farm that has given four generations of the Lester family pride in the legacy that continues to drive the tradition of farming. Carolyn, her two daughters, Lisa and Shelly, and their husbands and two sisters are actively engaged in the business of farming, fishing, cooking, and retailing. Lisa and Shelly prepare specialty products made on premises for the market. Carolyn's son-in-law Charles Niggles, both farmer and fisherman, manages the farm. He plants and harvests tomatoes, corn, squash, flowers, herbs, potatoes, beans, and tons of lettuce—including his "famous arugula." Carolyn's sisters, Claire and Dianna, hold the fort in the market on a regular basis. It is surely a family affair.

At the country market, shelves are laden with all manner of baked goods, breads, berry muffins, scones, coffee and pound cakes, pies, jams, jellies, chutneys, and relishes, with much of their own and other local produce going into their finished product. "In the old days people had to grow and prepare their own food to survive; this holds true today with Round Swamp Farm growing and preparing all manner of food for their appreciative customers," said Carolyn.

The Round Swamp Farm family is a proud family of farmers and fisherman. They are a family that believes in giving back to the community that has given so much to them.

QUAHAUG CLAM AND CORN CHOWDER

THE MEAT OF THE LARGE, HARD-SHELL CHOWDER CLAM, MORE PROPERLY KNOWN BY ITS Algonquian Indian name quahaug (pronounced co-hog), is more strongly flavored. This hard-shell clam however, gives off a salty fragrance to make superb chowder.

YIELD: 6 SERVINGS

12 quahaug chowder clams

2 tablespoons extra-virgin olive oil

2 onions, finely chopped

2 carrots, cut into small dice

2 Yukon Gold potatoes, diced

1 large bay leaf

Kosher salt and freshly ground black pepper

2 ears fresh corn kernels

1 cup half-and-half

1 tablespoon fresh thyme leaves

1 tablespoon chopped flat-leaf Italian parsley

Scrub the clams vigorously, one against the other, in a bowl of cold water. Transfer the clams to a 4 to 5-quart saucepan filled with $1^1/_2$ quarts fresh water. Cover and bring to a boil. Reduce the heat to medium and simmer the clams until they open, 8 to 10 minutes. With a slotted spoon, transfer the clams to a large colander set over a bowl to reserve the clam broth. Pour the broth back into the saucepan and cook over medium-high heat until reduced to 4 to $4^1/_2$ cups; set aside. Remove the meat from the clamshells, discarding the shells. Mince the clams and reserve.

Meanwhile, heat the oil in a separate saucepan over medium-high heat and sauté the onions for 3 to 4 minutes. Add the carrots and potatoes and sauté for 2 to 3 minutes longer. Add the reduced clam broth, the bay leaf, and salt and pepper to taste and simmer for 8 to 10 minutes. Stir in the corn kernels and simmer for 2 to 3 minutes longer. Add the half-and-half and the minced clams to the broth, stir to mix, and simmer gently for 8 to 10 minutes.

Before serving, discard the bay leaf. Stir in the thyme and parsley. Adjust the seasonings to taste and serve hot. The chowder can be prepared up to one day before using. Refrigerate in a suitable container. Bring to room temperature and reheat gently before serving.

CLASSIC GAZPACHO WITH VERJUS

WHEN I DECIDED TO RECREATE A GAZPACHO RECIPE THAT HAD BEEN IN MY SOUP FILE FOR a long time, I was inspired to incorporate Wolffer Estate's verjus. Verjus is made from the unfermented juice of wine grapes that are picked at half ripeness. It is milder than vinegar and provides a fresh and delicate acidity to the soup.

YIELD: 6 TO 8 SERVINGS

1 1/2 cups cubed day-old bread, crusts removed

1/2 cup extra-virgin olive oil

2 1/2 pounds ripe tomatoes

1 medium red onion, coarsely chopped

1 Kirby cucumber, trimmed and seeded

1 red bell pepper, trimmed, seeded, and coarsely chopped

2 large garlic cloves, peeled and coarsely chopped

1 1/4 teaspoons kosher salt

Freshly ground black pepper

2 or 3 dashes Tabasco sauce

6 tablespoons verjus

2 tablespoons sherry wine vinegar

Snipped chives, for garnish

Put the cubed bread in a small bowl and pour the olive oil over it. Toss to coat.

To peel the tomatoes, cut an X in the rounded end and plunge into boiling water for 30 seconds. Immediately transfer to a bowl of ice water; drain. When cool enough to handle, peel, seed, and coarsely chop.

In the work bowl of a food processor fitted with the steel blade, combine the onion, cucumber, bell pepper, and garlic. Process for a few seconds, scraping down the sides of the bowl with a rubber spatula as necessary. Add the tomatoes, salt, and pepper to taste, Tabasco, verjus, and sherry vinegar. Process for 10 to 15 seconds, until the mixture is puréed. Add the oil-soaked bread cubes, scraping any excess oil into the work bowl with a rubber spatula. Process for 15 to 20 seconds, until the bread resembles a fine crumb and gives texture to the mixture. Let rest for 15 to 20 minutes and then adjust the seasonings to taste. Pulse to mix. Pour the gazpacho into a covered container and refrigerate for several hours or up to 2 days.

When ready to serve, ladle into soup bowls or mugs and sprinkle with snipped chives. Serve chilled.

THE NORTH FORK TABLE & INN
Southold

GERRY HAYDEN AND CLAUDIA FLEMING RETURNED TO THEIR ROOTS WHEN THEY founded the North Fork Table & Inn, in Southold, Long Island. Gerry Hayden, who hails from Setaucket, knew as a young boy that he would have a culinary career. He graduated from the Culinary Institute of America in Hyde Park in 1986. He worked with many impressive chefs including Charlie Palmer, David Burke, and Drew Nieporent of Montrachet, Tribeca Grill, and Nobu fame. Through these contacts he also learned the importance of the front of the house and excellent service—salient points in running a restaurant. It was while at Tribeca Grill in Manhattan that he met and worked with Claudia Fleming from Brentwood, Long Island.

In 1993 Gerry Hayden became executive chef of East Hampton Point. There he proved his mettle for straightforward food with uncompromising high standards. In 1999 he was asked to take the executive chef position at Charlie Palmer's Aureole, which provided the incentive for him to move back to Manhattan, where he reconnected with Claudia Fleming, and, as they say, the rest is history. They dated briefly and then married in 2001. In 2005 they purchased a home and then a restaurant with a history reputed to date back to the late 1700s. They completely renovated the statuesque white-pillared building in Southold using colors inspired by sand, sky, and earth, while keeping true to its historical nature. Claudia worked with architect Ian Haspel, who happened to be the husband of K. K. Haspel. K. K., as Gerry calls her, is a farmer in Southold not far from the restaurant. The nine-acre farm is completely self-sustainable and biodynamic, and at least 70 percent of the produce used at the North Fork Table & Inn comes from K. K.'s farm. "It's like living in a small town," said Gerry.

For Claudia and Gerry, being on the North Fork surrounded by water, farmland, and the vineyards; the produce, the fish from the sea, and the local duck farms; and the sheer beauty of the place continually offers inspiration to stay true to the fundamentals of cooking. Gerry has contact with numerous local fishermen who have become his friends. They fish from the inlet where the Haydens' home is, catching local Peconic bay scallops, fluke, monkfish, and more. It can't get much fresher than that!

GREEN GRAPE GAZPACHO

GERRY HAYDEN, THE EXECUTIVE CHEF AND OWNER OF THE NORTH FORK TABLE & INN, incorporates Catapano Dairy Farm's goat's milk yogurt for this delectable milky soup.

YIELD: 6 SERVINGS

1 pint plain yogurt, preferably goat's yogurt

$^1/_2$ pound seedless green grapes, washed

$^1/_4$ cup blanched and toasted almonds

4 ounces goat cheese

1 teaspoon toasted coriander seeds

3 tablespoons extra-virgin olive oil, divided

16 Marcona almonds,* roasted, salted, and coarsely chopped

Place the yogurt, grapes, almonds, goat cheese, coriander seeds, and 1 tablespoon of the olive oil in a blender. Blend until thoroughly puréed and smooth. Refrigerate the soup for 3 to 4 hours or overnight until ready to serve.

Serve well chilled with the remaining 2 tablespoons of olive oil drizzed on top and the chopped Marcona almonds.

* NOTE: Marcona almonds, known as the "queen of almonds," are imported from Spain. They may be difficult to find and are a bit pricey. Blanch 1 cup almonds for 1 minute, peel, and, while still wet, transfer to a parchment-lined baking sheet. Add 2 tablespoons kosher salt, toss, and let dry on the sheet pan for 48 hours. Roast the almonds at 225°F for 1 hour to 1 hour and 15 minutes until toasty beige. Use what you need to garnish the soup; then store the remaining almonds in a covered tin. They will keep for weeks and make a wonderful snack at cocktail time.

MESCLUN SALAD WITH BASIC VINAIGRETTE

"MESCLUN" COMES FROM MECLA, THE OLD FRENCH WORD FOR MIXTURE. THE CONCEPT originated in the Provence region of France where farmers would offer mixtures of young, tender lettuces and other greens that were unique to each farm. Today the mix is grown together to include an assortment of greens to accommodate a variety of color, texture, and flavor. Mesclun is generally dressed with a light dressing of oil, vinegar, salt, and pepper so as not to obscure its delicate flavors.

YIELD: 2 TO 4 SERVINGS

$^1/_4$ to $^1/_2$ pound mesclun, washed and spun dry

2 to 3 tablespoons extra-virgin olive oil

Kosher salt

$^3/_4$ to 1 tablespoon imported red wine or balsamic vinegar

Freshly ground black pepper

Spread the greens on a double length of paper towels. Roll up and wrap the greens to absorb any excess moisture. If preparing ahead, place in a zip-top bag and chill until ready to serve.

When ready to serve, transfer the greens to a salad bowl to dress. Add the oil in a slow steady stream beginning at the outer perimeter of the greens towards the center. Toss the greens with the oil and let stand for up to 10 minutes without getting soggy. Just before serving, add about $^1/_4$ teaspoon salt into a tablespoon measure. Add enough vinegar to fill the tablespoon. Agitate the vinegar to dissolve the salt and pour over the greens in a circular movement. Add several grinds of pepper to taste and toss well to mix. Serve at once.

GIRL FARMER
Sagaponack

MARILEE FOSTER GREW UP IN A FARMING FAMILY, BUT AS A GIRL WAS NOT expected to get "Dirt Under Her Nails"—the title of her book published by Bridge Works in 2002. Marilee graduated from Benoit College with a liberal arts degree and a passion for the English language. Nevertheless, Marilee, a fifth-generation farmer, found herself moving irrigation at 2:00 a.m. and learning the workings of the farm from her brother, Dean She no doubt felt the tug of her heritage and has found farming to be her calling. Her father, Clifford Foster, and brother run the larger, three-hundred-acre farm of potatoes, grain crops, and field corn in Sagaponack. Initially, Marilee's father gave her some space to farm, but she found herself becoming more committed to organic farming. She rents a ten-acre parcel of land behind the Sagaponack general store. The bulk of Marilee's business comes from the side of the road in front of the family home. She packages her own line of potato chips and sells them along with her produce at the Sag Harbor Farmers' Market. Local restaurants are another source of revenue.

She plants asparagus crowns in March in the greenhouse and then nurses them along when she moves them outdoors in the warmer weather. "Rule of thumb," says Marilee. "Asparagus can't be cut for two years or you risk killing the crown, the node of the asparagus. After three years the asparagus can be harvested." She has a particular penchant for growing tomatoes. Starting with just a few, today Marilee grows several varieties of heirloom tomatoes that come in all shapes, colors, and flavors, including the beautiful dark burgundy Black Krim, which she describes as sensuous. Tomatoes like hot and dry conditions for optimal growth, and weather, of course, is always a factor. She prefers to sell her heirlooms at the moment of ripening. A charming aside—Marilee recalls a note of thanks once left at her farm stand. It read, "This is the second best tomato I ever had in my life." (Marilee thought, *why the second best?*) The customer continued, "the first tomato I shared with someone I was madly in love with, a long time ago, in Italy."

ROASTED CHIOGGIA BEETS AND HEIRLOOM TOMATOES

WITH BASIL AND PARMESAN

ROASTED BEETS WILL KEEP WELL IN THE REFRIGERATOR FOR ABOUT A WEEK. WHEN TRIMMING, be sure to leave a bit of the root and about one inch of the stem so they will maintain their moisture while roasting. This visually beautiful and savory salad is a summertime favorite when heirloom tomatoes are at their best.

YIELD: 6 SERVINGS

1 bunch farm fresh beets, preferably Chioggia beets, trimmed

3 to 4 large ripe yellow or red heirloom tomatoes, sliced about $1/4$ inch thick

Kosher salt and freshly ground black pepper

3 to 4 tablespoons extra-virgin olive oil

1 to $1/2$ tablespoons sherry vinegar

Large handful basil leaves, cut into chiffonade (see note on page 104)

Shaved Parmesan cheese

Preheat the oven to 400°F.

Scrub, rinse, and pat the trimmed beets dry with paper towels. Center the beets in a square of heavy-duty foil large enough to wrap securely. Fold over the corners of the foil to make a tight package and transfer to a sheet pan. Roast about 1 hour to $1^1/4$ hours, depending on their size. Remove from the oven and let cool. The beets can be stored, unpeeled and still wrapped in the foil, in the refrigerator for up to one week. When ready to use, trim the tops from the beets and peel.

To serve, cut the peeled beets into $1/4$-inch-thick slices. Slice the tomatoes to an even thickness. Overlap the beet and tomato slices on individual salad plates. Sprinkle with salt and pepper to taste and then drizzle the oil and vinegar on top. Scatter the basil and the Parmesan cheese shavings over the beets and tomatoes. This salad can be prepared up to an hour or so ahead and served at room temperature.

NOTE: In the summer, local farmers grow the sweet Chioggia yellow and pink beets that when sliced reveal their beautiful stripes. They may generally be smaller in size than regular beets and may require a little less cooking time. When the knife goes through easily, they are done. Early seasonal pear tomatoes can be substituted for the heirloom tomatoes, which come into season in August and September.

HEIRLOOM TOMATO AND MELON SALAD
WITH GOAT'S MILK YOGURT DRESSING

ALTHOUGH THE LAUNDRY WAS A HAMPTONS HOT SPOT, THE RESTAURANT ITSELF HAD A warm, comfy feel when you walked in, a fire roaring and the presence of its original site, a Laundromat. Andrew Engle was the executive chef at the Laundry and gave us this wonderful salad. It's as local as local can get and is made with Catapano goat's milk yogurt and locally grown melon and heirloom tomatoes.

YIELD: 6 TO 8 SERVINGS

FOR THE DRESSING

1 cup goat's milk yogurt

2 tablespoons white balsamic vinegar

2 tablespoons freshly squeezed lemon juice

Kosher salt and freshly ground black pepper

2 tablespoons extra-virgin olive oil

FOR THE SALAD

1 large ripe melon, such as Galia or Crenshaw

2 pounds assorted heirloom tomatoes

1/4 cup micro arugula or fresh basil chiffonade, washed and spun dry

2 tablespoons lemon zest

Freshly ground black pepper and fleur de sel or other sea salt

For the dressing, place the yogurt, vinegar, and lemon juice in a mixing bowl. Season with salt and pepper to taste and whisk to mix. Slowly whisk in the olive oil until the mixture is emulsified.

For the salad, peel and seed the melon and cut into narrow wedges. Cut the tomatoes into wedges. When ready to serve, divide the greens among six to eight salad plates. Divide evenly the wedges of melon and tomatoes and the julienned strips of preserved lemon over the greens. Drizzle the dressing over the top of each salad and finish with a few turns of the pepper mill and a dash of fleur de sel. Serve at room temperature.

NOTE: Catapano goat's milk yogurt of Catapano Dairy Farm on the North Fork is available on the South Fork at The Green Thumb organic market in Water Mill and Lucy's Whey, American artisanal cheese shop in East Hampton and at farmers' markets.

SUMMER CORN AND SCALLOP SALAD

WHEN MY DEAR FRIEND AND TALENTED COOK LYNN ROGERS RABINEAU VISITED ONE SUMMER, she whipped up this uncommonly delicious and visually beautiful corn and scallop salad. Like Lynn, this dish is a winner.

YIELD: 6 SERVINGS

FOR THE VINAIGRETTE

2 shallots, finely chopped

1 to 1½ teaspoons Dijon mustard

2 teaspoons sherry wine vinegar

2 teaspoons freshly squeezed lemon juice

3 tablespoons extra-virgin olive oil

Kosher salt and freshly ground white pepper

FOR THE SALAD

4 or 5 ears fresh corn, shucked

3 scallions, trimmed and thinly sliced (white and light green parts)

18 diver or large sea scallops, side muscle removed

Kosher salt and freshly ground white pepper

2 tablespoons butter

1 tablespoon extra-virgin olive oil

Bunch baby arugula, washed and spun dry

½ cup pear or cherry tomatoes, halved

Chive stems, for garnish

For the vinaigrette, put the shallots in a mixing bowl. Whisk in the mustard, vinegar, and lemon juice. Slowly whisk in the olive oil and season to taste with salt and white pepper.

For the salad, cook the corn in a pot of boiling salted water for 2 minutes. Drain and cool. Cut the kernels from the cobs into a mixing bowl. Add the scallions and about 1½ tablespoons of the vinaigrette; toss to mix. The salad up to this point can be prepared up to a couple of hours ahead.

Rinse the scallops. Pat them dry with a paper towel and season with salt and pepper to taste. Melt the butter with the oil in a skillet, preferably cast iron, over medium-high heat until hot and the butter is a light golden brown. Working in batches, put the scallops into the hot pan and cook, basting with the foaming butter, for about 1½ minutes on each side, until a golden crust is formed. Transfer to a warm platter.

To serve, toss the arugula with about 1½ tablespoons dressing and place on a serving platter or divide equally among six individual salad plates. Spoon the corn and scallion mixture over the arugula and artfully arrange the scallops and tomato halves around the platter or plates. Drizzle the remaining dressing over the scallops and tomatoes. Garnish the platter or plates with chives and serve at room temperature.

HOMEMADE MOZZARELLA

PASQUALE LANGELLA, MOZZARELLA CHEESE MAKER EXTRAORDINAIRE, HOLDS COURT every Friday, Saturday, and Sunday at Tutto Italiano, a Citarella specialty food store in East Hampton where he makes fresh mozzarella.

From start to finish, Pasquale's hands are poetry in motion as he works the special curd in several additions of hot (140°F) water in a huge vat until the curds melt into supple sheets of what appears to be voluminous yards of white velvet stretched over a stainless steel paddle. As Pasquale's hands work the melting, smooth curd into the familiar mozzarella shape, the pieces are transferred to cold water to hold their shape.

Pasquale prepares mini balls of mozzarella to share with his audience. Still warm from the hot liquid bath, the small bites, creamy and smooth, just slide down your throat, leaving a rich, slightly salty aftertaste. It is heaven in a bite.

CAPRESE SALAD

EVERYONE IS FAMILIAR WITH THE TOMATO, BASIL, AND MOZZARELLA SALAD KNOWN AS caprese. The twist is to prepare a basil purée to dress the salad, which is made with freshly made mozzarella and seasonal heirloom tomatoes.

YIELD: 6 SERVINGS

2 red locally grown
   tomatoes, thinly sliced

2 yellow tomatoes, thinly
   sliced

1 pound good quality fresh
   mozzarella (not Buffalo),
   thinly sliced

12 to 14 large basil leaves,
   divided

$1/4$ cup extra-virgin olive oil

2 tablespoons sherry wine
   vinegar

Kosher salt and freshly
   ground black pepper

Black Gaeta olives,
   for garnish

3 to 4 tablespoons basil
   purée, for garnish
   (optional)*

Alternate layers of the tomato slices, mozzarella slices, and 6 basil leaves, dividing equally among six salad plates. Dress each dish with olive oil and a light drizzle of vinegar, salt, and pepper.

Stack the remaining basil leaves, roll them like a cigar, and slice crosswise into a chiffonade. Scatter the basil chiffonade over the tomato and mozzarella. Garnish each plate with 2 or 3 olives for serving.

If using the basil purée, dress the edge of each plate "Jackson Pollack style," gently splattering it for presentation.

*NOTE: For the basil purée, place 1 cup packed basil leaves and $1/3$ cup extra-virgin olive oil in a food processor. Season with salt and pepper and purée until smooth.

FRESNO

East Hampton

GRETCHEN MENSER WAS BORN IN LA PAZ, BOLIVIA, WHERE HER PARENTS WERE in the Peace Corps. She left when very young to live abroad, where she had the good fortune to experience many different cultures and cuisine. Back in the states she attended Boston University and studied art history. After graduation she visited a friend at the Culinary Institute of America in Hyde Park, New York. As soon as she entered the building, she knew that she would not continue her work at a gallery. The career change was an epiphany.

After graduating from the CIA, she went to work at fashionable East Hampton restaurants—Nick & Toni's, Rowdy Hall, and 1770 House. Prior to becoming executive chef at Fresno, she was chef de cuisine at 1770 House for three years. She has been at Fresno since 2006 and couldn't be happier working on the East End. Fresno, with its sky-lit room, zinc bar, and wall of French doors overlooking a landscaped patio for dining outdoors in season, is a little gem of a restaurant. Here, Gretchen cooks with a European sensibility, creating clean and exciting flavors and cooking with the local bounty as much as possible. This philosophy aligns with Fresno's tradition of offering a spectrum of new American fare, emphasizing simple but sophisticated preparations.

Highlights of Gretchen's menus include sautéed black sea bass with fennel, beets, blood oranges, and quinoa, cataplana, a Portuguese shellfish stew fresh from the local sea, and a chocolate brioche bread pudding with dried cherries, pistachios, and Bourbon sauce guaranteed to make grown men cry.

DUCK CONFIT WITH CORN, HEIRLOOM TOMATOES, AND PEACH GASTRIQUE

GRETCHEN MENSER, EXECUTIVE CHEF OF FRESNO RESTAURANT IN EAST HAMPTON, PREPARES this deliciously piquant summer salad with local, farm-fresh ingredients. The peach gastrique can be made weeks in advance. And you can use more or less duck confit, depending on how generous you would like to be.

YIELD: 4 SERVINGS

FOR THE PEACH GASTRIQUE

1/2 cup good quality red wine vinegar

1/2 cup sugar

1/2 teaspoon vanilla extract

3 ripe peaches, peeled and sliced

FOR THE SALAD

Kernels from 3 ears of corns

2 or 3 heirloom tomatoes, cut into wedges or 1/2 pint grape tomatoes, halved

1 or 2 duck leg confit (see page 333)

For the gastrique, combine the vinegar and sugar in a small nonreactive saucepan and stir to mix. Bring to a boil, reduce the heat to medium low and simmer briskly until the mixture is reduced by half or is a light syrup. Watch carefully as the mixture could caramelize. Remove from the heat and stir in the vanilla. Cool completely and then pour into a food processor or blender. Add the peaches to the food processor or blender and purée. The gastrique can be prepared ahead and refrigerated in a suitable container for several weeks.

For the salad, blanch the corn kernels in a pot of boiling salted water for 2 minutes. Drain well and spread on a plate to cool. Transfer the kernels to a mixing bowl. If using grape tomatoes, add to the corn kernels. Trim the duck legs of excess fat and cut the meat into large shreds.

To serve, equally divide the corn kernels and tomato wedges, or the corn and tomato mixture, among four salad plates. Divide the shredded duck confit over the corn mixture and spoon the peach gastrique on top to dress the salad. Enjoy at room temperature.

CONFIT (pronounced con-fee) is a method of preserving meat with salt and its own cooking fat to last for months without refrigeration. For duck confit, duck legs with thighs attached are the most desirable part for preserving. You can purchase prepared duck confit at Cromer's in Sag Harbor and Catena's in Southampton.

GRILLED CALAMARI AND SWEET ONION SALAD
WITH SPICY VINAIGRETTE

FRYING CALAMARI SEEMS INTIMIDATING TO ME. BREADED AND FRIED IS A REAL CHALLENGE, but in the right hands it is a delicious and popular appetizer. The very talented Starr Boggs, of the restaurant of the same name in Westhampton Beach, prepares grilled calamari to serve in a composed salad. I fell in love with the different textures and level of flavors to adapt the recipe below.

YIELD: 5 TO 6 SERVINGS

FOR THE GARLIC OIL

$^1/_2$ cup extra-virgin olive oil

4 garlic cloves, peeled

FOR THE CALAMARI

1 pound calamari with tentacles, thoroughly cleaned and left whole

2 garlic cloves, finely chopped

2 tablespoons extra-virgin olive oil

3 or 4 dashes chili oil or Tabasco sauce

Kosher salt and freshly ground black pepper

FOR THE VINAIGRETTE

$^1/_3$ cup garlic oil

3 tablespoons rice wine vinegar

$^1/_4$ cup lemon juice

3 or 4 dashes chili oil or Tabasco, or more to taste

Kosher salt

For the garlic oil, pour the oil into a small saucepan over low heat and add the garlic. Cook until the garlic is golden brown, about 10 minutes, being careful not to burn it. Let cool and strain the oil into a clean mason jar, reserving $^1/_3$ cup to use in the vinaigrette. The garlic oil will keep for a week or so at room temperature.

For the calamari, check the tubes of the calamari to be sure they are clean within. Rinse the calamari and tentacles and pat dry with a paper towel. Combine the garlic, olive oil, chili oil, and salt and pepper to taste in a bowl. Add the calamari and marinate about 10 minutes.

For the vinaigrette, combine the reserved garlic oil, vinegar, lemon juice, chili oil, and salt to taste. Mix well and adjust the chili oil to your taste.

For the salad, preheat a grill to medium high and grease the grill rack with 1 tablespoon of the canola oil. Toss the onions in a mixing bowl with the remaining 1 tablespoon of canola oil. Grill the onions until slightly charred and still a bit crispy, 4 to 6 minutes, turning once. Transfer to a bowl.

Drain the calamari, discarding the marinade. Grill in batches as necessary, turning once with tongs, just until slightly charred and no longer translucent, 3 to 4 minutes. Be careful not to overcook or the calamari will become rubbery. Transfer the calamari to a cutting board and slice each calamari tube lengthwise into strips about $^1/_2$ inch wide. Leave the tentacles whole. Add the calamari to the

2 tablespoons canola oil,
divided

2 Spanish onions, sliced $\frac{1}{2}$
inch thick

6 to 8 cups mesclun greens,
washed and spun dry

Chopped fresh parsley or
julienned fresh basil, for
garnish

onions and toss to mix with 4 to 6 tablespoons of the vinaigrette.

To serve, toss the mesclun with the remaining vinaigrette and divide among five or six salad plates. Divide the calamari and onions evenly over the greens. Garnish with parsley or basil and serve at room temperature.

NOTE: The garlic oil, vinaigrette, and greens can all be prepared ahead of time for this unusual and tasty salad. Just refrigerate in separate containers for up to one day ahead and everything is ready when you are.

STARR BOGGS

To grow up on a farm of more than a thousand acres, where animals are bred and butter is churned daily, would be a fantasy for any child. Starr Boggs, the founder of the notable restaurant in Westhampton Beach by the same name, was that child. He grew up on the eastern shore of Virginia on the Chesapeake Bay. According to Starr, it was "an area not unlike the East End of Long Island." At about the age of seven, he worked in the fields planting and harvesting the "truck crops." He helped in the kitchen while watching family members freezing, canning, and "putting up." These deep-rooted traditions left an indelible mark on Starr.

Starr Boggs went to William and Mary College on a football scholarship. Due to a knee injury, he ended up pursuing what would be a successful culinary career.

After several stints at restaurants in Florida and Nantucket, in 1981 he became the chef at the Inn of Quogue, in Quogue, Long Island. In 1986, he opened his highly esteemed Starr Boggs restaurant at 23 Sunset Avenue in Westhampton Beach. After moving it and then selling it, he reopened his namesake restaurant in a charming Victorian home on Parlato Place in Westhampton Beach in 2004. The spacious dining room was completely renovated to give the space a casual elegance. The extensive outdoor dining garden is indeed a popular place in the warm summer months.

Starr Boggs loves the freshness of the produce available from both the North and South Fork farms, the fish from the sea, and the wines of the vineyards. His philosophy, like any great chef, is to offer the very best product he can find and to prepare food that's simple and flavorful while keeping its integrity intact. Starr is serious about food and aware of the need to preserve natural resources. He works closely with the Long Island Seafood Council to help maintain clean waters in the surrounding bays and encourages good farming practices. Starr has been on Long Island for thirty years and is encouraged by new and younger chefs that have come to the area to create inspired dishes using local ingredients. He has seen the East End grow into a significant food and wine destination.

PANZANELLA WITH GRILLED CROUTONS

PANZANELLA IS THE CLASSIC ITALIAN BREAD SALAD INCORPORATING SWEET SEASONAL tomatoes, fresh basil, and fragrant olive oil. Dry Tuscan bread is traditionally used. To capture the same quality of the bread, grill cubes of day-old crusty baguette.

YIELD: 6 TO 8 SERVINGS

1/2 pound loaf day-old crusty Italian bread

1/3 cup plus 2 tablespoons extra-virgin olive oil, divided

1 1/2 tablespoons red wine vinegar

1 1/2 pounds red and yellow summer tomatoes

1 small red onion, sliced paper thin

15 to 20 large fresh basil leaves, cut into chiffonade (see note on page 104)

Kosher salt and freshly ground black pepper

Cut the bread into 1 1/2-inch cubes. In a bowl, toss the cubes with 2 tablespoons of the olive oil and grill on a rack in a preheated grill or in a grill pan until toasted on both sides, turning as necessary. Transfer to a bowl, toss with the vinegar, and set aside.

Cut the tomatoes into bite-size wedges. Place on a wire rack one layer deep over a plate and drain about 20 minutes. Meanwhile, place the onions in a bowl of cold water and soak for 15 minutes. Drain the onions and squeeze dry in a clean kitchen towel.

To assemble the salad, add the tomatoes, onion, basil, and the remaining 1/3 cup olive oil to the grilled bread in the bowl. Season with the salt and pepper to taste and toss to mix. Cover the bowl with plastic wrap and let stand for 1 to 2 hours before serving.

PANZANELLA, a lunchtime salad, comes from the Roman word meaning "hilly." Because of its keeping qualities, Michelangelo dined on the salad while chipping away on the mountain.

HERB NEW POTATO SALAD

FRESH DUG POTATOES WITH THE BRIGHTNESS OF HERBS ADD AROMA AND FLAVOR TO THIS do-ahead potato salad.

YIELD: 8 TO 10 SERVINGS

$2^1/_2$ to 3 pounds new red potatoes with skin

2 teaspoons kosher salt

$^1/_4$ cup dry white wine

$^1/_3$ to $^1/_2$ cup extra-virgin olive oil

Kosher salt and freshly ground pepper

$^1/_2$ cup mixed fresh herbs (basil, thyme, oregano, mint)

Scrub the potatoes clean, put into a large pot, and cover with water. Bring to a boil and add salt. With cover slightly off, cook at a brisk simmer for 16 to 18 minutes, or until tender. Drain, pat dry, and cut in half. Transfer the potatoes to a large bowl and drizzle with the wine and oil while still warm. Season to taste with salt and pepper.

Meanwhile, rinse the herbs and pat them dry with a clean kitchen towel. Stack the basil leaves, roll them up like a cigar, and cut crosswise into chiffonade or "ribbons." Remove the leaves from the stems of the remaining herbs and chop coarsely. Sprinkle the herb mixture over the potatoes. With a large rubber spatula, carefully mix the ingredients until well coated. The salad can be prepared up to one day ahead. Refrigerate, covered, in a suitable container. Transfer to a serving dish and bring to room temperature before serving.

WHEAT BERRY SALAD
WITH SUGAR SNAP PEAS AND CHERRY TOMATOES

I LOVE THE WHOLESOME CRUNCH AND TEXTURE OF WHEAT BERRIES IN SALADS. THIS MARvelous grain can be purchased in natural food stores or specialty markets. Just keep in mind that you will need to soak the wheat berries for three to four hours, or even overnight, before cooking.

YIELD: 6 TO 8 SERVINGS

1½ cups whole wheat berries

Pinch of kosher salt

4 large scallions, trimmed and thinly sliced

2 tablespoons snipped chives

2 tablespoons chopped flat-leaf Italian parsley

2 tablespoons chopped fresh cilantro

2 ounces sugar snap peas, trimmed and cut into thirds (about ¾ cup)

10 to 12 cherry tomatoes, rinsed and halved

Freshly ground black pepper

3 tablespoons extra-virgin olive oil

1 tablespoon good quality balsamic vinegar

Boston lettuce leaves, for serving (optional)

Toast the wheat berries in a skillet over medium heat about 5 minutes, gently shaking the pan occasionally, until they give off a pleasant aroma and the grains begin to pop. Transfer to a strainer and rinse under cold running water. Put the wheat berries in a saucepan with enough water to cover the wheat berries by 2 inches and let sit at room temperature for 3 to 4 hours. Place the pan over high heat. Add the salt, cover, and bring to a boil. Reduce the heat to medium and cook at a brisk simmer for 1 hour or just until the wheat berries are tender but toothsome to the bite, making certain that the water doesn't evaporate before the wheat berries are done. Add more water if necessary. Remove from the heat and let rest for a few minutes and then drain in a colander and cool.

Combine the scallions, chives, parsley, cilantro, snap peas, tomatoes, and wheat berries in a salad bowl. Season with the pepper to taste. Toss with the oil and vinegar. Taste and adjust seasoning as necessary. The salad may be prepared up to one day ahead and refrigerated, covered.

When ready to serve, bring the salad to room temperature. If desired, arrange washed and dried whole leaves of lettuce on six to eight serving plates and spoon equal amounts of the salad over the leaves. I also like to serve it buffet style at a summer barbeque or party buffet.

PIKE FARM
Sagaponack

THERE IS A RATHER QUAINT FEELING ABOUT JENNIFER AND JIM PIKE'S ROAD-side farm stand on Sagg Main Street in Sagaponack. Several rustic wood counters with covered-wagon-style wood roof tops shade the mounds of corn spilling out of burlap bags, boxes of colorful sweet berries, and the multitude of greens that are set back from the stretch of road. Smaller box-like counters show off the variety of multicolored heirloom and field tomatoes, potatoes, apples, peaches, and melons in season. Look beyond the counters to view the vast field of farmland where an occasional tractor is visible from behind this picturesque farm stand.

One almost always runs into a familiar face or two at Pike's farm stand, whether they are celebrity or friend. Situated south of the highway, the farm is easily accessible from Route 27, the Hamptons' main highway, as Sagg Main is also a passageway to the area's beaches.

Jim Pike, a first-generation farmer, began farming in 1987. In 1998 he met Jennifer, who hails from Pittsburgh. She happily left her office job in order to farm. To get a jump on the season and to ensure sturdy, quality plants, she and Jim begin their crops in the green-house before moving them outside in warmer weather to plant in the fields.

The Pikes are always on the lookout for new and better products, such as heirloom tomatoes and artichokes. Artichokes typically only produce on perennial plants, and since they would not survive northeastern winters, they are not grown in New York. But some-one discovered a variety that produces the first year, and Jim tried growing artichokes. "It was a hit, especially among people who have enjoyed baby artichokes in their travels abroad. Unfortunately, they are unpredictable. Some years there are bumper crops, and other years they can be scarce or not produce at all. Our customers have learned not to go to the farm stand and insist on a specific ingredient for a recipe but to purchase what is appealing and available that day," said Jennifer.

Jim and Jennifer plant twenty-six varieties of tomatoes, eight varieties of corn, and many other fruits and vegetables over the course of the season, more than twenty-one thousand plants. They go to great lengths to have the first corn and tomatoes locally. Pike's farm stand is open from strawberry season through the fall harvest.

GRILLED CORN ON THE COB WITH CAYENNE

STUDENTS FREQUENTLY ASK ME FOR THE BEST WAY TO GRILL CORN. I LOVE THE FOLLOWING suggestion from a dear friend and colleague, Bonnie Barnes of Atlanta, Georgia.

YIELD: AS MANY AS YOU LIKE

Fresh ears of corn
Extra-virgin olive oil
Kosher salt
Cayenne pepper

Carefully pull back the corn husks, keeping them attached at the base, and discard the silks. Remove one or two outer husks from each ear of corn and set aside.

Brush the corn with a light coating of olive oil and a sprinkle of salt and cayenne. Fold the husks back over the corn and tie the open ends together with a long strip of outer husk to secure it. This procedure may be done up to several hours ahead.

Brush the husks with olive oil and grill over hot coals or a gas grill heated to medium-high for $3^1/_2$ minutes on each side, until the husks are grilled and charred. Serve hot.

BRAISED BABY ARTICHOKES WITH GARLIC AND OLIVE OIL

LOCAL FARMERS ON THE EAST END HAVE EXPERIMENTED WITH ARTICHOKE SEED SINCE 2002 and now even artichokes are a local crop.

YIELD: 4 TO 6 SERVINGS

Juice of 1 lemon

6 to 8 baby artichokes

3 tablespoons extra-virgin olive oil

2 shallots, finely chopped

2 garlic cloves, finely chopped

$^1/_2$ to $^3/_4$ cup dry white wine

$^1/_2$ cup water

2 sprigs fresh thyme

2 sprigs fresh rosemary

Kosher salt and freshly ground black pepper

Fill a large bowl with cold water and squeeze the lemon juice into it. Snap off the tough outer leaves of the artichokes, leaving only the tender inner yellow leaves. Trim the pointed tips of the leaves and the tip of the stem. Slice each artichoke in half and cut the artichokes in half lengthwise. Remove the fuzzy inner choke with a teaspoon and discard. Place the artichoke hearts into the lemon water.

Drain the chokes and pat dry with paper towels. Heat the oil in a skillet over medium-high heat and sauté the shallots and garlic for 1 to 2 minutes, being careful not to brown them. Put the artichokes in the skillet with the wine and water. There should be enough liquid to barely cover the artichokes. Add the thyme and rosemary and season with salt and pepper to taste. Bring the liquid to a boil and then reduce the heat to medium low. Cook, partially covered, until the artichokes are tender when pricked with a fork, 30 to 35 minutes. Check for evaporation, adding a bit more wine or water as necessary.

Wine suggestion: Macari Vineyards Early Wine (white table wine)

SUMMER VEGETABLE RAGOÛT

THIS RECIPE HAS ROOTS IN SPAIN, WHERE THEY PRODUCE VERY GOOD OLIVE OILS. USE A great tasting olive oil to prepare this seasonal ragoût made with farm-fresh vegetables.

YIELD: 6 SERVINGS

3 to 4 ripe tomatoes

3 to 4 tablespoons extra-virgin olive oil

2 medium Spanish onions, halved and thinly sliced

3 garlic cloves, thinly sliced

2 large red bell peppers, trimmed and cut into $1/2$-inch-wide strips

2 large yellow bell peppers, trimmed and cut into $1/2$-inch-wide strips

Kosher salt and freshly ground black pepper

1 bay leaf

2 tablespoons finely chopped flat-leaf Italian parsley

2 teaspoons fresh thyme leaves

2 teaspoons imported red wine vinegar

To peel the tomatoes, make an X in the rounded end and plunge into boiling water for 30 to 40 seconds and drain. Immediately transfer to a bowl of ice water. When cool enough to handle, peel, seed, and coarsely chop; set aside.

Warm the oil in a large heavy skillet over medium heat. Add the onion slices, toss to coat, and sauté for 4 to 5 minutes, stirring occasionally until tender. Add the garlic and sauté for 1 to 2 minutes. Add the bell peppers and season to taste with salt and pepper. Cover and cook for 5 minutes, stirring occasionally. Add the chopped tomatoes and bay leaf and simmer, uncovered, for 20 to 25 minutes, stirring occasionally. The ragoût can be prepared and stored, covered, in the refrigerator up to two days in advance. Bring to room temperature before completing the dish.

Add the parsley, thyme, and vinegar to the vegetables and stir to mix. Before serving, remove the bay leaf. Serve warm or at room temperature.

MACARI VINEYARDS
Mattituck and Cutchogue

THE PREVAILING MANTRA OF JOSEPH MACARI JR. OF MACARI VINEYARDS IS TO "do right by the land." Joseph Macari Sr. bought farmland out in Mattituck from the North Road out to Long Island Sound in 1964 and bided his time while contemplating what to do on it. By the late 1980s, Joseph Macarai Jr. decided growing grapes was a good idea. While he had enjoyed drinking Italian wines with his family, farming a vineyard and making wine were new concepts. "I had no idea about farming, but I fell in love with it. I love the soil in particular and feel like everything good comes from having good soil."

This devotion to maintaining healthy soil for his vines has led Macari to try to follow biodynamic practices as much as he can. The pressures of fungus during the growing season mean that Macari has found that he still has to spray, but he maintains a herd of cattle just to have a steady supply of manure to fertilize his land. As Macari says, "cow manure can heal the whole earth. They give us biodynamic compost, and the stuff is beautiful. . . . If you feed the soil, the plant will get what it needs." He hasn't used chemical fertilizer or herbicide in ten years.

In describing the idea of a model for his wines, Macari says, "I try to live up to the French (Bordeaux in particular), but after thirteen years of making wines, this is Long Island, and our wines can stand on their own two feet now. We don't need a model, because our wines are what they are. I did get some viticultural ideas from California, but they needed to be adapted to our unique situation here."

There are now close to two hundred acres of vines planted at Macari, in both Cutchogue and Mattituck. His children are also involved in the process. His son Joey is studying viticulture.

He considers having his children grow up on Long Island to be the greatest benefit of being here. "To have my family here and to be part of nature is the greatest thing. We also take the water around us for granted, but the maritime climate, sandy soil, and beautiful farmland all make this a very special place."

PEPPERONATA

LOCAL FLAVORS ARE SO EVIDENT IN THIS DELECTABLE ITALIAN IMPORT. THE BONUS IS THAT it benefits from being prepared up to one or two days ahead.

YIELD: 6 TO 8 SERVINGS

4 to 6 seasonal ripe tomatoes

3 tablespoons extra-virgin olive oil

2 medium red onions, halved and thinly sliced

2 large garlic cloves, finely chopped

4 red and yellow peppers, cut into ¼-inch-thick slices

2 teaspoons kosher salt

Freshly ground black pepper

To peel the tomatoes, make an X in the rounded end and plunge into boiling water for 30 seconds to 1 minute, depending on their size. Immediately transfer to a bowl of ice water. When cool enough to handle, peel, seed, and slice into wedges; set aside.

Heat the oil in a 12-inch skillet over medium heat. Add the onions and sauté until translucent, 2 to 3 minutes, stirring occasionally. Add the garlic and cook for 30 to 40 seconds. Arrange the peppers in a layer over the onions. Top with the tomato wedges. Do not mix the vegetables. Sprinkle with the salt and the pepper to taste, cover the pan, and simmer for about 20 minutes.

Remove the cover and toss the vegetables gently to mix. Taste to adjust the seasonings if necessary. With a slotted spoon, transfer the vegetables to an ovenproof serving dish and then simmer the liquid in the skillet until slightly thickened. Pour the reduced liquid over the vegetables and serve.

NOTE: You can prepare the dish ahead of time and store in the refrigerator for up to two days. To serve, bring the pepperonata to room temperature. Preheat the oven to 375°F and cook about 10 to 15 minutes to heat through before serving.

POTATOES SAUTÉED WITH SAGE

THESE EASY-TO-PREPARE, "STIR-SAUTÉED" POTATOES GO WELL WITH ALMOST ANY ENTRÉE.

YIELD: 6 TO 8 SERVINGS

2^1/$_2$ pounds new or Yukon
    Gold potatoes

3 tablespoons extra-virgin
    olive oil

10 to 12 fresh sage leaves

1 large garlic clove, peeled

Kosher salt

Freshly ground black pepper

Peel the potatoes and cut them into 1-inch pieces. Pat dry on paper towels.

Heat the olive oil in a large nonstick skillet over medium heat and then add the sage leaves and garlic clove. Sauté for 1^1/$_2$ to 2 minutes. Add the potatoes and toss to coat. Cover, reduce the heat to low, and cook for 18 to 20 minutes. Season with salt to taste and continue to cook the potatoes until tender, about 10 minutes, stirring every 2 to 3 minutes. (Keep the pan covered between stirring.)

To serve, remove and discard the garlic clove. Transfer to a warm serving dish and sprinkle with pepper to taste. Serve immediately.

PAPPARDELLE OF ZUCCHINI AND SUMMER SQUASH

IN SUMMER, ZUCCHINI AND SUMMER SQUASH ARE BEST WHEN THEY ARE NARROW IN SIZE, so select them carefully. The vegetables are shaved with a vegetable peeler into long thin strips to resemble pappardelle pasta.

YIELD: 4 SERVINGS

2 farm-fresh zucchini

1 to 2 farm-fresh summer squash

1/4 cup extra-virgin olive oil

4 slices pancetta (about 1/4 pound), coarsely chopped (optional)

6 garlic cloves, roasted (see page 334), puréed

1/2 cup half-and-half

4 tablespoons grated Parmigiano-Reggiano cheese, divided

Pinch of grated nutmeg

1/2 teaspoon Tabasco sauce

8 fresh basil leaves, torn

Freshly ground black pepper

Scrub the zucchini and summer squash clean and pat dry with paper towels. Using a vegetable peeler, peel the zucchini and squash lengthwise into thin wide slices.

Heat the olive oil in a 12-inch skillet over medium-high heat. Add the pancetta, if using, and sauté until golden and crispy, 3 to 4 minutes. Add the garlic purée and sauté about 30 seconds. Toss in the zucchini and squash and sauté for 2 to 3 minutes. Add the half-and-half with 2 tablespoons of the Parmigiano-Reggiano and toss thoroughly to coat. Season with the nutmeg, Tabasco, and basil and stir to mix. Taste to adjust the seasonings, if necessary.

Transfer to a serving dish, season with the remaining 2 tablespoons Parmigiano-Reggiano and black pepper to taste, and serve.

SANG LEE FARMS
Peconic

IF YOU LOVE TO COOK WITH ASIAN INGREDIENTS, THERE'S NOTHING LIKE COOKING with ones that are available from the source that grows the product. Karen Lee of Sang Lee Farms in Peconic, on the North Fork of Long Island, has created an inspired list of products made with the fresh, seasonal, organic produce that is grown on the farm.

Karen Lee grew up in Boston with an Irish-Catholic upbringing, where food was burnt steak and canned beans. "Maybe that was part of my attraction to the Hamptons where fresh food was so available and so beautiful that it totally inspired me. And it was a combination of marrying a farmer who is producing these beautiful fresh vegetables and his Chinese background with such tremendous respect for food, for cooking the food, for the presentation of food, and for families that gather around the food—I had never been part of that. The whole thing was so memorable that I just became immersed in it," Karen said with enthusiasm.

Fred Lee had not planned to go into the family farming business; circumstances changed when Fred's father took ill and shortly thereafter passed on. Fred's father began growing Asian vegetables in Huntington, Long Island, in the 1940s. (He moved the farm from Huntington to East Moriches in 1964.) He supplied the Chinatown market in Manhattan and eventually sold to other cities along the East Coast from Montreal to Florida and as far west as Chicago. The business was changing, but Fred needed time to sort things out—how he could be responsive to and be involved in the business. The company also had a farm in Florida, and when Fred and Karen were first married, they were going back and forth for several years to take care of both farms.

"When we started a family of our own," said Karen, "we had to make a choice; it was one farm or the other, and the choice was New York. It made more sense since that's where the markets are. . . The business had changed over the years. Originally we were wholesale Chinese producers and only sold to Chinatown markets. In the early 1990s we started to work with wholesale brokers who wanted mesclun, which was coming into its time for the high-end restaurants. And that's when mesclun production began along with an Asian mesclun mix, which includes Chrysanthemum leaf (called tung ho), mizuna, tatsoi, pea shoots, and much more."

Karen started a farm stand in 1998 and began to add to their line of produce. "We decided we would do specialty carrots," said Karen. "From that point on anything new we grew we grew organically, and in 2007 we became formally certified organic by NOFA–NY. We are at a point in time where people are taking more of an interest in local, seasonal organic foods. We hold cooking class demonstrations to teach people how to use the unusual products we grow. We developed a line of prepared foods, such as dressings for our beautiful mesclun; one explosively addictive Asian vinaigrette has really taken off. We make a line of pesto sauces, dips, and soups. We hold a tomato festival dinner every year in mid-August to showcase our forty varieties of heirloom tomatoes."

In the last ten years, Sang Lee Farms went from being 100 percent wholesale to less than 1 percent. They now have a community-supported agriculture program (CSA) in several communities in Brooklyn and farm stands at the farm and three farmers' markets in East Hampton, Westhampton Beach, and Northport. "We are in the right place at the right time," said Karen Lee.

STUFFED ZUCCHINI BLOSSOMS

ORDER THESE PRIZED AND TENDER ZUCCHINI BLOSSOMS FROM YOUR LOCAL FARMER WHEN they are in season. The blossoms are used only when very fresh. You may find them with the tiniest zucchini attached to the blossom. Catapano's chèvre goat cheese adds a special zing to the stuffing.

YIELD: 4 TO 6 SERVINGS

8 fresh zucchini blossoms

1 green or yellow zucchini

$1/4$ pound softened goat cheese chèvre

3 tablespoons fresh basil chiffonade (see note on page 104)

Kosher salt and freshly ground white pepper

1 tablespoon extra-virgin olive oil

Preheat the oven to 375°F.

Open the zucchini blossoms and remove the pistils. If the tiny zucchini is attached to the blossom, slice it lengthwise from below the blossom in thirds so it cooks evenly. Gently wipe the zucchini clean with a damp paper towel; then trim the ends, and grate on the large holes of a box grater. Transfer to a mixing bowl with the goat cheese and basil and season to taste with salt and pepper; stir to mix. With a teaspoon, spoon the filling into each blossom and then gently twist the end of the blossom to enclose the filling. Arrange the blossoms in a buttered shallow baking or serving dish. (The blossoms can be prepared to this point and refrigerated, covered with plastic wrap, for a day. Bring to room temperature before baking.)

Drizzle the stuffed blossoms with the olive oil and bake for 20 minutes. Serve hot or warm.

MARINATED SUMMER VEGETABLES ON THE GRILL

A GRILLED VEGETABLE PLATTER MADE WITH THE BEST SELECTIONS FROM YOUR LOCAL FARM stand is au courant and colorful and can be made ahead and served at room temperature.

YIELD: 6 TO 8 SERVINGS

3 to 4 narrow zucchini and summer squash, rinsed, trimmed, and cut into thirds on the diagonal

2 to 3 red onions, sliced into 1-inch rounds

3 to 4 unpeeled baby eggplants, rinsed and cut in half lengthwise

2 to 3 red or yellow bell peppers, rinsed, seeded, and cut into thirds

6 to 8 whole plum tomatoes, rinsed

FOR THE MARINADE

3 garlic cloves, finely chopped

1 tablespoon white wine vinegar

2 tablespoons freshly squeezed lemon juice

1 tablespoon finely chopped flat-leaf Italian parsley

3 tablespoons fresh basil chiffonade (see note on page 104)

3 tablespoons fresh rosemary leaves

Kosher salt and freshly ground black pepper

$^1/_2$ cup extra-virgin olive oil

Place the zucchini, squash, onions, eggplants, bell peppers, and tomatoes in a large glass or ceramic bowl and set aside.

For the marinade, combine the garlic, vinegar, lemon juice, parsley, basil, rosemary, and salt and pepper to taste in a mixing bowl and stir to mix. Add the oil in a slow steady stream and whisk until the mixture is emulsified. Pour over the vegetables and carefully stir to coat with the marinade. Allow to marinate for several hours or overnight, turning the mixture once or twice.

When ready to cook, preheat a charcoal grill until the coals are a gray ash, 20 to 25 minutes, or preheat a gas grill to medium-high heat for 10 minutes. Arrange the vegetables in a hinged broiling rack or on an oiled mesh grill rack and grill 3 to 4 inches from the source of heat. If using a hinged broiler, grill 8 to 10 minutes on one side and 6 to 8 minutes on other side. If cooking directly on the grill, use long-handled tongs to move the vegetables around as necessary. The total cooking time is 12 to 18 minutes, depending on the vegetable. Brush with marinade several times while grilling. Timing is approximate and should be done to your taste and according to how hot the coals are. Serve warm or at room temperature.

COUSCOUS WITH FRESH ROSEMARY

COUSCOUS CAN BE PURCHASED IN EITHER INSTANT FORM OR ONE THAT REQUIRES LENGTHY cooking. The instant is easier to use and is more consistent.

YIELD: 6 SERVINGS

$1/2$ cup chicken stock, preferably homemade

1 tablespoon finely chopped fresh rosemary leaves

1 red bell pepper, seeded, ribbed, and diced

2 tablespoons unsalted butter

Kosher salt and freshly ground black pepper

2 cups dry couscous

In a saucepan, bring the chicken stock to a boil over high heat and add the rosemary. Add the bell pepper, butter, and salt and pepper to taste. Reduce the heat to medium low and simmer for 10 to 12 minutes.

Add the couscous to the hot broth and return to a boil. Once boiling, remove from the heat and cover pan. Let it rest for 10 to 15 minutes. Fluff with two forks, taste, and adjust the seasoning as necessary. Serve with grilled fish or chicken.

ANGEL HAIR PASTA WITH TOMATO COULIS

TOMATO COULIS IS A BRIEFLY COOKED SAUCE MADE WITH BLANCHED, PEELED, AND SEEDED tomatoes. Fresh seasonal tomatoes can be frozen whole. The peel slips off the tomatoes easily without blanching them when microwaved on high for 20 to 30 seconds.

YIELD: 4 SERVINGS

FOR THE TOMATO COULIS

6 to 8 plum tomatoes

2 tablespoons extra-virgin olive oil

2 shallots, finely chopped

2 garlic cloves, finely chopped

2 tablespoons fresh basil chiffonade (see note on page 104)

2 tablespoons finely chopped flat-leaf Italian parsley

Kosher salt and freshly ground black pepper to taste

FOR THE PASTA

1 pound angel hair pasta

1 to 2 tablespoons kosher salt

Grated Parmigiano-Reggiano (optional)

For the coulis, make an X in the rounded end of the tomatoes and plunge into boiling water for 30 for 40 seconds. Immediately transfer to a bowl of ice water to stop the cooking. When cool enough to handle, peel, seed, and coarsely chop the tomatoes.

In a saucepan, heat the oil over medium heat and sauté the shallots for 1 to 2 minutes until translucent. Add the garlic and sauté for 40 to 50 seconds until tender. Stir in the tomatoes, basil, parsley, and salt and pepper to taste. Simmer for about 5 minutes. Taste to adjust the seasonings if necessary.

Meanwhile, cook the pasta in a large saucepan of boiling water with the salt for 9 to 12 minutes according to the package, or until al dente or firm to the bite. Drain and toss with the tomato mixture. Serve with grated cheese, if desired.

FETTUCCINE WITH RED PEPPER AND HERBS

SEVERAL SUMMERS AGO, I DINED AT GARGA, A TINY RESTAURANT, IN FLORENCE, ITALY. THE chef, barely twenty feet away in his small kitchen, prepared everything to order. The pasta was simply topped with an abundance of fresh herbs and a shower of diced red bell pepper. The flavor was pure summer.

YIELD: 4 TO 5 SERVINGS

8 garlic cloves

3 tablespoons extra-virgin olive oil

3 tablespoons unsalted butter

1 large or 2 medium sweet red bell peppers, rinsed and cut into small dice

1/2 pound shiitake mushrooms, stemmed, rinsed, and sliced

1 cup heavy cream

1 tablespoon kosher salt

1 pound homemade fettuccine (see page 334) or fresh store-bought fettuccine

Freshly ground black pepper

1 cup fresh mint, basil, and sage leaves

1/2 cup grated Parmigiano-Reggiano cheese, plus more for serving (optional)

Poach the whole, unpeeled garlic cloves in simmering water until tender, 10 to 12 minutes. Drain and pat dry with paper towels; then peel and cut in half lengthwise.

Heat the oil with the butter in a 12-inch skillet over medium heat. Add the poached garlic halves and sauté until the butter sizzles. Add the bell peppers and mushrooms and sauté for 4 to 5 minutes. Add the cream and stir to mix.

Meanwhile, bring 4 to 5 quarts of water in a large saucepan to a boil and add the salt. When the water comes to a boil, add the pasta and cover the pot. When the water returns to a boil, cook, uncovered, for 2 to 3 minutes for homemade pasta or 4 to 5 minutes for "fresh" store-bought pasta.

Before draining the pasta, stir 1 ladleful of cooking water into the warm sauce in the skillet. Drain the pasta and add to the skillet. Toss with tongs to mix. Season to taste with salt and pepper. Transfer to a warm serving platter and sprinkle with the fresh herbs and cheese. Serve immediately on warm plates. Pass additional cheese at the table, if desired.

FUSILLI WITH PESTO SAUCE

AS A RULE, I AM NOT A FAN OF COLD PASTA SALADS. I HAVE, HOWEVER, USED THE FOLLOWING pesto recipe with fusilli, a short twisted-shaped pasta that holds the sauce very well. It's a perfect dish for warm weather buffet entertaining.

YIELD: 8 TO 10

FOR THE PESTO

3 cups fresh basil leaves, rinsed and patted dry

2 to 3 garlic cloves, peeled

1/3 cup pine nuts

1/2 teaspoon kosher salt

Freshly ground black pepper

1/2 to 2/3 cup extra-virgin olive oil

1/2 cup freshly grated Parmigiano-Reggiano cheese

2 tablespoons butter, softened

FOR THE PASTA

1 to 2 tablespoons kosher salt

1 pound fusilli pasta

Fresh basil sprigs, for garnish

Wash the basil leaves and gently pat dry. Without crushing the basil, lightly pack into a measuring cup. Set aside.

Put the garlic cloves into the work bowl of a food processor fitted with a steel blade or into a blender and process until finely chopped. Add the basil leaves, pine nuts, salt, and pepper to taste and pulse until the ingredients are combined. Scrape the mixture down the side of the bowl with a rubber spatula as necessary.

With the motor running, add the oil in a thin stream and blend until the mixture is smooth. The pesto can be made ahead to this point. When ready to sauce your pasta, stir in the cheese and butter.

Meanwhile, bring 5 to 6 quarts of water to a boil. Add the salt and pasta. Stir with a fork to separate the pasta and return to a boil. Cook for 9 to 12 minutes, until al dente or firm to the bite. Be careful to not overcook. Just before draining the pasta, add 2 to 3 tablespoons of the cooking water to the pesto to soften and stir to mix.

Drain the pasta and cool under running water. Transfer to a clean kitchen towel and pat dry. Put the pasta in a large serving bowl, add the pesto, and stir to coat. Garnish with sprigs of fresh basil. This dish can be prepared ahead and served at room temperature.

LINGUINE WITH LEEKS, TOMATO, AND MOZZARELLA

AS I VIEW BUNCHES OF LEEKS ON LOCAL FARM STAND SHELVES, THEY HAVE THE LOOK OF A prize-winning vegetable. Team them with tomatoes bursting with sweet summer flavor and marry with locally made fresh mozzarella for an excellent pasta dish.

YIELD: 4 TO 6 SERVINGS

2 large leeks

2 tomatoes

2 tablespoons extra-virgin olive oil, plus more for drizzling

Kosher salt and freshly ground black pepper

1 pound linguine

2 to 3 tablespoons chopped fresh mint

$^3/_4$ cup chopped fresh mozzarella

Remove any bruised outer layers of the leeks. Cut the large green tops of the leeks at an angle, exposing the light green layers underneath. Holding on to the root ends, halve or quarter each leek lengthwise. Rinse away the sand between the layers under running water and then soak in a bowl of cold water for about 15 minutes. Pat the leeks dry with paper towels and slice thin.

Meanwhile, make an X in the rounded end of the tomatoes. Blanch in boiling water for 30 to 40 minutes and then drain. Immediately transfer to a bowl of ice water to stop the cooking. When cool enough to handle, peel, seed, and coarsely chop.

Heat the oil in a skillet over low heat. Sauté the leeks, stirring occasionally, 6 to 8 minutes until tender. Add the chopped tomatoes and stir to mix. Season to taste with salt and pepper and cook for 3 to 4 minutes to blend the flavors. Keep warm.

Meanwhile, bring a large pot of salted water to a boil. Add the pasta, return to a boil, and cook until al dente, 9 to 11 minutes.

Before draining the pasta, add $^1/_4$ cup pasta water to the leek and tomato sauce in the skillet. Drain the pasta and return to the pot. Pour in the sauce and add the mint and mozzarella; toss to mix. Taste and adjust the seasoning as necessary; then serve on warm plates. Drizzle a tiny bit of olive oil over each serving.

BALSAM FARMS
Amagansett

ALEX BALSAM AND IAN CALDER-PIEDMONTE MET AT CORNELL WHEN ALEX studied agriculture and Ian studied philosophy. Ian's grandfather and uncle were dairy farmers in Michigan where he grew up. After college he went abroad for two years. When he returned he connected with Alex, who had started a small boutique farm in Amagansett, leasing land from the Peconic Land Trust and a small farm stand on their property. For Alex it was a seasonal business until Ian came along. When Ian began working on the farm, he realized how much he loved the area, the satisfaction of growing food, the relationships he developed with chefs, and customers and has made a full commitment to the farm.

Calder-Piedmonte doesn't use chemical fertilizers or pesticides. His fertilizers are organically approved and derived from natural sources: composted manure, bone meal, and fish emulsion.

Working primarily with local chefs, Calder-Piedmonte has built a unique business and supplies upscale restaurants such as Della Femina and Nick & Toni's, both in East Hampton. The restaurants and specialty food shops make up a good part of his business, and, most importantly, the farm supplies the Ross School in East Hampton. Founded in 1991, the Ross School is a private co-educational boarding and day school serving more than five hundred students from pre-kindergarten through twelfth grade, and it promotes and prepares only local and organic foods.

Balsam Farms participated in the East Hampton farmers' market initially and today it is represented in four farmers' markets: East Hampton, Bridgehampton, Southampton, and Montauk. The Balsam Farms farm stand is located on the corner of Town Lane and Windmill Lane in Amagansett.

PASTA IN THE MANNER OF PANZANELLA

PANZANELLA IS THE NAME OF A FAMOUS BREAD SALAD MADE WITH TOMATO, BASIL, AND onions. The ingredients are uncooked and served cold over very hot pasta—homemade spaghetti is the traditional cut for this light and fresh summer dish. Giuliano Bugialli, award-wining Italian cookbook author and educator, has been a great influence in my culinary life. This recipe is my tribute to him.

YIELD: 5 TO 6 SERVINGS

1 large red onion, coarsely chopped

1 1/2 pounds ripe fresh tomatoes (not overripe), cut into 1-inch pieces

2 garlic cloves, finely chopped

3/4 cup extra-virgin olive oil

Kosher salt and freshly ground black pepper

1 pound fresh pasta, cut into spaghetti (see page 334)* or 1 pound dried store-bought spaghetti

2 bunches arugula, large stems removed, washed very well and spun dry

20 to 25 large fresh basil leaves, washed very well and gently towel dried

Soak the onion in a bowl of cold water for 20 to 30 minutes. Drain and squeeze out any excess moisture with a clean kitchen towel.

Meanwhile, put the tomatoes in a glass bowl. Place the onions over the tomatoes. Scatter the garlic over the onions and top with the olive oil. Season with salt and pepper to taste. Do not mix. Cover the bowl and refrigerate for 1 hour or longer.

When ready to serve, bring 4 to 5 quarts of water to a rolling boil with 2 tablespoons salt. Add the spaghetti all at once, stirring gently to separate. Cover and return the water to a boil. Cook 30 seconds to 2 minutes for fresh pasta and 9 to 12 minutes for store-bought pasta, until firm to the bite. Drain in a colander, shaking off the excess moisture.

Arrange the arugula and basil leaves on a large platter. Place the hot pasta over the greens. Immediately distribute the cold sauce over the pasta and toss to mix everything together before serving.

* NOTE: If using fresh pasta, prepare according to the recipe on page 334, taking it to the fourth notch; then insert the length of pasta into the taglierini (narrow) cutter for fresh spaghetti.

SPAGHETTI WITH TOMATOES, PARSLEY, AND WINE

USE THE VERY FRESHEST AND SWEETEST TOMATOES FOR BEST RESULTS. I SUBSTITUTED FRESH basil for the parsley one day when preparing this dish in mid-September. It was the height of tomato season and, with basil still abundant in my herb garden, it made an excellent substitution. If it is not growing in your garden, it is in good supply at the farmers' markets this time of the year.

YIELD: 4 TO 6 SERVINGS

2 pounds tomatoes

1 tablespoon kosher salt, plus more to taste

1 pound thin or regular spaghetti

2 garlic cloves, finely chopped

$1/2$ cup extra-virgin olive oil

$3/4$ cup dry white wine

Freshly ground black pepper

3 to 4 tablespoons chopped flat-leaf Italian parsley

Freshly grated Parmigiano-Reggiano cheese, for serving (optional)

Make an X in the rounded end of the tomatoes and plunge into boiling water for 30 for 40 seconds. Immediately transfer to a bowl of water to stop the cooking. When cool enough to handle, peel, seed, and coarsely chop the tomatoes.

Meanwhile, bring a large saucepan of water to a rolling boil and add 1 tablespoon of the salt. Add the spaghetti all at once, stirring to separate the strands. Return the water to a boil and then cook at a brisk simmer for about 8 minutes, until al dente or firm to the bite; drain.

While the spaghetti is cooking, in a 3-quart saucepan over medium heat, sauté the garlic in the oil for 30 to 40 seconds. Add the white wine and bring to a boil. Add the tomatoes, season with salt and pepper to taste, and stir to mix. Reduce the heat to low and simmer for 5 minutes. Add the parsley and stir to mix. Taste and adjust the seasonings if necessary.

To serve, pour the sauce over the spaghetti on a warm serving platter, toss well, and serve immediately on heated plates. Sprinkle with cheese, if desired, and serve hot.

Wine suggestion: Macari Vineyard Sauvignon Blanc

BLUEFISH FRESH FROM THE SEA

WHEN THE BLUES ARE RUNNING AND FRESHNESS IS GUARANTEED, THEY ARE AT THEIR BEST. A bluefish must be dressed as soon as possible after being taken from the waters because it has a high oil content. The tomatoes and onions contain neutralizing acids, which give the fish a milder flavor.

YIELD: 6 SERVINGS

2 (1-pound) bluefish fillets

Kosher salt and freshly ground black pepper

3 to 4 ripe tomatoes, peeled (see note on page 000), seeded, and diced

1/3 pound mushrooms, wiped clean and thinly sliced

2 large shallots, finely chopped

2 to 3 tablespoons chopped fresh tarragon leaves

1 tablespoon lemon juice

1/4 cup dry white wine

1 tablespoon extra-virgin olive oil

Lemon wedges, for garnish (optional)

Preheat the oven to 400°F.

Place the fish, skin side down, on a work surface. Cut away the dark meat that runs down the center of the fillets. Rinse the fillets and pat dry with paper towels.

Lightly grease a baking dish large enough to hold the fillets in one layer. Place the fillets, skin side down, in the dish and sprinkle with salt and pepper to taste.

Mix the tomatoes, mushrooms, shallots, tarragon, lemon juice, and white wine in a bowl and stir to mix. Season with salt and pepper to taste. Spoon the mixture evenly over the fillets. Drizzle with the olive oil. (This can be done up to several hours ahead to this point, if necessary. Cover with plastic wrap, and place in the refrigerator. Bring to room temperature, about 30 minutes before baking.)

Place in the oven and bake for 12 to 15 minutes. Remove the fish from the oven, turn on the broiler, and adjust the rack to 3 to 4 inches from the heat source. Return the fish to the oven and broil about 5 minutes until the fish is opaque. Garnish with lemon wedges, if using, and serve warm or at room temperature.

Wine suggestion: Pellegrini Vineyards Gewurztraminer

STUART'S SEAFOOD MARKET
Montauk

BRUCE SASSO FROM MASSACHUSETTS LOVED TO VACATION IN MONTAUK SO THAT HE could indulge in his favorite sport: fishing. Fishing was his love, and in the early 1980s he got involved with a friend selling fish. It wasn't long after that that he began his wholesale business on the East End of Long Island with just a van and a phone. Charlotte Klein, a political science student from New Jersey, worked at Gosman's fish market in the summer in Montauk, where her parents had a vacation home.

Bruce lived and breathed fish. He literally worked by the sweat of his brow to learn everything he could about the fish business. He had been renting space at Stuart's fish market in Amagansett for his lobster tanks and freezer for the wholesale business he had created. At about the same time, Charlotte moved out to Montauk full time in 1986 to manage Gosman's market for the next ten years. It was sometime in the late '80s that Bruce and Charlotte met, and their meeting was fortuitous. Charlotte loves food, loves to cook, and loves feeding people—going back to her college days. She learned by doing from her stash of cookbooks and cooking magazines. Charlotte and Bruce married in 1993, and in 1997, they bought Stuart's Seafood Market.

Stuart Vorpahl was a fisherman who started the market to sell fresh fish to the locals, and, as a kind of way station for New York City trucks, taking fresh fish for the Fulton Fish Market.

When Bruce and Charlotte bought Stuart's, they had only two trucks and rented warehouse and freezer space. Today they own two retail establishments, Stuarts in Amagansett and Claws on Wheels in East Hampton, and two catering establishments, and sell to local restaurants and other fish markets—all out on the East End of Long Island.

Charlotte keeps their retail store supplied with a side pantry stocking whole grains, extra-virgin olive oils, vinegars, honey, and fine quality breads. Through the season local farm produce from Balsam Farms, artisanal cheeses from Mecox Bay Dairy, and apples from Halsey's Milk Pail are also available. Customers can also pick up crab and fish cakes, clam pies, key-lime pies, and carrot cakes all made in house.

Charlotte is a bubbly front-of-the-house people person, complementing Bruce's behind-the-scenes temperament, busy purchasing fish directly off the boats and working with the restaurants, The Sassos are best friends and partners who love Stuart's and are committed to a tradition of being in a place where the baymen bring in their catch, as they have been doing now for sixty to seventy years.

STUART'S SEAFOOD MARKET'S STOVE-TOP CLAMBAKE

CLAMBAKES ARE AN AMERICAN INSTITUTION THAT CAN BE APPROACHED IN VARIOUS WAYS. From the beach to the backyard, they can be dug into a sand pit, on a barbecue grill over glowing coals, or even on a stove-top. Shaded in hats and high-rubber boots, outfitted with a clam rake and a basket, you are ready to go digging up clams yourself.

For a beach barbecue, you can forage a large pile of driftwood and seaweed along the shore line and select a dozen or more large stones to make a level surface. Pile on the driftwood and make a brisk fire to heat the stones. You can also fire up charcoal in an outdoor barbecue grill, or you can do a stove-top clambake with Stuart's recipe.

YIELD: 6 SERVINGS

16 to 20 new red potatoes, scrubbed and quartered

2 tablespoons salt

6 (1-pound) lobsters

$2^1/_2$ pounds steamers or littleneck clams, scrubbed clean

$2^1/_2$ pounds mussels, debearded and scrubbed clean

6 ears of corn, shucked

Put the potatoes in a saucepan with cold water to cover by at least an inch. Bring to a boil, add salt, and cook the potatoes with the pan partially covered for 6 to 8 minutes. Drain and cut in half.

In a large 20-quart kettle or lobster pot, layer the lobsters, clams, mussels, par-boiled potatoes, and corn in that order.

Pour about 6 inches of water into the kettle; the lobsters don't need to be submerged. Cover the kettle, place over high heat, bring to the edge of a boil. This could take about 20 minutes. Then, adjust the heat to a brisk simmer and cook for another 10 minutes, or until the lobsters have turned red, the clams and mussels have opened, and the potatoes are tender when poked with the tip of a knife. Transfer the contents of the pot to a large serving platter. Remember the lobster forks, bibs, and lots of paper napkins.

FLUKE FILLETS WITH CILANTRO AND LIME

FLUKE, ALSO KNOWN AS SUMMER FLOUNDER, HAS A DESIRABLE MEATY TEXTURE AND IS prevalent in our local waters.

YIELD: 6 SERVINGS

FOR THE CILANTRO-LIME DRESSING

2 to 3 garlic cloves, finely chopped

Juice of 1 lime (about 4 tablespoons)

1/4 cup chopped fresh cilantro

Kosher salt and freshly ground black pepper

1/4 cup extra-virgin olive oil

FOR THE FISH

6 large fluke fillets with skin

2 tablespoons extra-virgin olive oil

Kosher salt and freshly ground black pepper

For the dressing, combine the garlic, lime juice, cilantro, and salt and pepper to taste in a small bowl. Whisk in the olive oil until the mixture is emulsified.

For the fish, preheat the broiler to high. Rinse the fillets and pat dry with paper towels. Place in a baking pan just large enough to hold them in a single layer. Drizzle the olive oil evenly over the fillets and season with salt and pepper to taste. Broil about 3 to 4 inches from the heat for 3 to 4 minutes. Remove from the oven and drizzle two-thirds of the dressing over the fillets. Return to the oven and continue broiling the fish for another 3 to 4 minutes, until springy to the touch. Spoon over the remaining dressing and serve.

NOTE: If you have any leftovers, the fluke is delicious cold the next day.

EAST END CLAM PIE

FROM AN OLD-TIMER CONCERNING CLAM PIES: "IF YOU LIKE POTATOES, ADD MORE POTATOES; if you like onions, add more onions; if you like clams, add more clams." In other words, what you want to put in, put in; what you want to leave out, leave out.

YIELD: 6 TO 8 SERVINGS

2 dozen freshly shucked littleneck clams, halved, broth reserved

3 tablespoons unsalted butter

1 small onion, finely chopped

1 celery rib, finely chopped

2 to 3 Yukon Gold potatoes (about 1 pound), diced

Kosher salt and freshly ground white pepper

$\frac{1}{2}$ cup half-and-half

2 teaspoons fresh thyme leaves

Dash Tabasco sauce

Basic piecrust (see page 337) or pastry for 2-crust pie

Preheat the oven to 425°F.

Halve the clams over a bowl, catching the liquid from the clams in the bowl. Strain the liquid through a cheese cloth–lined strainer and reserve. Set aside.

Melt the butter in a 10 to 12-inch skillet over medium heat. When the butter foam subsides, sauté the onion and celery for about 3 minutes. Add the potatoes and sauté for 2 to 3 minutes longer, stirring occasionally. Add salt and white pepper to taste. Add the half-and-half and the reserved clam liquid. Cook at a brisk simmer for 3 to 4 minutes, until the liquid thickens slightly. Add the clams, thyme leaves, and Tabasco. Taste and adjust the seasonings if necessary. Remove from the heat.

Divide the piecrust dough in half and roll out one of the halves until it is slightly larger than a 9-inch pie dish. Line a pie dish with the pastry and bring the edges up the side of the dish and trim, leaving a slight overhang. Prick the botom of the pastry with a fork in several places. Spoon the clam filling into the pastry. Roll out the remaining half of the dough and lay it over the clams. Crimp the edges and moisten with water. Poke holes in the surface of the pastry and bake for 15 minutes. Reduce the heat to 325°F and bake for about 20 minutes longer. Cut into wedges and serve hot or warm.

TASTE OF THE NORTH FORK

"I MAKE FOOD PRODUCTS," SAID GERRY WOODHOUSE PROUDLY, "WHAT IS characteristic about them is that we use local ingredients in making the products and that they all reflect our seasons here on the North Fork."

"For example, she continued, "I myself am a certified organic grower growing herbs and edible flowers. You might find products such as rugosa rose jelly made from the beach petals of the rose—the color of which is a natural brilliant pink. I grow lavender to infuse local honey for lavender honey. I will use other local growers for my products as well. For Christmas, for instance, we did some wonderful brandied peaches which came from Wickham Fruit Farm in Cutchogue. We also do private label for local chefs, wineries, and farmers. We'll make products using their ingredients—for example I make a chocolate wine sauce and an olive merlot tapenade for one of the vineyards on the South Fork, and an olive pinot noir for a local North Fork vineyard. Farmers will bring us their corn to make a corn relish or beets to pickle or other ingredients to make a variety of vegetable based and a traditional basil pesto which is a value-added item they can sell at their farm stands. . . . Our commercial kitchen is certified so that we are licensed to do organic products for organic growers such as Quail Hill Farm in Amagansett," said Gerry.

Gerry Woodhouse has created a niche market for her boutique style operation in her hands-on 1800 square foot facility in Peconic on the North Fork. Some of the space is being reconfigured so that more equipment and work space can be added since they still do almost everything by hand, including their own labeling and packaging.

There is also a small Taste of the North Fork retail store on Peconic Lane in Peconic. When you get there be sure to pick up a jar of their sweet and spicy pumpkin condiment.

CAFÉ MAX
East Hampton

MAX WEINTRAUB, OWNER OF CAFÉ MAX IN EAST HAMPTON, IS A CHEF IN THE classic tradition. He has set high standards for his kitchen. A peek into the walk-in refrigerator revealed a ten-gallon stock pot filled with aromatic vegetable trimmings: leeks, carrots, and onions, feathery bunches of dill, among others. This is just the first step in making a classic stock to create clear full-flavored broths and stock reductions for sauces that anoint his tasteful food.

Chef Max, a graduate of the Culinary Institute of America in Hyde Park, is a hands-on chef, moving between the stove and window where the food is readied for dining service.

As a small boy Max helped his dad deliver eggs from the family egg farm in New Jersey to local restaurants. When he was twelve he worked at a friend's parent's Neapolitan restaurant, where he stayed through his high school years, eventually becoming assistant chef. After Max graduated from the CIA, he worked with several excellent chefs, including classically trained Charles Granger, who became Max's mentor. Max moved with him to East Hampton to be sous chef at the Maidstone Club, where Max went on to become the executive chef and partner.

Nancy, Max's wife, had a strong interest in wine and accumulated a small library on the subject. She was in charge of the dining room, while Max ran the kitchen. The two fell in love and became partners in life and business. Nancy had a vision to open a restaurant of her own one day. In 1992, they opened Café Max, a fifty-seat restaurant in East Hampton where they reinvented themselves and created a more informal dining experience. Nancy immersed herself in the world of wine, and her diligence earned the restaurant the Award of Excellence from *Wine Spectator* magazine. The year-round restaurant attracts a steady local and summer clientele who come for the quality of the sophisticated food served, the unpretentious and attentive staff, and the cozy warmth of this pristine café with its white tablecloth service. It has been said of Café Max that it is an unHampton experience in the Hamptons.

CAFÉ MAX SCALLOPS PROVENÇAL

TO ENSURE SUCCESS WITH ANY SCALLOP PREPARATION, THE SCALLOPS SHOULD BE VERY DRY before sautéing, and make sure your oil is hot before adding the scallops. Brown them quickly and turn the scallops starting with the first scallop put into the pan.

YIELD: SERVES 6
AS A FIRST COURSE

FOR THE TOMATO SAUCE

8 ripe plum tomatoes, blanched, peeled, and seeded

2 tablespoons extra-virgin olive oil

1 medium red onion, finely chopped

$^1/_2$ teaspoon kosher salt

6 to 8 grinds freshly ground black pepper

$^1/_4$ teaspoon sugar

FOR THE SCALLOPS

$1^1/_2$ to $1^2/_3$ pounds large sea scallops

4 tablespoons canola oil

Kosher salt and freshly ground black pepper

2 tablespoons unsalted butter

2 garlic cloves, finely chopped

2 tablespoons fresh lemon juice

$^1/_2$ cup seasoned Tomato Sauce

1 tablespoon coarsely chopped flat-leaf Italian parsley

2 tablespoons snipped chives

For the tomato sauce, make an X in the rounded end of tomatoes and drop in boiling water, for 30 seconds. Immediately transfer to a bowl of ice water. When cool enough to handle, peel, seed, and coarsely chop the tomatoes.

Heat the oil in a saucepan over medium-low heat. Sauté the onion, stirring occasionally until translucent, 3 to 4 minutes. Add the prepared tomatoes, salt, and pepper and stir to mix. With the pan partially covered, simmer for about 15 minutes, or until tomatoes break down. Add the sugar and stir to mix. This will make about 2 cups of sauce. You will need only $^1/_2$ cup for the recipe. You can refrigerate the rest for up to one week or use for sauces or stews.

For the scallops, remove the side muscle from the scallops and discard. Rinse and then pat dry with a paper towel.

Heat a 12-inch sauté pan over medium heat for 2 to 3 minutes. Add the oil and after few seconds add the scallops; start in the center and then surround with the remaining scallops. Sauté until the scallops are golden brown, 30 to 40 seconds. Season the scallops with salt and pepper. Turn and cook for another 25 to 30 seconds to brown the other side. Transfer the scallops to a side dish one layer deep. Discard the fat in the skillet.

Return the skillet to medium-low heat and add the butter and garlic. Sauté the garlic for about 30 seconds and then stir in the lemon juice, seasoned tomatoes, and parsley. Taste and adjust the seasoning as necessary. Return the scallops to the pan and toss to coat with the sauce. Divide equally among six warm plates, garnish with chives, and serve at once.

MARINATED SWORDFISH AND SHRIMP BROCHETTE

IN THE NORTH ATLANTIC WATERS, SWORDFISH IS AT ITS BEST IN THE MONTHS OF AUGUST and September when the meat is very firm with a distinctive flavor. The brochettes team nicely with Slow Roasted Tomatoes (see page 195) and Couscous with Fresh Rosemary (see page 147).

YIELD: 6 SERVINGS

6 (1 to $1^1/_4$-inch-thick) sword-fish steaks (about $1^1/_2$ pounds)

$1^1/_2$ pounds jumbo shrimp

$^1/_2$ cup canola or corn oil

$^1/_2$ cup extra-virgin olive oil

2 garlic cloves, finely chopped

2 to 3 shallots, finely chopped

3 tablespoons finely chopped flat-leaf Italian parsley

3 tablespoons fresh basil leaves, cut into chiffonade

1 tablespoon fresh thyme leaves

Freshly ground black pepper

To trim the swordfish, remove and discard the skin and most of the red muscle. Cut the swordfish into $1^1/_2$-inch cubes; set aside.

Peel and devein the shrimp; set aside.

Combine the oils in a saucepan with the garlic and shallots and warm for 5 minutes over low heat. Remove from the heat and let sit for 20 to 30 minutes to infuse the garlic flavor. Transfer to a bowl and add the parsley, thyme, and basil and season with freshly ground pepper to taste. Marinate the swordfish and shrimp in three-quarters of this mixture for 1 to 2 hours. Refrigerate lightly covered with a tent of aluminum foil.

Before grilling, soak bamboo skewers in water for at least 20 minutes. Preheat a charcoal grill until the coals are ashen hot or a gas grill on high for 10 minutes; then adjust the heat to medium.

Drain the swordfish and shrimp from the marinade, discarding the marinade. Thread the swordfish and shrimp on skewers. Brush the grill with oil and place the skewers on the grill rack. Cook until the fish is opaque and just cooked through, about 3 minutes per side, turning once. Baste with the remaining marinade during cooking.

STRIPED BASS ON THE GRILL

STRIPED BASS—FLAKY, MILD, AND SWEET—EMERGING FROM THE COLD ATLANTIC OFF OF Montauk never ceases to please. I look forward with delight to the opening of striped bass season, generally around the first of July, as do commercial and sports fishermen. I'm ever grateful to Darryl Scalera, formerly of Bridgehampton, who loves to talk food. She shared this recipe with me over a haircut.

YIELD: 6 SERVINGS

1¹/₂ to 2 pounds center-cut
    striped bass fillets, with
    skin*

1 teaspoon garlic powder

1 teaspoon dried oregano

1 teaspoon kosher salt

1 teaspoon freshly ground
    black pepper

¹/₄ cup freshly squeezed
    lemon juice

¹/₄ cup extra-virgin olive oil

Cut the fillet into six even-sized portions. Rinse and pat dry with paper towels. Place the garlic powder, oregano, salt, and pepper in a small bowl and stir to mix. Rub the mixture generously into the fish on both sides and marinate for 20 to 30 minutes.

Meanwhile, combine the lemon juice and olive oil in a glass measuring cup; set aside.

Preheat a charcoal grill until the coals are ashen hot or a gas grill on high for 10 minutes; then adjust the heat to medium. Oil the grill rack. Place the fish on the prepared hot grill, skin side down, and cook for about 4 minutes. After about 2 minutes of grilling, spoon a quarter of the lemon juice mixture over the fish and continue to cook another 2 minutes. Carefully turn the fish with a metal spatula and cook 3 minutes more until springy to the touch. Spoon a quarter of additional lemon juice mixture over the fish. Continue to cook until the fish is springy to the touch. When done, transfer the fish to a warm platter and pour the remaining lemon juice mixture over the fish. Serve at once.

* NOTE: Center-cut fillets are quite thick and will probably need a little more cooking time on each side. You can also place a tent of foil over the fish to cook through for the last couple of minutes.

SEA BASS EN PAPILOTTE

WHEN THE FISH IS SERVED, THE HOST LEADS THE WAY BY SLITTING OPEN THE PACKAGE containing the fish and aromatics. Fragrant scents waft upwards to the delight of each guest.

YIELD: 6 SERVINGS

6 ($^{1}/_{2}$-pound) skinless sea bass fillets

2 tablespoons unsalted butter, softened and divided

$^{3}/_{4}$ pound sea scallops, side muscle removed, divided

$^{1}/_{4}$ cup dry white wine

2 to 3 ripe tomatoes, diced

$^{1}/_{2}$ teaspoon dried oregano, divided

Kosher salt and freshly ground pepper

2 tablespoons extra-virgin olive oil

6 sprigs fresh rosemary

Egg glaze: 1 egg yolk mixed with 1 teaspoon water

Have the fishmonger gut, scale, bone, and clean the sea bass fillets. Rinse the fish, pat dry with paper towels.

Fold six 16-inch squares of parchment paper in half, each large enough to accommodate the ingredients, and cut off the hard edges to round out the corners. Rub each parchment "package" with butter and place a fish fillet at the crease. Top each with two scallops and divide the wine equally among the packages. Top each fillet with equal amounts of diced tomatoes and then season each package with oregano and salt and pepper to taste. Drizzle equal amounts of olive oil over the top. Place a sprig of rosemary over each fillet and fold over the parchment to enclose packages.

Starting at the fold, overlap the paper, folding back the edges as you continue around. Each fold seals the one before. Brush the parchment with the egg glaze to seal. Repeat with the remaining packages. The packages can be prepared to this point several hours ahead of time and refrigerated on a baking sheet, one layer deep.

When ready to serve, preheat the oven to 375°F. When ready, bake for 12 minutes. Transfer the packages, unopened, to dinner plates. Pass around small kitchen shears and instruct each diner to slit the paper open in a criss-cross fashion from the center to fold back the edges. The food is eaten from inside the paper and not moved onto the plate.

NOTE: This is a perfect dish for entertaining because the filled packages can be prepared several hours before serving.

Wine suggestion: Roanoke Vineyard Chardonnay

CRISPY SOFT-SHELL CRAB SANDWICH IN BRIOCHE

THIS IS A SCRUMPTIOUS AND LOFTY SANDWICH WHEN PILED HIGH WITH LIGHTLY DRESSED greens on sliced brioche. The dressing benefits greatly when made with Catapano's goat cheese yogurt and Bees' Needs honey.

YIELD: 6 SANDWICHES

FOR THE SOFT-SHELL CRABS

6 large soft-shell crabs, cleaned

1/3 cup all-purpose flour

1 tablespoon dried mixed herbs, such as rosemary, thyme, and oregano

Kosher salt and freshly ground black pepper

1 egg, beaten with 2 tablespoons water

1/4 cup extra-virgin olive oil

FOR THE DRESSING

1/2 cup plain yogurt

1 tablespoon whole-grain Dijon mustard

2 teaspoons honey

FOR THE SANDWICHES

6 brioche rolls, halved

2 bunches arugula, washed well and spun dry

For the soft-shell crabs, rinse the crabs and pat dry with paper towels. In a bowl, combine the flour with the mixed herbs. Add salt and pepper to taste and stir to mix. Divide the flour mixture between two plates. Put the egg wash in a medium bowl.

Coat both sides of the crabs in the seasoned flour; then dip in the egg wash and then coat in the seasoned flour again, shaking off the excess.

Heat the oil until hot but not smoking in a nonstick skillet large enough to hold the crabs in one layer. (You may have to do this in two batches.) Cook for 2 to 3 minutes on each side. Set aside on paper towels.

For the dressing, combine the yogurt, mustard, and honey in a bowl and mix well.

For the sandwiches, spread a thin layer of the dressing on each brioche half. Divide the greens evenly among the sandwiches and arrange one crab on the bottom half of each sandwich. Top with the remaining halves of the bread. With a serrated bread knife, cut the sandwiches in half on the diagonal and serve.

FISHBAR ON THE LAKE
Montauk

JENNIFER MEADOWS IS EXECUTIVE CHEF/OWNER OF FISHBAR ON THE LAKE, inside the "Gone Fishing Marina" in Montauk. When you dine at this seaside restaurant, the fish is only hours out of the sea.

When just a teenager, Jennifer seemed to mangle anything she tried to cook in the kitchen. Determined to get it right, this enthusiastic young lady with a competitive edge went on to graduate from Johnson & Wales, in Providence, Rhode Island. Her culinary journey took her to a position as sous chef in San Diego, where she was absorbed with the West Coast sensibility for spa cuisine, and then to Hawaii, where she catered posh weddings held on the beach and used local products, such as taro root, in vegetable and fish dishes, such as *moi*, a delicate, sweet and buttery local fish.

Moving back east she worked at Nora's in Washington, DC, one of the first certified organic restaurants in the country. Jennifer then connected with the Inlet, a restaurant built by the Montauk Inlet Seafood Corporation and owned by a group of fisherman. Jennifer cooked a "test menu" for the restaurant and was hired the next day. At the Inlet she met Daniel Grimm, one of the Inlet owner's sons who tended bar and managed the restaurant. Some months later in 2008, Jennifer and Daniel, now a couple, opened Fishbar.

What makes the Fishbar unique is that Jennifer hand picks the fish off the fishing boats as they come in to dock. She calls their satellite phones before the boats arrive to make sure she's there to make her selections as soon as they show up. As much as she can, she sources produce from local farmers and growers. There are a few dishes that she can't source locally, like shrimp and steak, but customers expect these dishes to be available.

This small, fifty-seat restaurant has a cabana like feel with its sun-yellow canopy-draped ceiling. Its setting is on an inlet between Lake Montauk and the ocean, with a clear view to Star Island. This is a destination to look forward to visiting anytime between early May and into the beautiful autumn months of September and October.

GRILLED PORGY WITH SMOKY TOMATO CHUTNEY

JENNIFER MEADOWS, CHEF AND OWNER OF FISHBAR ON THE LAKE IN MONTAUK, GIVES US porgy, a sweet delicate fish that is perfect for grilling. She offers some good advice on grilling porgy. "Grilling a whole fish can be challenging. To help prevent your fish from sticking to the grill and ruining that beautiful crispy skin, don't try to move it around. Allow the grill to cook off some of the moisture before trying to move it. Take your tongs or spatula and slowly lift up the fish to peek underneath. If you see the skin sticking, give it another minute or two. Also, don't try to grill all the porgies at once! I generally only put two porgies on at a time in order to give the fish the heat and the space it needs for beautiful, crispy grill marks."

YIELD: 4 TO 6 SERVINGS

FOR THE CHUTNEY

4 tablespoons extra-virgin olive oil, divided

1 small white onion, thinly sliced

2 to 3 garlic cloves, thinly sliced

1 small jalapeño, ribbed, seeded, and chopped, about 1 tablespoon (optional)

6 ripe red tomatoes, cut into large dice

$1/3$ cup freshly squeezed orange juice

2 to 3 tablespoons freshly squeezed lime juice

$1/2$ teaspoon cumin (or more to taste)

$1/2$ teaspoon smoked paprika (or more to taste)

Kosher salt and freshly ground black pepper to taste

For the chutney, heat a 10 to 12-inch sauté pan over medium heat. Add 3 tablespoons of the oil. When the oil is hot, add the onion, garlic, and jalapeño, if using, and sauté until lightly golden, for 3 to 4 minutes. Add the tomatoes, orange juice, lime juice, cumin, and smoked paprika and bring to a boil. Reduce the heat to medium low and simmer briskly for 30 to 35 minutes, stirring occasionally to keep the ingredients from sticking to the pan. Most of the liquid will evaporate, and the chutney should be fairly thick. Season with salt and pepper to taste. Remove from the heat and swirl in the butter. If preparing ahead, let cool and refrigerate for several hours or overnight. The chutney can be served at room temperature or reheated to serve warm. Just before serving, garnish with the scallions and parsley.

For the porgy, have your fishmonger gut, scale, and remove the fins from each porgy. Rinse with cold water inside and out and dry thoroughly with paper towels.

When ready to grill, prepare a charcoal grill until the coals are ashen hot or preheat a gas grill to high. Brush the grill grates with oil to prevent the fish from sticking. Score the fish in two or three places on both sides with a sharp knife, being careful not to cut into the flesh. Rub a

2 tablespoons unsalted butter

4 scallions, trimmed, rinsed, and thinly sliced on the bias, for garnish

1/3 cup finely chopped flat-leaf Italian parsley, for garnish

FOR THE PORGY

4 to 6 jumbo porgies (about 1 1/2 pounds each)

Extra-virgin olive oil

Kosher salt and freshly ground black pepper

thin coat of olive oil on the skin and sprinkle both sides and the cavity with salt and pepper. Place the fish on the hottest section of your grill and leave it there for 4 to 5 minutes. Slowly lift the fish with your tongs or spatula, loosening any skin that may be stuck. Flip over and grill 4 to 5 minutes longer. To test for doneness, insert a cardboard match into the thickest part of the fish. The matchstick should go straight down without bending. If it bends, gently place the fish back on the grill for 1 to 2 more minutes, until cooked through. The fish can also be placed in a preheated 375°F oven with olive oil drizzled in the baking pan.

To serve, lift the meat free from the center bone; then remove the bone and discard. Serve the firm white meat with the tomato chutney and a drizzle of olive oil.

"SCUP" is the porgy of northeastern U.S. waters. It can grow up to 5 pounds, but fish of 1 pound are closer to average. Other species of porgy, such as Grassy, Jolthead, and Pacific, are from waters all around the United States.

OVEN-FRIED CHICKEN WITH PANKO BREADCRUMBS

THIS CHICKEN IS PERFECT FOR SUMMER PICNICS AND A SILPAT-LINED BAKING SHEET MAKES FOR easy cleanup. Panko are Japanese breadcrumbs readily available at supermarkets.

YIELD: 6 SERVINGS

1 (3$^1/_2$-pound) chicken, cut into eight pieces

Kosher salt

2 cups buttermilk

1$^1/_2$ cups panko breadcrumbs

1 tablespoon chopped fresh rosemary

1 tablespoon chopped fresh sage

1 teaspoon paprika

Freshly ground black pepper

Trim the chicken of excess fat and remove any pin feathers. Rinse well and pat dry with paper towels. Season with salt to taste. Place the chicken pieces in a bowl and pour the buttermilk over the chicken. Let soak for about 20 minutes.

Meanwhile, season the breadcrumbs with the rosemary, sage, paprika, and salt and pepper to taste; spread on a platter.

Preheat the oven to 450°F.

Lift the chicken, one piece at a time, from the buttermilk and coat both sides with the breadcrumbs. Transfer to a Silpat or parchment paper–lined baking sheet. Bake for 40 to 45 minutes, until the crumbs are golden brown and the chicken is done. Serve warm or at room temperature.

GRILLED CHICKEN WITH WHITE WINE AND SAGE

WHEN I PLANT MY HERB GARDEN EACH SPRING, FRESH LEAFY SAGE IS ALWAYS INCLUDED. Sage gives poultry a robust aromatic flavor and its gray-green leaves make an attractive garnish. This useful herb can be brought inside after the season and kept in a sunny window.

YIELD: 6 TO 8 SERVINGS

2 (3 to 3¼-pound) chickens, cut into eight pieces

2 garlic cloves, finely chopped

5 to 6 fresh sage leaves, stacked, rolled, and thinly sliced

½ cup extra-virgin olive oil

2 teaspoons kosher salt

Freshly ground black pepper to taste

½ cup dry white wine or ⅓ cup fresh lemon juice

Trim the chicken of excess fat and remove any pin feathers. Rinse well and pat dry with paper towels.

In a mixing bowl large enough to hold the chicken, combine the garlic, sage, oil, salt, pepper to taste, and wine or lemon juice. Stir to mix. Add the chicken, coating with the marinade. Cover and marinate in the refrigerator for several hours, turning the pieces from time to time so they are well coated. Remove from the refrigerator and bring to room temperature before grilling.

Preheat a charcoal grill until the coals are ashen hot or a gas grill on high for 10 minutes and then lower the heat to medium high. Oil the grill rack. Place the chicken, skin side down, over the hot coals. Have a squirt bottle of water nearby to douse the flames if there are any flare-ups. Sear the chicken until well browned, 5 to 6 minutes on each side, basting once or twice with the marinade. The dark meat will take 10 to 12 minutes longer to cook than the breast meat. Move the pieces to higher or lower heat levels as necessary. It may be necessary to cover the chicken for a few minutes to be sure the pieces are cooked through to an internal temperature of 160°F. Transfer to a serving platter and serve warm or at room temperature.

Wine suggestion: Macari Vineyards Viognier

GRILLED PORTERHOUSE WITH ROASTED GARLIC BUTTER

FOR STEAK LOVERS, A PORTERHOUSE IS THE STEAK OF CHOICE ON THE GRILL. WHEN teamed with the sweet deliciousness of roasted garlic butter melting into the crusted grilled steak, it gets the taste buds watering.

YIELD: 2 TO 3 SERVINGS

FOR THE GARLIC BUTTER

1 medium garlic head

1/2 pound (2 sticks) unsalted butter, softened

Kosher salt and freshly ground black pepper

FOR THE STEAK

1 (11/4-inch-thick) T-bone steak (about 11/4 pounds)

Kosher salt

1 tablespoon extra-virgin olive oil

A T-BONE STEAK is really two steaks in one. The leg of the T separates the small tenderloin portion from the longer top loin. Most beef die-hards profess that T-bones taste best when grilled.

For the garlic butter, preheat the oven to 400°F. Wrap the garlic head loosely in foil and bake for 45 to 50 minutes, until the garlic cloves feel soft to the touch. Remove from the oven, and when cool enough to handle, squeeze the flesh from each clove of garlic into a bowl. Add the softened butter and salt and pepper to taste and mash with a fork until well blended and smooth. Transfer the mixture to a square of wax paper. Shape the butter into a cylinder on the paper and securely wrap the paper around the log. Close with tape and freeze. When ready to use, slice frozen disks of the butter at serving time. Return the unused portion to the freezer; it will keep for up to one month.

For the steak, heat a charcoal grill until the coals are ashen hot or a gas grill to medium high. While the grill is preheating, generously season the steak on both sides with salt and a drizzle of the olive oil. Put the steak on the hot grill and do not move for at least 5 minutes. Turn and grill the other side for 4 to 5 minutes or until an instant thermometer inserted into the meat registers 125°F for rare, 135°F for medium rare, or 140°F for medium. Do not cook the steak beyond medium or else it will taste like the sole of a shoe. Transfer to a cutting board and allow to rest for about 5 minutes before serving.

Slice the meat and serve on warm plates. Top with the disks of garlic butter and allow the butter to melt into the crusty surface. Enjoy!

MARINATED SKEWERED SAUSAGE ON THE GRILL

A FARMER'S WIFE IN THE UMBRIAN HILL TOWN OF ASSISI, ITALY, PREPARED THIS DISH WHEN I escorted a cooking group there. In the context of the meal, the dish was served as a "*piatta de mezzo*" or a dish in-between. Served in small portions after the pasta course but before the main course, it was both appetizing and delicious. Students have also used the sausages as an outdoor grilled appetizer. The sausages may also be broiled.

YIELD: 4 TO 6 SERVINGS

$1^{1}/_{2}$ to 2 teaspoons fresh rosemary leaves

$1^{1}/_{2}$ to 2 teaspoons fresh sage leaves

$^{1}/_{2}$ teaspoon kosher salt

Freshly ground black pepper

$^{1}/_{4}$ cup extra-virgin olive oil

1 pound Italian sweet sausage, cut into $1^{1}/_{2}$-inch pieces

12 to 15 fresh bay leaves

In a mixing bowl, combine the rosemary, sage, salt, and pepper to taste. Gradually whisk in the olive oil in a thin steady stream. Add the sausage and toss to coat. Let marinate, covered, in the refrigerator for several hours or overnight.

Before grilling, soak bamboo skewers in water for at least 20 minutes.

Thread the sausage pieces onto the skewers alternating with a bay leaf. Arrange on a shallow platter or baking sheet.

Preheat a charcoal grill until the coals are ashen hot or a gas grill to high for 10 minutes and then reduce the heat to medium. Grill the sausage skewers for 8 to 10 minutes on each side. The sausage can also be broiled 4 inches from the source of heat, 3 to 4 minutes on each side. Baste with the marinade while grilling or broiling. Serve warm or at room temperature.

RED WINE MARINATED FLANK STEAK

THIS IS A DELICIOUS MARINATED STEAK, SERVED HOT OFF THE GRILL OR AT ROOM TEMPERATURE. It's total simplicity!

YIELD: 6 SERVINGS

3 cups dry red wine

4 sprigs fresh rosemary

4 sprigs fresh thyme

2 bay leaves

1 small onion, coarsely chopped

4 garlic cloves, coarsely chopped

3 tablespoons extra-virgin olive oil

1 (2-pound) flank steak

Kosher salt and freshly ground black pepper

Combine the wine, rosemary, thyme, bay leaves, onion, garlic, and olive oil in a large shallow baking dish or a large zip-top bag and stir. Add the steak and turn to coat both sides. Cover and refrigerate at least 4 hours or overnight, basting from time to time.

Preheat a charcoal grill until the coals are ashen hot or preheat a gas grill to high for about 10 minutes and then reduce the heat to medium. Oil the grill rack with paper towels. Remove the steak from the marinade and discard the marinade. Season both sides of the steak with salt and pepper. Grill 5 to 6 minutes on each side for medium rare. Transfer to a cutting board and let rest 6 to 8 minutes. Slice against the grain for serving.

Wine suggestion: Wolffer Estate Merlot for cooking; Wolffer Estate Lambardo Merlot for drinking

FAJITAS ON THE GRILL

THE NAME *FAJITA* COMES FROM THE SPANISH WORD *FAJA*. MEANING LITTLE SASH. THIS southwestern specialty, traditionally made with skirt steak, which is shaped like a belt, can be sautéed or grilled. When prepared in a similar manner, boneless, skinless chicken breasts and portobello mushrooms are equally delicious variations. Whichever you choose, fajitas are tasty, easy, and quick to prepare. Choose them all for a southwestern summer barbecue party!

YIELD: 6 TO 8 SERVINGS

3 to 4 pounds skirt steak, trimmed

3 garlic cloves, finely chopped

2 to 3 tablespoons chopped fresh cilantro

1 jalapeño, seeded and finely chopped

$^1/_3$ to $^1/_2$ cup freshly squeezed lime juice

1 teaspoon ground cumin

$^1/_4$ cup extra-virgin olive oil

Kosher salt and freshly ground black pepper

FOR SERVING

Large flour tortillas

Sautéed peppers and onions (recipe follows)

Tomatillo salsa (recipe follows)

Place the steak in a glass baking dish or a zip-top bag.

Combine the garlic, cilantro, jalapeño, lime juice, cumin, olive oil, and salt and pepper to taste in a mixing bowl and stir to mix until thoroughly incorporated. Pour the marinade over the steaks and let marinate, covered, in the refrigerator for several hours or overnight, turning occasionally.

Preheat a charcoal grill until the coals are ashen hot or a gas grill on high for 10 minutes and then reduce the heat to medium. Oil the grill rack with paper towels. Remove the steak from the marinade, reserving the marinade. Pat the steak dry with paper towels and place on the grill about three inches from the source of heat. Grill, turning once or twice, basting with the reserved marinade until the steak is well seared on the outside and rare on the inside and springy to the touch, 3 to 4 minutes on each side. Transfer to a cutting board and let the steak rest for 8 to 10 minutes.

To serve, slice the steak thinly on the diagonal. Fill the tortillas with sliced steak, grilled mushrooms, sautéed peppers and onions, and a dollop of tomatillo salsa. Roll up and enjoy.

VARIATION: For chicken fajitas, use 3 to 4 pounds boneless, skinless chicken breasts and marinate in the refrigerator for a couple of hours. Bring to room temperature and grill about 3 minutes on each side or until springy to the touch.

VARIATION: For grilled portobello fajitas, use 3 to 4

large, smooth portobello mushrooms. Remove the stems flush with the gills (use stems for a stock or discard). Rinse quickly under running water and wipe dry with a paper towel. Score the caps and the stubby cut surface of the stems and marinate for an hour or so. Grill for 3 to 4 minutes on each side until tender. Press down occasionally, with a flat spatula, as mushrooms grill to hold in the juices.

SAUTÉED PEPPERS AND ONIONS

2 tablespoons extra-virgin olive oil

2 large red onions, peeled and thinly sliced

2 red bell peppers, cored, deseeded, and thinly sliced

Kosher salt and freshly ground pepper

Warm the oil in a large skillet over medium heat and add the onions and peppers. Toss to coat in the oil and sauté for 3 to 4 minutes. Season with salt and pepper to taste. Cover the skillet, reduce the heat to low, and cook, stirring occasionally to redistribute the vegetables, for 5 to 6 minutes longer or until tender. Keep warm for serving.

TOMATILLO SALSA

TOMATILLO, KNOWN AS A MEXICAN GREEN TOMATO, IS A berry and not a tomato at all. Use it to make this tangy salsa.

3 tomatillos, papery outer skin removed

$1/2$ small red onion, finely chopped

2 garlic cloves, finely chopped

1 small zucchini, sliced and diced

1 jalapeño, seeded and finely diced

1 tablespoon extra-virgin olive oil

1 tablespoon rice wine vinegar

Kosher salt and freshly ground pepper to taste

Pour boiling water over tomatillos, dry, and coarsely chop. Soak onions in bowl of cold water for 15 minutes, drain and squeeze dry in a clean kitchen towel. Combine tomatillo and onion with remaining ingredients and season to taste with salt and pepper. Prepare up to one day ahead, refrigerate, covered, and bring to room temperature before serving.

MIXED BERRY MASCARPONE TRIFLE

JUST LAYER FRESH BERRIES THAT ARE IN SEASON IN A PRETTY GLASS DISH AND ENJOY THIS amazingly simple trifle!

YIELDS: 6 SERVINGS

$2^1/_2$ pints fresh mixed berries, such as raspberries, blackberries, and blueberries

$^1/_2$ cup superfine sugar

Pinch of salt and freshly ground black pepper

2 (8-ounce) containers mascarpone cheese

1 to 2 tablespoons framboise (raspberry liqueur)

6 to 8 prepared biscotti, depending on size, broken into coarse chunks

Mint leaves, for garnish (optional)

Rinse the berries in a colander and drain for several minutes. Transfer the berries to a mixing bowl and sprinkle with the sugar, salt, and pepper. With a rubber spatula, stir gently to mix, being careful not to bruise the berries. Marinate 10 to 15 minutes.

Place the mascarpone in a separate bowl and stir to soften. Add the framboise and mix until thoroughly blended. Set aside.

Place half the biscotti chunks on the bottom of a glass serving bowl or trifle dish. Spoon half the berries over the biscotti. Spread a layer of half the spiked mascarpone over the berries. Continue with another layer of the remaining biscotti, the remaining berries, and the remaining mascarpone. Sprinkle any leftover biscotti crumbs on top. Refrigerate, covered, for up to three hours until ready to serve. Garnish with fresh mint leaves before serving, if desired.

OYSTER POND FARM
Orient

IT WAS UNIQUE FOR RON APOSTLE AND HIS SON-IN-LAW TOM STEVENSON ALONG with their wives, Linda Apostle and Jill Stevenson, to move out to Orient, about three miles from Orient Point and almost the tip of the North Fork, to grow berries. They are the proprietors of Oyster Pond Farm in Orient.

The Apostles and the Stevensons are newcomers to the area. Tom is from New Jersey and studied viticulture at the University of California at Davis. He met Jill in New Jersey where her parents, Ron and Linda, were industry executives in the corporate world. When Tom returned from the West Coast in the late '90s, they were a couple then and settled on the North Fork, where Tom worked as a vineyard manager for one of the wineries.

When Ron and Linda retired in 2000, they knew nothing about farming but decided they wanted to be closer to their daughter and son-in-law. "We scoured the North Fork in the winter of 2001 looking for the right property," said Ron. "Jill, Tom, and I came out to walk the property. There was good soil for what we wanted to do, which after much deliberation is to grow a specialty fruit." They grow berries in what is called a permanent greenhouse, which gives them three seasons of protection.

"We grow strawberries, four kinds of raspberries and black berries," Tom said. They plant their strawberries in individual pots stacked six feet high in the greenhouse. When they're ready to be moved outside, they cover the entire orchard with black woven landscape fabric to control the weeds and temperature and to conserve moisture. Tom and Ron talked a great deal about the soil, about how they have to test it regularly to test the nutrients and pH levels. They use only sustainable methods and neutralize the soil with lime if it is too acidic. Tom and his brother run production; Ron is in sales; Linda and Jill deliver to local high-end restaurants and they make the jam from the fresh fruit to sell at their farm stand. "Whatever we sell is produced right here," said Tom. "Our thing is what you get from us is picked that day. The second day, if any fruit is left over it goes into making the jam. We're trying to do the very best quality—no matter who you are or what you're growing you've got to be looking at the quality level. That's where we believe the future is."

FOURTH OF JULY BLUEBERRY PIE

THIS IS A PERFECT NO-BAKE ALL-AMERICAN DESSERT FOR SERVING ON THE FOURTH OF JULY.

YIELD: 1 (9-INCH) PIE

$^2/_3$ cup granulated sugar

1 cup water

1 teaspoon grated lemon zest

2 tablespoons cornstarch

2 pints fresh blueberries, washed and well drained, divided

1 (9-inch) Basic Pate Brisée piecrust (see page 337)

1 cup heavy cream (optional)

2 teaspoons confectioners' sugar

Combine the sugar and water in an enamel or stainless saucepan and bring to a boil, stirring to dissolve the sugar. Add the lemon zest and cook at a brisk simmer for 15 minutes. Place the cornstarch in a small bowl and add 2 tablespoons of the simmering liquid. Stir to dissolve. Return to the saucepan. Add 1 cup of the blueberries and cook for 5 to 8 minutes, until the mixture is thick and glossy, stirring frequently to prevent the mixture to burn at the bottom of the pot. Transfer the sauce to a bowl to cool.

With a large rubber spatula, gently fold the cooled sauce into the remaining 3 cups of berries. The pie filling can be prepared ahead up to this point. Refrigerate, covered, with a tent of plastic wrap.

Preheat oven to 375°F.

Roll out pie dough on a lightly floured board to 10 inches in diameter and transfer to a glass (Pyrex) pie plate. Drape the dough into the plate to fit evenly around. Crimp the edges with a pastry crimper. Make indentations along the bottom of the dough with a fork. Refrigerate for 20 to 30 minutes to firm. Place a large square of parchment paper or foil over the pie shell and fill with pastry weights. Bake blind for 15 minutes. Remove the weights and parchment paper or foil. Return to the oven and bake for 8 minutes longer, until crust is lightly browned and crisp. Let cool and then spoon the filling into the prebaked crust. The pastry shell can be filled up to a day ahead and refrigerated, loosely covered, until ready to serve.

Whip the cream in a cold mixing bowl with cold beaters until it begins to thicken and then beat in the confectioners' sugar until the cream is stiff enough to form firm peaks. Serve slices of the pie with a dollop of whipped cream.

PEACH AND BERRY BAKE

BLESSED WITH AN ABUNDANCE OF LOCAL PEACHES IN LATE SUMMER, DON'T MISS THE opportunity to prepare this simple but sophisticated treat.

YIELD: 8 TO 10 SERVINGS

$^2/_3$ cup sugar

$^1/_2$ cup dry white wine

$^1/_4$ cup cold water

2 or 3 strips orange zest

$^1/_8$ teaspoon ground
   cinnamon

1 teaspoon vanilla extract

6 large ripe but firm
   peaches, preferably
   freestone

1 cup blueberries or
   blackberries

Vanilla ice cream or
   frozen yogurt

Preheat the oven to 375°F.

Combine the sugar, wine, water, and orange zest in a saucepan and bring to a boil. Adjust the heat to medium low and simmer briskly for 5 to 6 minutes, until syrupy. Remove from the heat and stir in the cinnamon and vanilla.

Meanwhile, rinse, halve, pit, and quarter the peaches and arrange cut side up, one layer deep, in a large oven-proof serving dish. Pour the syrup over the peaches and bake for 35 to 45 minutes, depending on the ripeness of the peaches. Scatter the berries over the peaches about 10 minutes before the peaches are done. Remove from the oven and baste with the pan juices several times while still warm. The peaches will look a bit caramelized when done. Serve warm with a scoop of ice cream or yogurt.

NOTE: I prefer to use freestone peaches for this recipe. The flesh of clingstone peaches is too firm for baking to tender juiciness.

Wine suggestion: Wolffer Estate Diosa Late Harvest chardonnay (ice wine)

CATAPANO DAIRY FARM
Mattituck

CATAPANO DAIRY FARM IS A SMALL FARM WITH A HERD OF EIGHTY-EIGHT GOATS, located on the North Fork of Long Island right in the heart of Long Island's wine country. Karen Catapano co-founded the Goat Cheese Dairy Farm in Mattituck, with her husband, Dr. Michael Catapano, in 2003. Dr. Catapano, whose specialty is "urgent care," was drawn to the land with his medical background and scientific understanding of the chemistry for artisanal cheese making.

Karen, a former nurse and avid horse rider, grew up with horses, dogs, cats, and just about every animal imaginable. After her son went off to Iraq in January 2003 and with the loss of a job that she dearly loved because of a hospital default, Karen was ready for a change. Her husband's family knew of a small one-acre goat farm with just eighteen goats that was for sale on the North Fork, where Dr. Catapano's family lived. Karen and her husband bought the dilapidated farm in March of 2003. With her son away and accustomed to taking care of people, being able to care for the neglected goats and to begin anew with the dairy farm gave Karen renewed purpose.

The Catapanos organically grow alfalfa on a farm exclusively for their goats in upstate New York. They even hired a goat nutritionist from Cornell to balance the nuances of nutrition to achieve maximum production from the goats while maintaining their health. Karen has found her passion in the dairy goat farm, and today, her son, who served admirably in Iraq and was officially discharged, works with her at the farm.

Karen and Michael entered the American Cheese Society's annual competition in Louisville in 2005. To their joy, their soft, fresh chévre won first place in the goat competition category. The thought process, the care, the feed, and their immaculate work conditions won them the competition.

The Catapanos' award-winning and popular chèvre varieties include garlic, fresh herb, and lemon-pepper. The Capatanos begin production of their goat cheese feta and light and lemony goat milk yogurt in late April. In May they begin producing their whole milk ricotta, a new favorite among local chefs.

CHÈVRE GOAT CHEESE CAKE WITH BERRY SYRUP

THE SUCCULENT TASTE OF BLACKBERRIES, THE SWEET CRUNCH OF BLUEBERRIES, AND THE mild tartness of raspberries give this unique cake, made with tangy Catapano chèvre goat cheese, a sweet finish.

YIELD: 8 SERVINGS

FOR THE CAKE

$4^1/2$ ounces fresh chèvre goat cheese, softened

8 ounces low-fat softened cream cheese

1 cup crème fraîche (see page 338)

$^3/4$ cup granulated sugar, plus extra for dusting

Zest of 1 lemon

1 tablespoon freshly squeezed lemon juice

1 teaspoon vanilla extract

4 large eggs

$^1/4$ cup cornstarch

FOR THE BERRY SYRUP

$^1/2$ cup sugar

1 cup cold water

2 teaspoons freshly squeezed lemon juice

3 cups mixed berries (such as blueberries, blackberries, and raspberries)

Confectioners' sugar, for dusting

For the cake, Preheat the oven to 350°F. Grease a 10 x 2-inch round cake pan with butter and dust with granulated sugar.

In a mixing bowl, combine the goat cheese, cream cheese, crème fraîche, granulated sugar, lemon zest, lemon juice, and vanilla. Using an electric mixer, beat at medium speed until smooth. Beat in the eggs, one at time, incorporating them completely before adding the next one. Beat in the cornstarch at low speed.

Spoon the batter into the prepared pan and bake for 35 to 40 minutes, or until a skewer inserted in the center of the cake comes out clean. Transfer to a wire rack to cool completely. The cake can be made up to one day ahead to this point, refrigerated, suitably wrapped.

For the syrup, combine the sugar, water, and lemon juice in a saucepan and bring to a boil over high heat. Stir to dissolve the sugar, reduce the heat to medium low, and cook at a brisk simmer for 10 to 12 minutes until it is a syrupy consistency; do not let the syrup color. Add the berries and return the mixture to a boil. Reduce the heat to medium and cook at a brisk simmer for 8 to 10 minutes, stirring frequently. Watch carefully that the berry mixture does not boil over. Pour into a pitcher. Cover with plastic wrap and refrigerate until ready to serve.

To serve, dust the top of the cake with confectioners' sugar. Cut into wedges and pour berries over the cake wedges.

CHERRY CLAFOUTIS

THIS TYPICAL FRENCH HOUSEWIVES FRUIT CAKE MADE WITH LOCAL CHERRIES (OR BERRIES) IS light, sweet, and delicious—and perfect for summer entertaining.

YIELD: 6 TO 8 SERVINGS

2 cups cherries or local raspberries and/or blueberries

3 tablespoons Kirsch

3 large eggs

1 cup half-and-half

1/3 cup granulated sugar

1 teaspoon lemon zest

Pinch of salt

1/2 teaspoon vanilla extract

1/3 cup all-purpose flour

Confectioners' sugar, for dusting

With a cherry pitter or a paring knife, remove the pits from the cherries. Place in a bowl with the Kirsch and macerate about 30 minutes. If using berries, rinse under cold water and drain, shaking to remove the excess water, before macerating.

Preheat the oven to 350°F.

In a separate mixing bowl, beat the eggs with the half-and-half until frothy. Add the sugar, lemon zest, salt, vanilla, and flour and mix well.

Pour about half the batter into a 2-quart well-buttered glass or porcelain "quiche" baking dish. Arrange the cherries or berries in a single layer over the batter and then pour the remaining batter over the berries. Place on the middle rack of the oven and bake for 40 to 45 minutes or until puffed and golden brown or when a knife inserted in the center comes out clean. Sprinkle confectioners' sugar through a sieve over the top and serve warm or at room temperature.

THIS RECIPE IS A perfect "taste of the Hamptons." Made with local ingredients, such as Iacona or North Sea Farms fresh eggs and Wickham Farms cherries or Oyster Pond Farms plump sweet berries, this French custard classic is tailor-made.

Savoring the Hamptons in
AUTUMN

M ost East Enders concur, "fall is the best time of the year in the Hamptons." For the locals, highways, streets, shops, and restaurants have been joyfully reclaimed. With a nip in the air and cooler days ahead there may be a touch of melancholy for the "fun in the sun" of summer is coming to an end, yet the farm stands are still vibrant, with autumn the most colorful of seasons.

The seasons project the way we think about food. They almost demand change. Autumn arrives with a new palette of colors and flavors. The late varieties of corn, tomatoes, leek, eggplant, and zucchini and the gorgeous hues of winter squash inspire a more robust and comforting style of cooking that includes warm soups, vegetable casseroles, simmering stews, and the sumptuous aromas of home baking.

Locals and visitors alike participate in apple picking at farms on the North and South Forks and the child-oriented adventures in a vast and colorful field of bright orange pumpkins at the area's pumpkin patch on the main road in Southampton.

Here on the East End, we have "true" free-range poultry and turkeys. It is where locals and weekenders pick up healthy, wholesome chickens and the freshest eggs through the year at Iacono Farm in East Hampton and Kings Farm in Southampton. Ludlow's turkey farm in Bridgehampton and Kings North Sea Farm in Southampton are decidedly busy places just before Thanksgiving.

Autumn is in the air, and the sun slips a little earlier each evening as it peeks over the trees, and the supply of the very best tomatoes will soon end for another year.

PORCINI AND WILD MUSHROOM PÂTÉ

THE ORIGINAL VERSION OF THIS MUSHROOM PÂTÉ PREPARED WITH FRESH PORCINI MUSH-
rooms was served to me at Carl Villa's home in Fiesole, Italy. Carl Villa was a close family friend who
shared his sense of great food. Dried porcini mixed with local "wild" mushrooms make a fine replica.
Here's to you, Carl!

YIELD: 10 TO 12 SERVINGS

2 ounces dried porcini
  mushrooms

$^1/_2$ pound shiitake
  mushrooms

$^1/_2$ pound oyster mushrooms

$^1/_2$ pound white button
  mushrooms

3 tablespoons extra-virgin
  olive oil

$^1/_4$ cup chopped scallions

2 garlic cloves, minced

$^1/_4$ cup finely chopped flat-
  leaf Italian parsley

1 teaspoon fresh snipped
  chives

2 teaspoons fresh marjoram
  leaves

1 to 2 teaspoons kosher salt

Freshly ground pepper

5 to 6 tablespoons unsalted
  butter, softened

$^1/_2$ cup chicken stock
  (see page 335) or low-
  sodium canned

1 ($^1/_4$-ounce) envelope
  unflavored gelatin

Chives or blanched scallion
  greens, for decoration
  (optional)

Soak the porcini mushrooms in a small bowl of enough
warm water to barely cover for 15 to 20 minutes. Place the
porcini mushrooms in a clean bowl, reserving the liquid.
Strain the reserved liquid through a fine sieve lined with
cheesecloth into a small bowl. Repeat this procedure back
and forth three or four times, discarding the sandy
residue left in the strainer each time. Reserve the concentrated mushroom liquid.

Place the shiitake, oyster, and button mushrooms in a
colander and rinse quickly under a spray of cool water.
Transfer to a clean kitchen towel and pat dry. Cut into $^1/_2$-
inch-wide slices.

Heat the oil in a 12-inch skillet over medium heat. Add
the scallions and sauté for 2 to 3 minutes. Add the garlic
and sauté 30 to 40 seconds without browning. Add the
mushrooms, parsley, chives, marjoram, salt, and pepper
to taste. Cook, stirring, for 2 to 3 minutes. Add $^1/_2$ cup of
the reserved porcini liquid and cover the pan. Simmer
for about 10 minutes. Remove the cover and cook, stirring occasionally, for about 5 minutes longer until the
moisture evaporates. Allow to cool; then transfer the
mixture to the work bowl of a food processor fitted with
the steel blade. Add the softened butter and pulse to a
coarse textured purée. Using a rubber spatula, transfer
the mixture to a ceramic pâté dish or loaf pan and
smooth over the top.

Heat the stock in a small saucepan over medium heat
and stir in the gelatin. Remove from the heat and let stand

for a few minutes until the liquid is absorbed by the gelatin. Do not stir. Return the pan to low heat and move the pan gently back and forth over the heat until the mixture is liquid again. Pour half the mixture over the top of the pâté. Create an artistic design with the chives or scallions, if desired, and pour over the remaining gelatin. Cover and refrigerate for up to two days. Bring to room temperature for serving. Serve with crostini (see page 99) or crackers of your choice.

SLOW ROASTED TOMATOES
WITH THYME AND GARLIC CONFIT

USE THIS TASTY AND COLORFUL ACCOMPANIMENT FOR APPETIZERS OR ENTRÉES.

YIELD: 6 TO 8 SERVINGS

FOR THE TOMATOES

20 ripe plum tomatoes (about 3 pounds)

2 to 3 tablespoons extra-virgin olive oil

1 tablespoon fresh thyme leaves

Kosher salt and freshly ground black pepper

FOR THE GARLIC CONFIT

1 cup peeled garlic cloves (about 25)

$1/2$ cup vegetable oil

Pinch of salt

Preheat the oven to 250°F. Line a baking sheet with parchment paper.

For the tomatoes, rinse the tomatoes and pat dry with paper towels. Cut the tomatoes in half lengthwise and place cut side up on the prepared baking sheet. Brush the tops with the olive oil and sprinkle with the thyme and salt and pepper to taste. Roast the tomatoes for 2 to $2^1/2$ hours.

Meanwhile, prepare the garlic confit. Place the garlic cloves in a small heavy saucepan. Pour enough oil over the garlic to barely cover and season with the salt. Simmer gently over medium heat for 30 minutes or until the garlic is very soft. Transfer the garlic with a slotted spoon to a bowl and mash to a fine purée.

Both the roasted tomatoes and the garlic confit can be prepared ahead of time and refrigerated in separate containers. Bring to room temperature and spread the garlic confit on the tomatoes before serving.

ARTISANAL CHEESE MAKER

THE WHITE WALLS AND CEILING ARE IMPERMEABLE SURFACES. ALL THE EQUIPMENT is sanitized so that bacterium doesn't grow. This is where the slender, boyish looking, and prematurely white-haired cheese maker Arthur Ludlow, in his long white apron and high white rubber boots, prepares his hands-on artisanal cheeses with passion.

Cheese always has been made in livestock-rearing countries to use up surplus milk. That is exactly what turned "Art" Ludlow into a professional cheese maker. Since 2003 Art, his wife, Stacy, and sons, Peter and John, have produced farmstead cheeses from their small herd of Jersey cows at their Mecox Bay Dairy farm in Bridgehampton. It all began with Stacy's lone cow, and there was just so much milk the family could drink. Potato farming had been the Ludlow family business for one hundred years, but Art broke from tradition when he decided to learn as much as he could about cheese making.

Art Ludlow prepares his cheeses twice a week through the year. He begins by adding a freeze-dried bacterial culture to the curd to convert the lactose, which is a milk sugar and the only sugar in milk, to lactic acid. The conversion can happen rapidly, but the process will go on for awhile. He uses two large vats for production: one that has a huge balloon whisk and another that requires hand stirring, and the curd must be stirred for a lengthy period of time. When the cheese is ready, he drains the whey into a slanted stainless table. Taking a break from stirring the curd, he skims the surface and scoops up the resulting butter, which he uses at home.

East End cheese retailers praise Art Ludlow's Atlantic Mist, a raw milk Camembert-style cheese packaged in the round. His Shawondasee, a semi-hard cheese with a protective natural rind and subtle flavors, pairs nicely with fruit, and Mecox sunrise, a washed-rind semi-hard cheese, aged two to four months, was awarded second place in its category in a 2004 American cheese competition. This semi-soft textured cheese with a pungent flavor makes a fine addition to a diverse cheese plate. In honor of, and named for his mother, Sigit, Art created a British-style Gruyère. The cheese is all at once sweet, delicate, full flavored, and nutty.

Art Ludlow surely gets into his cheese making, tasting as he cuts into his ripening cheeses—always looking for efficiency and quality as an artisanal hands-on cheese maker.

MECOX BAY GRUYÈRE GOUGÈRE

A GOUGÈRE IS A CLASSIC PÂTÉ CHOUX PASTRY DOUGH SIMPLY MADE IN A SAUCEPAN. GRUYÈRE cheese is a classic component for this savory hors d'oeuvre. I use Mecox Bay Dairy's Sigit, a Gruyère-like cheese, for an uncommonly delicious gougère.

YIELD: ABOUT 5 DOZEN PUFFS, OR 20 APPETIZER SERVINGS

1 cup water

¼ pound (1 stick) unsalted butter

1 cup all-purpose flour

4 large eggs

1½ cups coarsely grated Gruyère cheese

½ to 1 teaspoon kosher salt

2 teaspoons Dijon mustard

1 to 2 dashes of cayenne pepper

1 tablespoon chopped flat-leaf Italian parsley

1 tablespoon snipped fresh chives

Preheat the oven to 400°F.

In a heavy saucepan, combine the water and butter and bring to a boil over high heat. Reduce the heat to medium and add the flour, stirring vigorously with a wooden spoon until the dough forms into a ball. Continue to cook, stirring for 1 minute to dry the dough a bit. Remove from the heat and cool. Transfer the dough to a mixing bowl.

Add the eggs, one at a time, beating well after each addition. Add the cheese, salt, mustard, cayenne, parsley, and chives and stir until thoroughly combined.

Drop heaping teaspoons of the dough 1 inch apart onto a Silpat or parchment paper–lined baking sheet. Bake for 20 to 25 minutes until crisp and golden brown. Use two baking sheets, as it will be necessary to bake these puffs in batches. The gougères can be prepared up to one day ahead, or you can freeze them for later use. When ready to serve, thaw and reheat them in a 375°F oven for about 5 minutes.

MARINATED BRUSSELS SPROUTS

THE SECRET TO GREAT TASTING BRUSSELS SPROUTS IS TO BUY THEM FARM FRESH AND NOT overcook them. This piquant hors d'oeuvre can be prepared a couple of weeks before serving and would be a perfect appetizer for Thanksgiving.

YIELD: 6 TO 8 SERVINGS

1 branch Brussels sprouts (about 2 pints)

3 to 4 shallots, finely chopped

1 large garlic clove, finely chopped

2 teaspoons fresh tarragon leaves

1 teaspoon kosher salt

Freshly ground black pepper

$\frac{1}{2}$ cup tarragon vinegar

$\frac{1}{4}$ cup canola oil

$1\frac{1}{2}$ teaspoons whole-grain Dijon mustard

Pull the Brussels sprouts from their spiraled branch and thoroughly rinse. Trim the stem ends and remove and discard any discolored outer leaves. Cut a shallow X in the stem end and soak in salted water for 15 minutes; drain.

In a large saucepan, cook the Brussels sprouts in enough boiling salted water to cover for 15 to 18 minutes or until tender. Drain and rinse in cold water. Pat dry with a clean kitchen towel and set aside.

In a noncorrosive (stainless or enamel) saucepan, combine the shallots, garlic, tarragon, salt, pepper to taste, vinegar, and oil. Stir to mix and bring to a boil. Reduce the heat to medium low and gently simmer, partially covered, for 10 minutes. Remove from the heat, stir in the mustard, and let cool until room temperature.

Place the Brussels sprouts in a glass or ceramic mixing bowl. Pour over the marinade and gently stir to coat. Transfer to a suitable storage container and refrigerate for up to three weeks. Serve at room temperature.

PURÉE OF FENNEL SOUP

CRISP, WHITE BULBS OF FENNEL SPORTING FLUFFY GREEN FRONDS ARE AVAILABLE AT LOCAL FARMS in the fall and late spring. Fennel gives body, texture, and a haunting flavor to this seasonal soup.

YIELD: 6 TO 8 SERVINGS

2 fennel bulbs (about 1 pound each)

2 tablespoons unsalted butter

2 medium onions, thinly sliced

2 boiling potatoes (Yukon Gold or red potatoes), sliced thin

1 tablespoon freshly squeezed lemon juice

5$\frac{1}{2}$ to 6 cups chicken stock (see page 335) or low-sodium canned

Kosher salt and freshly ground black pepper to taste

1 tablespoon Pernod

6 to 8 fennel fronds, for garnish (optional)

Remove the tops of the fennel at the bulb. The fronds may be set aside and used for garnish. Remove and discard the tough or bruised outer leaves. Cut off and discard the base. Cut the bulb in thin, even vertical slices. Place in a bowl of cold water to soak for 10 to 15 minutes. Drain and pat dry with paper towels.

In a large saucepan, melt the butter over medium heat. When the foam subsides, add the onions, fennel, and potatoes and toss to coat. Press a square of wax paper over the vegetables and cover the pot. Sweat the vegetables 7 to 8 minutes over low heat. Remove the cover and discard the wax paper. Add the lemon juice, stock, and salt and pepper to taste and stir to mix. Bring to a boil over medium-high and then reduce the heat to low and simmer, partially covered, for 35 to 40 minutes, or until the vegetables are tender.

Purée the soup with a hand immersion blender directly in the saucepan or ladle the soup and vegetables in batches into the work bowl of a food processor fitted with the steel blade or into a blender and purée until smooth. Return to the rinsed saucepan. Add the Pernod, taste for seasonings and simmer over medium-low until hot. Cover and refrigerate.

When ready to serve, reheat and garnish with the reserved fennel fronds, if desired.

PURÉE OF LEEK AND PARSNIP SOUP

A FRIEND SERVED THIS DELICIOUS SOUP FOR DINNER ONE EVENING. IT SIMPLY CONSISTS OF LEEKS, parsnips, and chicken stock. I couldn't wait to try it!

YIELD: 6 TO 8 SERVINGS

3 large leeks

4 to 5 parsnips

3 tablespoons extra-virgin olive oil

Kosher salt and freshly ground black pepper

7 cups chicken stock (see page 335) or low-sodium canned

Toasted croutons (see page 335), for garnish

Hold the leeks at the root end and cut off the dark green stems at an angle; then cut each leek lengthwise. Discard any bruised outer leaves. Hold the leeks under running water to wash away any sand embedded between the layers. Squeeze dry with paper towels and cut the leeks into thin slices. Peel, trim, and slice the parsnips.

Heat the oil in a soup pot over low heat. Add the leeks and parsnips and season to taste with salt and pepper. Toss to coat and then cover with a square of wax paper and cover the pot. Sweat the vegetables for 7 minutes. Remove the cover and discard the wax paper. Add the chicken stock. Cover the pot and simmer over medium-low heat for 30 to 35 minutes, until the vegetables are tender. Taste for seasonings and let cool to room temperature.

Purée the soup directly in the pot with a hand immersion blender or in batches in a blender. The soup can be prepared a day or two ahead and stored in a suitable container in the refrigerator. Return the soup to the pot and simmer to heat through before serving. Serve garnished with toasted croutons.

WILD MUSHROOM SOUP
WITH CRÈME FRAÎCHE

COMBINING RECONSTITUTED DRIED MUSHROOMS WITH FRESH MUSHROOMS ADDS INTENSITY to this delectable soup.

YIELD: 8 SERVINGS

1 ounce dried porcini mushrooms

1 bunch scallions

$^3/_4$ pound wild mushrooms, such as shiitake and oyster

2 tablespoons unsalted butter

1 tablespoon extra-virgin olive oil

1 to 2 garlic cloves, finely chopped

4 cups low-sodium beef stock

Kosher salt and freshly ground black pepper

$^1/_2$ cup crème fraîche (see page 338)

Coarsely chopped chives or parsley, for garnish

Soak the porcini mushrooms in warm water for 30 minutes. Drain, reserving the liquid, and place them in a small clean bowl. Strain the reserved liquid through a cheesecloth-lined sieve into a small bowl. Rinse the cheesecloth under running water to remove any sand. Repeat this cleaning procedure two to three time. Reserve the concentrated mushroom liquid. Cut the porcini into julienne strips and set aside.

Trim and rinse the scallions well. Remove any bruised outer leaves and the root ends and discard. The best of the white and green parts of the scallions will be used. Cut the scallions into thin slices and set aside.

Remove and discard the woody stem ends from the wild mushrooms. Rinse the mushrooms to clean and wipe dry. Cut into $^1/_2$-inch slices.

Heat the butter and oil in a large saucepan over medium heat. When the butter has melted, sauté the scallions until translucent. Add the garlic and sauté for 30 to 40 seconds longer. Add the mushrooms and cook, stirring occasionally, for 1 to 2 minutes. Pour in the stock and $^1/_3$ cup of the reserved mushroom liquid. Season with salt and pepper to taste and bring to the edge of a boil. Reduce the heat to medium low and simmer partially covered, maintaining a lazy surface bubble, for about 20 minutes. Adjust the seasonings to taste. Prepare up to two days ahead and refrigerate, covered, in a suitable container. Bring to room temperature if refrigerated.

Before serving, add the crème fraîche and return to a simmer. Serve hot with chopped chives or parsley for garnish.

QUAIL HILL FARM
Amagansett

ORGANIC FARMER SCOTT CHASKEY IS THE GUIDING FORCE BEHIND QUAIL HILL Farm in Amagansett. Scott grew up in the suburbs of Buffalo, New York, and went off to England to study in Oxford in 1976. He worked as a gardener to earn extra money. He never set out to be an organic gardener. Yet the innate feeling he had for gardening was an epiphany that eventually led to Quail Hill Farm.

Scott met his wife, Megan, when they were both students at Antioch College in London. From there a kind of fairy tale story unfolded. At age thirteen, Megan was moved by Dorothy Yglesias's book *The Cry of a Bird*. Even at that early age, she wrote to Dorothy and ended up carrying on a correspondence with her for ten years. When Dorothy died, Megan visited the publisher to pay her respects. When the publisher found out that Scott's background was in agriculture, he declared, "Oh, the angels must have sent you" and suggested that the Chaskeys become caretakers of Dorothy's cottage in Cornwall. "There we were, in Love Lane Cottage, and we stayed for ten years. I started working with this eighty-year-old local chap named Edgar. The cottage was at the end of a peninsula, six miles from Lands End. There were farmer and fisherman folk and an artist colony where we experienced a kind of Bohemian culture.

"Here we are now at the end of an island. When we came back to visit Megan's artist mother and sculptor stepfather, we fell right into the artistic culture of the Hamptons, which also had a base of fishing and farming," said Scott.

Scott's in-laws introduced him to CSA (Community Supported Agriculture) when they participated in a ten-family farm on Butter Lane in Bridgehampton in 1988. "The reason I'm doing what I'm doing," said Scott, "is that I actually found a way that I could help realize social change."

Scott Chaskey is an employee of the Peconic Land Trust, a conservation organization. Peconic Land Trust owns the land and also actively manages it, by running a community farm, which is unusual for a land trust. That they have combined the two is a positive thing. They are preserving the land through farming. Together they started the first CSA in the state of New York, specifically with ten families in Bridgehampton. For two years it existed on privately owned land. "This could be a problem for the owners," said Scott.

"John v.H. Halsey, president of the Peconic Land trust, started preserving and protected over nine thousand acres of land since 1983. Mr. Halsey was open to the idea of a CSA project and partnering with the conservation land trust. Both the CSA and the land trust happened at the same time; it was a wonderful kind of blossoming."

Scott was able to continue with his work when Quail Hill was included in a grant made possible by Josephine Schooner Connelly, a doctor at Stony Brook's medical school, to specifically create community gardens in low-income areas in Suffolk County. Scott Chaskey is currently president of NOFA (North Fork Organic Farm Association), New York. "We're not-for-profit," he continued. "We're educating people to sustainable farming practices. The key," Scott continued, "is working in harmony with natural systems and that's the style of agriculture we are doing. When you're farming and taking things out of the soil, you're removing nutrients, so you have to put nutrients back into the soil. The cover crops (green manure), a natural fertilizer, are plowed back into the soil. The amazing thing for me is that I get to work outside on the land and grow vegetables."

BUTTERNUT SQUASH, LEEK, AND APPLE SOUP

CREATE A FRESH AND INVENTIVE SOUP WITH THIS AUTUMN VEGETABLE SELECTION.
The technique of "sweating" the vegetables is akin to steaming before the broth is added.

YIELD: 6 TO 8 SERVINGS

2 tablespoons canola oil

1 tablespoon unsalted butter

1 butternut squash (2 to 2$\frac{1}{2}$ pounds), peeled and cut into 1-inch pieces

2 leeks, trimmed, washed well, and thinly sliced

1 onion, thinly sliced

1 tart apple, peeled, cored, and coarsely chopped

6 cups homemade chicken stock (see page 335) or low-sodium canned

Kosher salt and freshly ground black pepper

$\frac{1}{3}$ to $\frac{1}{2}$ cup freshly squeezed orange juice

$\frac{1}{4}$ cup finely chopped flat-leaf Italian parsley

2 to 3 tablespoons chopped fresh sage leaves

Croutons (see page 335), for garnish (optional)

Heat the oil and butter in a large saucepan over medium heat. When the butter foams, add the butternut squash, leeks, onion, and apple and sauté. Place a square of wax paper over the vegetables and then cover the saucepan. Sweat the vegetables for 7 minutes. Remove and discard the wax paper. Add the stock and bring to a boil. Add salt and pepper to taste. Add the orange juice and cook the soup over medium heat at a steady simmer for 25 to 30 minutes.

Purée the soup in the saucepan with an immersion blender or in batches in a blender. Prepare the soup ahead to this point and refrigerate, covered, in a suitable container. Return the soup to the saucepan when ready to serve. Add the parsley and sage and bring to a simmer. Serve hot, garnished with croutons, if using.

PUMPKIN SOUP WITH SPICY CROUTONS

ADD THIS PUMPKIN SOUP TO YOUR THANKSGIVING TABLE AND SERVE WITH SPICY CROUTONS that are seasoned with nutmeg, cinnamon, allspice, and pepper. I highly recommend making your own croutons; they are fresher and crisper than store-bought ones.

YIELD: 6 TO 8 SERVINGS

FOR THE SPICY CROUTONS

2 cups ($^1/_4$-inch cubes) crustless whole-grain bread

$^1/_2$ teaspoon freshly grated nutmeg

$^1/_2$ teaspoon ground cinnamon

$^1/_4$ teaspoon allspice

$^1/_8$ teaspoon freshly ground black pepper

$^1/_4$ cup extra-virgin olive oil

FOR THE SOUP

1 tablespoon unsalted butter

2 tablespoons vegetable oil (canola or corn)

1 large onion, thinly sliced

3 medium potatoes, cut into chunks

2 to 3 teaspoons fresh tarragon leaves

Kosher salt and freshly ground black pepper

$1^1/_2$ quarts chicken stock (see page 335) or low-sodium canned

1 (16-ounce) can pumpkin

$^1/_2$ cup heavy cream

For the croutons, put the bread cubes on a baking sheet and let dry overnight.

The next day, combine the nutmeg, cinnamon, allspice, and pepper in a large bowl and mix well. Heat the oil in a large skillet over medium-high heat to about 375°F. Add the bread to the oil in batches and sauté, stirring occasionally, until golden brown. Remove the bread cubes with a slotted spoon, allowing the oil to drip off, and put into the bowl with the spice mixture. Toss to mix. When cool, transfer to a wax paper–lined cookie tin to store and use as needed. Makes about 2 cups.

For the soup, in a large saucepan, heat the butter and oil over medium heat. When the butter foam subsides, sauté the onion about 3 minutes until tender, stirring occasionally. Add the potatoes, cover the pan tightly, and cook over low heat for about 5 minutes. Shake the pan occasionally to redistribute the potatoes. Add the tarragon, salt and pepper to taste, and stock; stir to mix. Partially cover and cook the soup over medium heat at a brisk simmer for 30 minutes.

Allow the soup to cool slightly and then purée in a blender or food mill until smooth. Return the puréed soup to the rinsed out saucepan and stir in the pumpkin. Simmer over medium heat for 20 to 30 minutes. Taste to adjust the seasonings if necessary. The soup can be prepared the day before and refrigerated, or up to a week ahead and placed in the freezer.

When ready to serve, add the cream, stir to mix, and reheat gently before serving. Serve immediately, garnished with croutons, if desired.

OPEN MINDED ORGANICS
Bridgehampton

THE FEW TENDRILS FALLING ONTO THE SIDE OF HIS BROW AND LONG WIRY braided hair dangling down his broad back don't detract from the warm personality of David Falkowski, or from his serious passion for the unique craft of growing mushrooms.

The Falkowski farm took roots in Bridgehampton about one hundred years ago with David's grandfather, Joseph-pop Falkowski. While in school, David took some time to go to Costa Rica to attend a seminar on agro-ecological design theory and a loosely defined philosophy of lifestyle ethic. Interested in sustainable agriculture and specialty crops, he went on to attend mushroom seminars and to study with Paul Stamets, a world-renowned mycologist in Shelton, Washington.

David returned to Bridgehampton in 2003 and built a 10 x 20-foot lab in the attic of his family home. Late that summer, with the advent of the Sag Harbor's Farmers' Market, David successfully marketed his first crop of blue oyster mushrooms along with some shiitake. In a timely manner he aggressively approached local restaurants, many of whom were delighted to showcase his locally grown, organic mushrooms.

David is a certified organic mushroom grower. He buys certified organic straw to grow his variety of oyster mushrooms. Shiitake mushrooms start in blocks and grow on oak logs in sawdust that is purchased with written statements that no chemicals are used in its production. Production begins in March for shiitake and April for his variety of oyster mushrooms, which includes blue, yellow, and white in quarter-pound clusters. When asked about morels, a celebrated and pricy mushroom, David eschews growing them but will find them in the wild in early spring and into July.

Production rotates and generally continues until late fall. You can grill, sauté, and braise them and serve them in salads, soups, and risottos, or you can let your imagination run wild as you enjoy one of the healthiest vegetables on the planet. Mushrooms are noted for containing more protein and vitamin B-12 than many other produce.

One of David's favorite ways to prepare oyster mushrooms is grilled with a sprinkle of a dressing of extra-virgin olive oil, salt, pepper, a bit of garlic, and Worcestershire sauce and served over a bed of greens "An occasional flare-up from the oil hitting the flames adds to the depth of flavor," says David.

For David, farming is a grown-up hobby for people with heart, pride, and passion, always working to make it better.

BRAISED WILD MUSHROOM AND GREENS SALAD

BRAISING, GENERALLY RESERVED FOR COOKING LESS TENDER CUTS OF MEAT SUCH AS SHORT ribs and shanks, is used here to cook a mix of flavorful mushrooms with balsamic vinegar. This inspired salad is topped with tender mushrooms and toasted pine nuts.

YIELD: 4 TO 6 SERVINGS

FOR THE MUSHROOMS

$^1/_2$ pound mixed mushrooms, such as shiitake and oyster

2 tablespoons extra-virgin olive oil

1 large leek, trimmed, washed well, and thinly sliced

2 garlic cloves, finely chopped

$^1/_4$ cup balsamic vinegar

2 tablespoons water

Kosher salt and freshly ground black pepper

**FOR THE GREENS
AND VINAIGRETTE**

4 cups mesclun or mixed salad greens, washed and spun dry

3 tablespoons extra-virgin olive oil

Kosher salt and freshly ground black pepper to taste

1 tablespoon balsamic vinegar

$^1/_4$ cup toasted pine nuts, for garnish

For the mushrooms, cut off and discard the coarse stems of the mushrooms. Rinse the caps in a colander, tossing them under a spray of cool water. Transfer to paper towels and pat dry. Cut the shiitake mushrooms into $^1/_4$-inch slices. Separate the oyster mushrooms at the stem end.

Heat the oil in a 10 to 12-inch nonstick skillet over medium heat. Add the leek and garlic and sauté, stirring 1 to 2 minutes. Add the mushrooms, toss to mix, and cook, stirring occasionally, for 3 to 4 minutes, until the mushrooms are slightly tender. Add the vinegar and water. Cover the pan, reduce the heat to low, and simmer for 8 to 10 minutes. This preparation can be prepared up to several hours ahead.

For the greens and vinaigrette, place the prepared greens in a large mixing bowl. Add the olive oil, circling the bowl, and sprinkle with salt to taste; toss to coat. Pour the vinegar, circling the bowl, and then add several grinds of black pepper. Toss to distribute the dressing. Adjust the seasonings to taste. Divide the greens among four to six plates, top with the mushrooms, and sprinkle on the pine nuts. Serve at once.

CRANBERRY COMPOTE WITH FIGS AND PECANS

MOST COOKS HAVE MADE A BASIC CRANBERRY SAUCE AT ONE TIME OR ANOTHER. HERE IS another flavorful way to accompany your Thanksgiving menu.

YIELD: ABOUT 2 CUPS

$^3/_4$ cup chopped dry figs

1 cup freshly squeezed
  orange juice

$^1/_2$ cup water

$^1/_2$ cup granulated sugar

$^1/_4$ cup turbinado sugar

1 (12-ounce) package
  fresh cranberries

$^1/_3$ cup toasted pecans,
  chopped (optional)

Combine the figs, orange juice, and water in a saucepan over medium-high heat and bring to a boil. Reduce the heat to low and simmer, stirring occasionally, for about 5 minutes. Add the sugars and cranberries and stir to mix. Simmer the mixture over medium heat, stirring frequently, about 10 minutes or until the mixture thickens. Add the nuts, if using, and stir to mix. Cool and transfer to a suitable container.

NOTE: The compote can be prepared up to a week ahead. Refrigerate in a suitable container until ready to serve.

THE KEEPER OF THE BEES

MARY WOLTZ'S BEEKEEPING CAREER BEGAN IN 2003 WHEN SHE BECAME THE manager of a garden facility that had a number of hives on the property. When Mary learned that the United States had lost well over half of its bee colonies in the late 1980s as a result of the inadvertent introduction of two parasitic mites and that the bees were still in a great deal of distress, she chose to devote her life to bees and beekeeping.

It is suggested that one needs to manage two thousand colonies in order to be economically viable. A single colony can grow to fifty thousand or more bees. Mary started her company Bees' Needs in 2007, to see if managing just one hundred colonies could be economically viable. The hives are scattered on farms along the North and South Forks of Long Island. Creatively she developed her own CSA, in her case, Community Supported Apiculture (beekeeping)—and doesn't believe there is another one like it in the country. Limited production meant she couldn't afford to wholesale her honey, and direct sales seemed the best route.

The seasons predictably determine the style of honey. Mary sells three different varieties: Marvelous May, Juicy July, and Fabulous Fall and could vary considerably from year to year. The honey becomes more complex over the course of the year, early being the lightest and late being the strongest.

The honeys the bees produce reflect the locality and what the farmers are growing. "If something is blooming the bees will find it," said Mary. "The range of honey varieties is infinite and each season is different, and it's always going to be different." When I asked Mary if she has a particular preparation for her honey, she replied, "Personally, I use it on my morning toast, in my hot cereal or just straight from the spoon."

Mary takes good care of her bees. She actually leaves them honey to sustain them, whereas many beekeepers feed the bee's sugar and water instead. Mary leaves as much honey on the hives for the winter that she feels the bees will require and will keep extra on hand to fill in should it be necessary. "It makes sense," said Mary, "bees do not actually make honey for us, but for themselves!"

FIGS, PINE NUTS, CHEESE, AND A DRIZZLE OF HONEY

THE INSPIRATION FOR THIS SALAD CAME WHEN A LOCAL FRIEND BROUGHT ME A BASKET OF ripe luscious figs from her Hampton Bays backyard fig tree.

YIELD: 6 SERVINGS

6 large fresh figs

$^{1}/_{4}$ cup pine nuts, lightly toasted

$^{1}/_{4}$ pound natural-rind nutty cheese*, shaved

Honey to drizzle

Rinse the figs and pat dry with paper towels. Cut in half lengthwise and divide equally among six salad plates. Top the fig halves with toasted pine nuts and shavings of cheese. Drizzle about 1 teaspoon of honey over each serving. Serve at room temperature.

* SHAWONDASEE, a natural, semi-hard rind tome cheese that pairs nicely with fruit, is made by Art Ludlow, artisanal cheese maker of Mecox Bay Dairy Cheese in Bridgehampton, New York. For this recipe I use honey from Mary Woltz's Bees' Needs, which has hives all over the East End of Long Island.

MIZUNA WITH ROASTED BEETS AND GOAT CHEESE

MIZUNA, AN ASIAN GREEN, IS GROWN LOCALLY ON THE EAST END OF LONG ISLAND. SWEET roasted beets and the salty tang of goat cheese complement the peppery bite of the greens. When preparing the beets, reserve the beet greens to sauté and serve as a side like you would spinach.

YIELD: 6 TO 8 SERVINGS

FOR THE VINAIGRETTE

2 to 3 shallots, finely chopped

1 tablespoon whole-grain Dijon mustard

$1^1/_2$ to 2 tablespoons sherry wine vinegar

Kosher salt and freshly ground black pepper

4 to 5 tablespoons extra-virgin olive oil

FOR THE BEETS

1 bunch fresh beets with greens attached

1 large bunch fresh mizuna

4 ounces fresh chèvre

$^1/_3$ cup walnuts, toasted

JUST TWO YEARS AFTER

Karen Catapano co-founded the Goat Cheese Dairy Farm on the North Fork in Mattituck, Long Island, with her husband, Dr. Michael Catapano, their soft fresh chèvre won first place in the American Cheese Society's annual goat cheese competition.

For the vinaigrette, in a mixing bowl combine the shallots, mustard, vinegar, and salt and pepper to taste. Whisk the ingredients together and then gradually add the oil, whisking until the ingredients are thoroughly incorporated. Adjust the seasonings as necessary.

For the beets, preheat the oven to 400°F. Trim the greens from the beets. Scrub the beets with a vegetable brush and pat dry with paper towels. Wrap the beets in heavy-duty foil and close tightly. Place on a baking sheet and roast for $1^1/_4$ hours. Remove from the oven and, when cool enough to handle, peel and discard the skin from the beets. Roasted unpeeled beets may be refrigerated in a suitable container until ready to use.

Wash and spin dry the mizuna. Roll up in paper towels to absorb any excess moisture. The mizuna may be prepared ahead and stored in a zip-top bag. Refrigerate up to 24 hours until ready to use.

When ready to serve, toss the mizuna with about two-thirds of the vinaigrette and divide equally among six to eight salad plates. Cut three to four beets into thin slices and arrange, overlapping each other, on the greens. Drizzle the remaining vinaigrette over the beets and top with crumbled chèvre. Sprinkle with toasted walnuts and serve.

NOTE: Roasted unpeeled beets will keep in the refrigerator for up to a week. Peel when ready to use in salads or slice and sauté to serve as a warm vegetable.

WARM DUCK CONFIT SALAD
WITH FENNEL HASH AND BEET VINAIGRETTE

THE SWEETNESS OF CARAMELIZED FENNEL, THE PEPPERINESS OF ARUGULA, AND THE RICHNESS richness of duck balance a whole bouquet of flavors with the acidity of the beet vinaigrette. Michael Rozzi of Della Femina affords us this delectable recipe.

YIELD: 4 SERVINGS

FOR THE BEET VINAIGRETTE

1 shallot, peeled

1 roasted or boiled beet, peeled

Kosher salt and freshly ground black pepper

1 teaspoon sherry wine vinegar

1 tablespoon extra-virgin olive oil

FOR THE FENNEL HASH

1 firm fennel bulb, trimmed

1 leek (white and light green parts only), trimmed and washed well

2 tablespoons extra-virgin olive oil

Kosher salt and freshly ground black pepper

1 teaspoon fresh thyme leaves

FOR SERVING

1 duck leg confit (see page 333), skin removed for cracklings (optional)*

1 bunch arugula, washed and spun dry

For the vinaigrette, finely mince the shallot in a food processor fitted with the steel blade. Cut the roasted beet into chunks, add to the minced shallot and process until puréed, scraping down the sides with a rubber spatula as necessary. Add salt and pepper to taste and the vinegar and process to mix. Add the oil slowly through the feed tube and process until mixed into the purée. Taste and adjust the seasonings. Transfer to a small bowl and reserve.

For the fennel hash, remove the large fennel stalks and chop some of the fronds to reserve for garnish. Rinse and dry the fennel and then shave with a mandolin or slice very thinly, discarding the heavy core. Cut the leek into thin slices. Heat the oil in a skillet over medium-high heat and sauté the fennel and leek for 5 to 6 minutes, turning occasionally, until lightly caramelized. Season with salt and pepper to taste and the thyme.

For serving, shred the duck confit meat and toss with the fennel hash. Divide the arugula among four salad plates and spoon the fennel hash over the greens.

Sprinkle with the reserved chopped fennel fronds and the duck cracklings, if using, and drizzle the beet vinaigrette in a circle around the plate.

*NOTE: For crunchy duck skin cracklings, cut the skin into 1/2-inch pieces and place on a parchment paper-lined baking sheet. Bake in a 350°F oven until brown and crisp, 12 to 15 minutes. Drain on paper towels and then toss over the salad like bacon bits.

DELLA FEMINA
East Hampton

AS A THIRD-GENERATION EAST ENDER, MICHAEL ROZZI ALWAYS DREAMED THAT he would not only become a chef, but an accomplished chef defining "Hampton's cuisine." Dreams really do come true.

Michael Rozzi graduated with honors from Johnson and Wales University in Rhode Island and did graduate work on occupational education at New York's Institute of Technology. He then traveled extensively, honing his skills and defining his distinguished regional cooking. Since 1996, Michael was sous chef to Kevin Penner and James Carpenter at Della Femina. In 2004 he became the executive chef of Della Femina restaurant.

Familiar to patrons, Della Femina, founded by adman Jerry Della Femina, is well known for its excellent cuisine and service, its wall of celebrity and noncelebrity caricatures at the entrance and bar area, and the large airy dining room with its natural reed sconce lighting that gives off the mellow effect of a visual oasis.

At Della Femina, Michael makes good use of local purveyors who grow crops in sustainable ways, such as Ian Calder-Piedomonte's boutique farm, Balsam Farm, in Amagansett on the South Fork and Paulette Satur of Satur farm in Cutchogue on the North Fork. Local ingredients have been a part of Michael's heritage—clamming down at Devon on the back bays of East Hampton and hunting pheasant in the fields of Bridgehampton, or fluke fishing in Shinnecock inlet. He grew up with fresh chickens from Schleicher farm—no longer in existence—and local apples from the popular Milk Pail in Water Mill. Michael has always understood that fresh is best.

ROASTED RED ONION AND FENNEL SALAD

THE CARAMELIZED SWEETNESS OF ROASTED ONIONS MINGLES WITH THE DISTINCTIVE FLAVOR of fennel, chiffonade of basil, and shavings of Parmigiano-Reggiano, making for a beautifully presented do-ahead salad.

YIELD: 8 TO 10 SERVINGS

2 large fennels, fronds removed

1 large red onion, unpeeled

Kosher salt and freshly ground black pepper

4 to 4^1/$_2$ tablespoons extra-virgin olive oil, divided

2 tablespoons freshly squeezed lemon juice

^{1}/$_2$ cup fresh basil chiffonade

Shaved Parmigiano-Reggiano cheese

Preheat the oven to 400°F.

Rinse the fennel, trim the bottom and top, and then slice lengthwise into ^{1}/$_2$-inch-thick pieces. Soak in a bowl of cold water for about 10 minutes. Drain and pat dry in a clean kitchen towel. Cut the onion in half and then cut each half into quarters. Place the fennel and onion in a large heavy roasting pan. Sprinkle with salt and pepper and toss to coat with 2 tablespoons of the olive oil. Roast 20 to 25 minutes, until tender and lightly glazed. Remove the fennel from the roasting pan and return the onions to the oven to roast 10 to 12 minutes longer, if necessary. They should be firm yet tender when pierced with the tip of a paring knife. Remove and discard the onion peel.

Place overlapping layers of onion and fennel in a round or oval gratin dish, sprinkling each layer with salt and pepper. Coat with the remaining 2 to 2^1/$_2$ tablespoons olive oil and the lemon juice and toss gently to mix. Cover with plastic wrap and refrigerate until ready to serve.

Bring to room temperature for serving and top with the basil chiffonade. Shave a generous amount of Parmigiano-Reggiano cheese over the top of the salad.

BAKED FENNEL AND PARMESAN GRATIN

THIS MAKE-AHEAD, ITALIAN-INSPIRED DISH IS A REAL CROWD PLEASER. IT CAN BE PREPARED ahead and baked when ready to serve!

YIELD: 6 TO 8 SERVINGS

2 to 3 large fennel bulbs

1 teaspoon kosher salt, plus more to taste

3 to 4 tablespoons extra-virgin olive oil

$^1/_3$ to $^1/_2$ cup freshly grated Parmesan cheese

Freshly grated nutmeg

Freshly ground black pepper

Trim the fennel bulbs of the stalks and feathery fronds and discard. Cut the bulb in half lengthwise and cut out the knob-like core at the base. Cut the bulb into vertical slices about $^1/_2$ inch thick. Place in a bowl of cold water to soak for 10 to 15 minutes.

Bring a large pot of water to a boil and add 1 teaspoon salt. Add the fennel and simmer briskly over medium-high heat until cooked but still firm, 12 to 14 minutes. Drain the fennel and rinse under a spray of cool water. Transfer to a clean kitchen towel to absorb excess moisture.

Butter a shallow baking or gratin dish. Layer the cooked fennel with a drizzle of oil, a third of the cheese, and a light sprinkle of salt, pepper, and nutmeg. Repeat the layering two more times, ending with the cheese. If preparing ahead, cover with plastic wrap and refrigerate.

If refrigerated, bring the fennel gratin to room temperature. Preheat the oven to 375°F, and bake for 20 to 25 minutes, until golden and crusty.

PEAR AND SWEET POTATO CASSEROLE

THIS FLAVORFUL MAKE-AHEAD SIDE DISH WILL ADD ANOTHER DIMENSION TO YOUR
Thanksgiving table.

YIELD: 8 TO 10 SERVINGS

3 cups water

$1/2$ cup sugar

2 cinnamon sticks

Juice of 1 lemon

4 medium-ripe Bartlett
    or Anjou pears

4 pounds sweet potatoes

4 tablespoons butter, melted

$1/2$ teaspoon ground
    cinnamon

$1/4$ teaspoon ground nutmeg

$1/2$ cup maple syrup

Place the water in a 5 to $5^1/2$-quart saucepan and bring to a boil over medium-high heat. Add the sugar and stir to dissolve. Add the cinnamon sticks, reduce the heat, and simmer slowly for 15 to 20 minutes until the liquid becomes a syrup and falls in a steady stream from a spoon.

Meanwhile, squeeze the lemon juice into a bowl. Peel, core, and halve the pears and add to the lemon juice. Remove the pear halves from the lemon juice and add to the syrup. Cover with a square of cheesecloth or clean kitchen towel to prevent them from darkening. Cover the pan tightly and poach gently over medium heat for 10 to 15 minutes or until tender when tested with the point of a knife. Remove the pears with a slotted spoon and set aside. Reduce the pear liquid over medium-high heat to about $1/2$ cup. Watch carefully and do not let the liquid burn. Discard the cinnamon sticks and reserve the syrup.

Cook the sweet potatoes in 4 quarts of boiling salted water until tender, 35 to 40 minutes. Drain and, when cool enough to handle, peel. Cut the sweet potatoes in half lengthwise. In a wide, buttered, shallow gratin dish, arrange the sweet potato and pear halves in alternating layers, cut side down. Pour the butter over the layers and season with the cinnamon and nutmeg. The casserole can be prepared up to two days ahead. Cover and refrigerate.

Preheat the oven to 350°F. If the casserole is refrigerated, bring to room temperature before baking. Mix the maple syrup with the reserved $1/2$ cup pear syrup and pour over the top of the casserole. Bake for 25 to 30 minutes and serve.

ROASTED BABY CARROTS WITH GARLIC AND THYME

WHEN NICELY TAPERED BABY CARROTS, ABOUT THREE INCHES LONG, ARE AVAILABLE FRESH AT the farm stand, use them for this sweet roasted carrot recipe.

YIELD: 6 TO 8 SERVINGS

12 to 15 farm-fresh baby carrots or 1 bunch regular carrots

3 to 4 tablespoons extra-virgin olive oil

Kosher salt and freshly ground black pepper

2 tablespoons fresh thyme leaves

6 to 8 whole garlic cloves

Preheat the oven to 400°F.

If using baby carrots, peel and trim the green tops to ³/₄ inch. (If organic, simply scrub them.) If using large carrots, peel and cut in half lengthwise. Rinse and pat dry with paper towels.

Place the carrots in an ovenproof serving dish and season with the olive oil and salt and pepper to taste. Toss the garlic cloves here and there. Toss the carrots to evenly coat and sprinkle with the thyme. Cover the pan with foil and roast 20 to 25 minutes. Remove the foil and turn the carrots, spooning over the pan juices. Continue to roast another 20 to 25 minutes, until the carrots are tender and lightly caramelized. The recipe may be prepared up to two to three hours ahead and reheated before serving. If you catch one of the garlic cloves in your serving just squeeze the garlic from the clove and enjoy the sweet puree. Serve warm.

NOTE: A tin-lined copper baking dish has excellent heat distribution and will cook the ingredients faster. If using a stainless steel or glass baking dish, cook the carrots for 5 minutes longer both covered and uncovered.

KOHLRABI WITH GARLIC AND DILL

FOR MANY, KOHLRABI IS A BIT OF A MYSTERY. THIS SMALL, PALE GREEN, SLIGHTLY KNOBBY, turnip-shaped vegetable is sometimes called a cabbage turnip. The vegetable, extremely popular all over Europe, is more like fresh and crunchy broccoli stems, touched with a hint of radish and cucumber. It is certainly worth a try.

YIELD: 4 TO 6 SERVINGS

4 kohlrabi, trimmed and peeled

2 tablespoons canola or vegetable oil

1 tablespoon unsalted butter

1 garlic clove, finely chopped

2 to 3 tablespoons chopped fresh dill

Kosher salt and freshly ground black pepper

$^1/_4$ to $^1/_3$ cup heavy cream or crème fraîche (see page 338)

$^1/_2$ teaspoon sugar

Cut each kohlrabi in half. Thinly slice and then stack the slices and cut into julienne sticks. Set aside.

Heat the oil and butter in a large saucepan over medium heat. When the butter melts and the foam subsides, add the garlic and sauté for 30 to 40 seconds and then add the kohlrabi. Toss to coat with the butter. Add the dill and season with salt and pepper. Sauté for 6 to 7 minutes, until barely tender. Add the cream and sugar and stir to mix. Taste to adjust the seasonings. The kohlrabi should be tender with a bit of crunch. The recipe can be prepared up to several hours ahead. Reheat if desired or serve at room temperature.

NOTE: According to Elizabeth Schneider's comments in her respectable tome on vegetables, *Uncommon Fruits and Vegetables*, "It is the enlarged stem of the kohlrabi (from which spring collard-like leaves) that gives the 'turnip' name to the crispy green vegetable; but it does not taste like a turnip, nor is it a root. It is sweeter, juicier, crisper, and more delicate that any turnip."

SAUTÉED SWISS CHARD WITH PINE NUTS

JOSEPH REALMUTO, EXECUTIVE CHEF OF NICK & TONI'S IN EAST HAMPTON, DESCRIBED THIS dish during an interview. The appeal was immediate. I hardly skipped a beat going to the stove to recreate the dish.

YIELDS: 4 TO 6 SERVINGS

1 bunch Swiss chard
(about 1 pound)

2 tablespoons extra-virgin
olive oil

2 medium shallots, finely
chopped

1 large garlic clove, peeled

2 to 3 anchovies, cut into
pieces

$1/4$ cup chicken stock
(see page 335) or low-
sodium canned

Kosher salt and freshly
ground black pepper

3 tablespoons toasted
pine nuts

$1^1/2$ tablespoons balsamic
vinegar

Cut the stems from the leaves of the chard, discarding any discolored stems or leaves. Rinse the stems and leaves in a colander under cold running water. Stack the leaves and slice crosswise into 2-inch widths and cut the stems into $1^1/2$-inch pieces.

Pour the olive oil into a 12-inch skillet and warm over low heat. Add the shallots, garlic, and anchovies and sauté for 2 to 3 minutes, until the garlic clove begins to color; discard the garlic. Add the chard leaves and stems, pushing the greens down into the pan, and pour over the stock. Season the greens with salt and pepper to taste and then cover and cook until tender, 8 to 10 minutes. Add the pine nuts and vinegar. Stir to mix and serve.

CAULIFLOWER WITH TOMATOES AND PARMESAN

THIS TIMELY RECIPE IS A REMINDER THAT CAULIFLOWER CAN BE A LUXURIOUS VEGETABLE when paired with the last of summer tomatoes and garden fresh basil.

YIELD: 6 TO 8 SERVINGS

1 medium farm-fresh cauli-flower (1½ to 2 pounds)

5 ripe tomatoes, peeled (see note on page 57), seeded, and coarsely chopped

3 tablespoons fresh basil chiffonade

Kosher salt and freshly ground black pepper

2 tablespoons extra-virgin olive oil

⅓ cup grated Parmesan cheese

2 tablespoons plain bread-crumbs (see page 335)

2 tablespoons unsalted butter, cut into small dice

Remove the outer leaves of the cauliflower, cut away the hard core, and then remove the florets from the base. Put the florets in a colander and rinse under cold running water.

Preheat the oven to 375°F.

Arrange the florets in a buttered baking dish. In a bowl, mix the tomatoes, basil, and salt and pepper to taste and spoon over the cauliflower. Pour the olive oil over and toss to coat. Mix the cheese and breadcrumbs and sprinkle evenly over the mixture. Add the butter on top and bake for 25 minutes until hot and bubbly. Serve at once. This dish may be frozen for up to a month.

NOTE: The cauliflower can be prepared ahead of time and refrigerated, covered, for several hours or overnight. When ready to bake, bring to room temperature.

CELERY ROOT AND CAULIFLOWER PURÉE

WHEN YOU SERVE THIS DISH TO COMPANY, NO DOUBT THEY'LL BE CERTAIN YOU ARE SERVING mashed potatoes. The slight piquant taste from the celery root and horseradish and the knowledge that it is a vegetarian dish will astonish your guests.

YIELD: 8 SERVINGS

1 head cauliflower (about 2$\frac{1}{2}$ pounds)

1 celery root (about 1$\frac{1}{2}$ pounds)

2 to 2$\frac{1}{2}$ tablespoons unsalted butter

2 teaspoons salt

1$\frac{3}{4}$ to 2 teaspoons prepared horseradish

Freshly ground black pepper

Remove the outer leaves of the cauliflower, cut away the hard core, and then remove the florets from the base. Put the florets in a colander and rinse under cold running water. Peel the celery root with a sharp knife and then cut into $\frac{1}{4}$-inch-thick slices. Stack the slices and cut into dice. Bring a large pot of salted water to a boil and add the vegetables. Cook, partially covered, over medium heat for 16 to 18 minutes or until the vegetables are tender when pierced with the tip of a knife. Drain well in a colander.

Put the vegetables into the work bowl of a food processor fitted with the steel blade and process to purée the mixture, stopping the processor from time to time to push the vegetables back down into the work bowl with a rubber spatula. Pulse until the mixture is smooth. Add the butter, salt, horseradish, and pepper to taste and process to mix thoroughly. Taste to adjust the seasonings if necessary. This can be made one day ahead up to this point. With a rubber spatula, transfer the purée to a stainless steel or enamel saucepan with a cover to reheat when ready to serve.

To serve, if the purée is refrigerated, bring to room temperature. Put the saucepan in a large shallow pan half-filled with warm water to create a water bath. Keep warm over medium-low heat, stirring from time to time until heated through. Serve hot.

MASHED POTATOES WITH ROSEMARY AND OLIVE OIL

ONE OF MY FAVORITE COMFORT FOODS IS MASHED POTATOES IN ANY FORM. THIS LOW-FAT, highly flavored potato side dish scented with aromatic rosemary hits a high note.

YIELD: 4 TO 5 SERVINGS

2 to 2¼ pounds russet potatoes, peeled and cut into 1-inch pieces

3 garlic cloves, peeled

1 teaspoon salt

½ cup chicken stock (see page 335) or low-sodium canned

1 tablespoon chopped fresh rosemary leaves

2 to 3 tablespoons extra-virgin olive oil

Kosher salt and freshly ground black pepper

Rinse the potatoes in a 3-quart saucepan. Drain and add enough cold fresh water to cover the potatoes. Add the garlic cloves and bring the water to a boil over high heat. Add the salt to the boiling water and reduce the heat to a brisk simmer. Cook, partially covered, for 16 to 18 minutes until the potatoes are tender when pierced with a knife.

Meanwhile, simmer the stock with the rosemary in a small saucepan over low heat for 4 to 5 minutes to infuse the stock.

Drain the potatoes and garlic. Return to the dry but still warm saucepan and swirl over low heat to dry the potatoes for 1 to 2 minutes. Mash with a potato masher or purée through a food mill over a bowl. Stir in the olive oil; then gradually add the rosemary-infused stock and continue to stir until light and fluffy. Season with salt and pepper to taste and serve hot.

NOTE: You may prepare the mashed potatoes up to several hours ahead and then reheat in a water bath (place the saucepan in a larger pan of hot water over low heat). Stir the mashed potatoes every so often to retain the smooth texture and to keep warm.

1770 HOUSE
East Hampton

KEVIN PENNER WAS BORN IN THE UNIVERSITY TOWN OF IOWA CITY, IOWA. While majoring in philosophy and nineteenth-century European history, with a minor in physics, Kevin detassled corn, picked rows of soy beans, and bailed hay. Much of this was done at his uncle's fifteen-hundred-acre farm. Kevin, soft spoken and scholarly, enjoyed school and worked at a pastry shop to pay his tuition. The Swiss woman who owned the pastry shop had a strong influence on Kevin. He worked a thirty-hour week, preparing classic pastries in the European tradition, in addition to maintaining his school schedule. Upon graduation Kevin applied for the job of pastry chef at the University of Iowa's Memorial Food Service, where he headed a large staff.

With his neverending quest for knowledge and wanting to explore new territory, Kevin moved to Seattle in 1988. He secured the pastry chef position at a Nordstrom's. Kevin kept his ear tuned into the right places. It was the beginning of the restaurant boom in Chicago, and he decided to move east. "Food trends", he said, "have moved from West to East," citing Alice Waters and her mission to work with locally grown foods. After working at some high-end Chicago restaurants, he made is way further east to work as sous chef at Della Femina in East Hampton. When the chef left in 1995, Kevin slipped right into the executive chef's position. Kevin eventually moved into the top chef position at 1770 House—a charming eighteenth-century country manor inn—where he has become an icon of the Hamptons restaurant scene, introducing a new standard of fine dining with his contemporary American cuisine and internationally inspired flavors.

A TALE OF TWO ROASTED FINGERLING POTATOES

THIS WONDERFUL RECIPE COMES FROM EXECUTIVE CHEF KEVIN PENNER AND CHEF DE CUISINE Matt Birnstill of the 1770 House in East Hampton. Fingerling potatoes are knobby, finger-sized potatoes with a buttery flesh and a rich heirloom flavor. They are delicious boiled or roasted with herbs and garlic. They needn't be peeled, just scrubbed clean with a vegetable brush.

ROASTED FINGERLING POTATOES WITH ROSEMARY AND THYME

YIELD: 6 TO 8 SERVINGS

1 to 1 1/2 pounds fingerling potatoes, scrubbed and halved lengthwise

3 tablespoons extra-virgin olive oil

Kosher salt and freshly ground black pepper

1/4 cup water

4 garlic cloves, sliced into slivers

1 to 1 1/2 tablespoons roughly chopped fresh rosemary leaves

1 to 1 1/2 tablespoons roughly chopped fresh thyme leaves

Sea salt

A CLASSIC WAY TO COOK SEVERAL VARIETIES OF POTATOES is to roast at high heat with a savory fresh herb finish.

Preheat the oven to 400°F.

Place the potatoes in a bowl with the oil and toss to thoroughly coat. Season with salt and pepper to taste. Place the potatoes in a shallow roasting pan just large enough to hold them in a single layer and add the water. Scatter over the garlic slices. Cover with a tent of foil and roast 40 minutes. Uncover and roast for 15 to 20 minutes longer, or until tender. Toss the potatoes in a warm serving dish with the rosemary, thyme, and sea salt to taste and serve.

NOTE: Chefs suggest serving these roasted fingerlings with any roast meat.

ROASTED FINGERLING POTATOES IN BUTTERY BROTH

YIELD: 4 TO 6 SERVINGS

1 pound fingerling potatoes, scrubbed clean

2 teaspoons kosher salt

3 tablespoons extra-virgin olive oil

3 garlic cloves, finely chopped

COOKED WITH A LITTLE STOCK, BUTTER, AND ROSEMARY, these fingerling potatoes are a little richer but nice.

Put the potatoes in a saucepan with enough cold water to cover and bring to a boil over high heat. Add the salt, reduce the heat to medium, and cook the potatoes until barely tender, 16 to 20 minutes, depending on their size.

$^1/_3$ cup chicken stock
(see page 335) or low-
sodium canned

2 tablespoons unsalted
butter, sliced thin

1 tablespoon coarsely
chopped fresh rosemary
leaves

Kosher or sea salt, as needed

Drain the potatoes and dry well in a clean kitchen towel. Slice in half lengthwise.

Preheat the oven to 450°F.

Place the fingerling halves in a lightly buttered shallow roasting pan large enough to hold them in a single layer. Pour over the oil, garlic, stock, butter slices, and rosemary. If the broth is unsalted, season the potatoes with kosher or sea salt. Roast 20 to 25 minutes or until the stock is absorbed and the potatoes are crisp.

NOTE: The chef suggests serving the buttery fingerlings with flounder, fluke, or striped bass.

CARAMELIZED ROOT VEGETABLES

WHENEVER I SERVE THIS VEGETABLE ROAST, I GET RAVES FOR THE SLIGHTLY SWEET FLAVOR derived from the mix of winter root vegetables. This dish can feed a crowd at a festive fall buffet such as Thanksgiving.

YIELD: 12 TO 14 SERVINGS

1 celery root

4 large parsnips

1 bunch carrots

2 large turnips or 1 rutabaga

4 sweet potatoes

12 garlic cloves, unpeeled

4 to 6 sprigs fresh thyme or $^{1}/_{2}$ teaspoon dried

$^{1}/_{3}$ cup plus 3 tablespoons extra-virgin olive oil, divided

Kosher salt and freshly ground black pepper to taste (optional)

3 tablespoons balsamic vinegar

Preheat the oven to 375°F.

Trim and peel the celery root, parsnips, carrots, turnips, and sweet potatoes. Cut into 1-inch chunks.

Place the vegetables in a shallow roasting pan, no higher than 2 inches and large enough to hold them. Add the garlic, thyme, $^{1}/_{3}$ cup of the olive oil, and salt and pepper to taste, if using, and toss well. Cover the pan with a tent of aluminum foil and roast for 25 to 30 minutes. Remove the foil, toss the vegetables, and continue roasting another 20 to 25 minutes, until the vegetables are tender and slightly crisp.

Heat the remaining 3 tablespoons olive oil and the balsamic vinegar together in a skillet over medium heat until hot and pour over the vegetables. Serve warm or at room temperature.

NOTE: This root vegetable roast is a perfect side dish for late fall, Thanksgiving, and winter holiday dinners. The vegetable roast can be prepared up to several hours ahead and reheated in a warm oven. Just before serving, heat the olive oil and vinegar to pour over the vegetables.

LINGUINE WITH ESCAROLE AND COCKLES

I LOVE TO PREPARE THIS DISH IN COOLER WEATHER WHEN LOCAL CLAMS ARE ESPECIALLY fresh and escarole is crisp and abundant.

YIELD: 4 TO 5 SERVINGS

2 pounds cockles

Kosher salt

1 bunch escarole
(about 1 pound)

1 pound linguine

$^1/_2$ cup extra-virgin olive oil

4 to 5 garlic cloves, sliced
paper thin

$^1/_8$ to $^1/_4$ teaspoon red
pepper flakes

$^2/_3$ cup dry white wine

3 tablespoons chopped flat-
leaf Italian parsley, divided

Scrub the cockles vigorously, one against the other, in a bowl of cold water, transferring the cleaned cockles to a bowl of fresh water. Repeat several times until the water is free of sand.

Meanwhile, bring a large pot of water to a boil and add salt to taste. Push the escarole leaves into the boiling water and cook over medium-high heat, partially covered, for 3 to 4 minutes. Drain in a colander and squeeze dry. Add fresh cold water to the pot and bring to a boil. Add the linguine and salt to taste. Cover the pot and return to a boil. Uncover and cook for 9 to 12 minutes until al dente. Drain, reserving $^1/_4$ cup pasta water

Meanwhile, warm the oil in a 12-inch skillet over medium-high heat. Add the garlic and red pepper flakes and sauté for 30 to 40 seconds. Add the wine and cook until reduced by half. Add salt to taste and 1 tablespoon of the parsley. Bring to a boil and add the cockles. Reduce the heat to a simmer and cook for about 8 minutes or until the cockles open. Add the escarole and reserved pasta water to the skillet, stir to mix, and keep warm over very low heat. Add the linguini to the skillet. Toss with the sauce and serve on warm plates, distributing the cockles and escarole evenly. Garnish with the remaining 2 table-spoons of parsley.

Wine suggestion : Channing Daughters Winery Mosaic

CHANNING DAUGHTERS
Bridgehampton

WINEMAKER AND PARTNER CHRISTOPHER TRACY WAS EXPOSED TO THE DELIGHTS of food and wine as a young man on his family's vineyard in St. Helena, California. He first came to Channing Daughters as a customer, though he quickly became more interested and involved in actually making wine at the vineyard. In 2002, Tracy was named winemaker at Channing Daughters, and he and his wife, Allison Dubin (who is now also a partner and winery manager), moved to Long Island.

The first vines at Channing were planted in 1982 by Walter Channing, a venture capitalist, sculptor, and wine aficionado. Channing Daughters has created a gallery of wines, including single varietal wines, multiple varietal wines, and field blends in which a number of compatible varietals are planted in one block and then harvested and fermented together to make an "expression of one plot of land." As Tracy describes it, he "makes decisions on the crush pad like a chef at the green market," adapting his approach according to the fruit available to him.

Tracy revels in their "capacity for diversity in wine. There is so much possibility in our fields." While he firmly believes that, as a winemaker on Long Island, his wines must first and foremost be of and for this place, his is inspired by the world of wines, including those of Northeastern Italy (Friuli-Venezia Giulia in particular) as well as Bordeaux, Burgundy, and Germany. When Tracy lists these far-reaching regions as inspiration, he speaks with deep knowledge of their wines and is currently a candidate to become a "Master of Wine," considered the holy grail of accreditation for sommeliers.

In thinking of what makes his wines distinctive, Tracy brings up the unique culture at Channing, describing the "instinctive, creative, passionate group of people tending, making, bottling, and selling the wines. We are also working with varietals that no one else is growing [on Long Island]," listing varietals such as Tocai Friulano, Muscat Ottonel, Malvasia, Blaufrankisch, and Dornfelder.

Beyond working with unusual varietals, Tracy also experiments with winemaking techniques. While white wines are traditionally fermented after the juice is pressed from the skin, Tracy ferments some of his white varietals on the skins to create "orange wine," a wine with more color, richer flavor, and more phenolics than an average white wine. "I'm really interested in symphonic wines. They have more weight and complexity and can be paired with more dishes."

Tracy seeks to make wines that will suit many different occasions and meals and currently has some two dozen wines available. He describes wines that "are light and ephemeral and then some that are richer and barrel influenced."

According to Tracy, the greatest advantage to being on Long Island "starts with the vineyards and the grapes, and our maritime macroclimate. This promotes wines with moderate alcohols in the 11 to 13 percent range, and with a crisp natural acidity. Tracy sees the South Fork of Long Island as a marvelous combination of "an agricultural, urban—not suburban—resort community. "It's unbelievable, and no other wine growing community has all three of these aspects in one place."

As for the greatest obstacles to growing wine on Long Island, Tracy promptly fingers "the rain and humidity. This promotes fungus, which can be a big problem. The birds, deer, and other critters are a real hassle, since there is no predatory hunting. Every row has to be netted and fenced, which means huge labor and time costs. This is not for the faint of heart."

LINGUINE WITH SLOW-ROASTED PLUM TOMATOES

ROASTING LATE SUMMER OR EARLY FALL PLUM TOMATOES HEIGHTENS THEIR SWEETNESS FOR this simple pasta dish. The tomatoes are slowly roasted in a low oven and can be completely prepared ahead for your convenience.

YIELD: 4 TO 6 SERVINGS

6 to 8 plum tomatoes

2 teaspoons fresh thyme leaves

1 to 2 garlic cloves, finely chopped

2 tablespoons kosher salt, plus more to taste

Freshly ground black pepper

3 to 4 tablespoons extra-virgin olive oil

1 pound linguine

5 to 6 tablespoons freshly grated Parmigiano-Reggiano, plus more for serving

Preheat the oven to 250°F.

Rinse the tomatoes, pat dry with paper towels, and cut in half lengthwise. Line a baking sheet with parchment paper or Silpat and place the tomatoes cut side up on the baking sheet. In a small bowl, mix the thyme, garlic, and salt and pepper to taste and sprinkle over the top of the tomatoes. Drizzle with the oil and bake for 2 to 2^1/$_2$ hours. The tomatoes can be roasted up to several days ahead and refrigerated in a suitable container.

If the tomatoes are refrigerated, bring to room temperature. When ready to cook the pasta, in a large saucepan bring about 5 quarts of water to boil and add 2 tablespoons of the salt. Add the linguine, stirring gently to separate the pasta. Cover and return to a rolling boil. Uncover and cook for 9 to 12 minutes until al dente, according to the package directions. Drain, reserving 2 to 3 tablespoons pasta water. Spoon the reserved pasta water over the tomatoes. Return the pasta to the pot and toss with the roasted tomatoes and the grated cheese. Serve on warm plates and pass additional cheese at the table, if desired.

PENNE WITH EGGPLANT, TOMATO SAUCE, AND RICOTTA SALATA

THIS CLASSIC PASTA RECIPE FROM SICILY, WHERE EGGPLANTS GROW AS ABUNDANTLY AS they do on the East End, is also known as Pasta alla Norma.

YIELD: 6 TO 8 SERVINGS

FOR THE EGGPLANT

2 medium eggplants
(about 2 pounds)

2 garlic cloves, coarsely
chopped

1/4 cup extra-virgin olive oil

FOR THE SAUCE

3 tablespoons extra-
virgin olive oil

2 to 3 shallots, finely
chopped

2 garlic cloves, finely
chopped

Pinch of red pepper flakes

1 (28-ounce) can Italian
peeled tomatoes

2 tablespoons kosher salt,
plus more to taste

Freshly ground black pepper

15 large fresh basil leaves,
cut into chiffonade

3 to 4 tablespoons finely
chopped flat-leaf Italian
parsley

1 pound penne rigate

1 cup grated ricotta salata or
mozzarella, for serving

Preheat the oven to 400°F. Line a baking sheet with parchment paper or Silpat.

For the eggplant, slice the ends from the eggplants and rub the cut surfaces with salt to draw out the indigestible juices. Peel the eggplants and slice crosswise into rounds about 1/2 inch thick. Cut the rounds into thick cubes. Place the eggplant in a large bowl. Sprinkle the garlic over the eggplant and drizzle with the oil; toss well. Arrange the eggplant on the prepared baking sheet in a single layer and bake for 10 to 12 minutes, turning once, or until lightly browned on both sides. Set aside.

Meanwhile, prepare the sauce. Heat the oil in a heavy saucepan over medium heat. Add the shallots and sauté for 2 to 3 minutes, until transparent. Add the garlic and red pepper flakes and sauté for 30 to 40 seconds longer. Crush the tomatoes with clean hands or purée in a food mill. Add to the saucepan and season with the salt and pepper. Simmer for about 25 minutes. Stir in the basil and parsley and remove from heat. Add the eggplant to the sauce and cover to keep warm. The eggplant and sauce can be prepared ahead, cooled, and refrigerated in a suitable container. Bring to room temperature and reheat while cooking the pasta.

Bring a large saucepan of water to a rolling boil over medium-high heat and add 2 tablespoons of the salt. Add the penne, stirring gently to separate. Cover and return the water to a boil and cook until al dente, 8 to 12 minutes. Drain the pasta and transfer to a warm serving dish. Pour the sauce over the pasta and toss very well. Sprinkle with the cheese and serve at once.

BOW-TIE PASTA WITH CRANBERRY BEANS AND GREENS

I HAD ABOUT HALF A POUND OF FRESH CRANBERRY BEANS IN MY REFRIGERATOR ALONG WITH beet greens, cut from the tops of fresh beets, and about half a cup of peeled and seeded tomatoes. It was just enough to combine with the half box of bow-tie pasta in my cupboard. With a sprinkle of Parmesan and some grated mozzarella, my dinner for two worked like a charm.

YIELD: 4 TO 5 SERVINGS

³/₄ pound fresh or dried cranberry beans

1 pound beet greens from two bunches of beets or 1 pound spinach, Swiss chard, or escarole

1 pound bow-tie pasta or other small shaped pasta

1 tablespoon kosher salt, plus more to taste

3 tablespoons extra-virgin olive oil

2 to 3 garlic cloves, finely chopped

1¹/₂ cups peeled and diced fresh tomatoes (see note on page 57)

Freshly ground black pepper

¹/₃ cup grated fresh mozzarella, plus more for serving

¹/₃ cup grated Parmigiano-Reggiano, plus more for serving

Shell the fresh cranberry beans from their pods and cook in boiling salted water for about 30 minutes. If using dried cranberry beans, cook for about 50 minutes. Drain the water from the cooked beans into a 4 to 5-quart saucepan. Add enough fresh cold water to the saucepan to equal about 4¹/₂ quarts and bring to a boil. Set the cranberry beans aside.

Meanwhile, trim and discard the tough stems from the greens. Rinse the greens well, then drain and coarsely chop.

Add the pasta and 1 tablespoon of the salt to the boiling water. Return to a boil and cook for about 5 minutes. Stir to separate the pasta. Add the greens to the pasta and cook for about 5 minutes longer, until the pasta is al dente. Drain, reserving ¹/₂ cup of the pasta water.

Heat the oil in a 10 to 12-inch nonstick skillet over medium heat and sauté the garlic 30 to 40 seconds. Add the beans and toss with the garlic for 1 to 2 minutes. Add the tomatoes and simmer over low heat, stirring occasionally, for about 5 minutes. Add the reserved pasta water, pasta, and greens and mix well. Add the cheeses and toss to mix thoroughly. Taste and adjust the salt and pepper as necessary. Serve on warm plates and pass additional cheese at the table, if desired.

ORECCHIETTE WITH BROCCOLI RABE, GARLIC, AND CAPERS

THEIR TIMING IS PERFECT TOGETHER—ORECCHIETTE, LITTLE EAR-SHAPED PASTA, COOKS with the broccoli rabe in the same amount of time. The garlic, capers, and olive oil dressing offset the slightly bitter taste of the vegetable.

YIELD: 4 TO 5 SERVINGS

1 large bunch broccoli rabe

Kosher salt

1 pound orecchiette

$1/3$ cup extra-virgin olive oil

2 large garlic cloves, finely chopped

Kosher salt and freshly ground black pepper

Pinch of red pepper flakes

4 tablespoons capers packed in wine vinegar, drained

3 to 4 tablespoons coarsely chopped flat-leaf Italian parsley

Trim the broccoli rabe, discarding the tough bottom stems. Separate the stems from the florets and place in two separate bowls of cold water to soak for 20 minutes; drain. The vegetables may be prepped up to several hours ahead if desired.

Bring a large pot of cold water to a boil. Add salt to taste; then add the pasta and broccoli rabe stems. Boil for 2 minutes and then add the florets. Cook for 7 to 10 minutes longer, until the pasta is al dente. Drain, reserving $1/2$ cup of the pasta water.

Meanwhile, warm the oil in a skillet over medium heat and sauté the garlic for 40 to 50 seconds, until barely golden. Season with salt, pepper, and red pepper flakes. Add the capers and sauté for 2 minutes longer. Add the reserved pasta water and continue to simmer.

Spoon the pasta and the broccoli rabe into a large warm serving dish. Pour over the sauce and mix well. Sprinkle with the parsley and serve immediately.

ISRAELI COUSCOUS WITH SHIITAKE AND PORCINI MUSHROOMS

THIS HUMBLE STAPLE, ISRAELI COUSCOUS, IS PASTA MADE FROM SEMOLINA FLOUR AND WATER. Like regular pasta, couscous has a neutral flavor. I have found its soothing texture to be an excellent foil for sautéed mushrooms and fresh herbs.

YIELD: 6 SERVINGS

1 ounce dried porcini mushrooms

1 cup Israeli couscous

2 to 3 tablespoons extra-virgin olive oil

1 small red onion, finely chopped

$^1/_2$ pound shiitake mushrooms, stemmed and sliced $^1/_4$-inch thick

$1^1/_4$ cups chicken stock (see page 335) or low-sodium canned

2 to 3 tablespoons finely chopped flat-leaf Italian parsley

Kosher salt and freshly ground black pepper

Soak the porcini mushrooms in a small bowl of enough hot water to cover for 15 to 20 minutes. Place the mushrooms in a clean bowl, reserving the liquid. Strain the reserved liquid over the mushrooms slowly through a sieve lined with cheesecloth. Repeat this procedure back and forth three or four times, discarding the sandy residue left in the strainer and the previous bowl each time. Reserve $^1/_2$ cup of the concentrated porcini liquid. Slice the porcini and set aside. This process may be done several days ahead. Refrigerate the mushrooms and liquid in separate containers.

In a dry 10 to 12-inch skillet toast the couscous over medium heat, shaking the pan for 3 to 4 minutes to color slightly. Remove from the pan and set aside. Heat the oil in the same skillet over medium-high heat and sauté the onion for 3 to 4 minutes until tender. If more oil is necessary to cook the shiitakes, push the onion to one side of the skillet, tip the skillet, and heat the remaining 1 tablespoon oil. Add the shiitakes and sauté for 4 to 5 minutes, tossing carefully to cook evenly. Add the toasted couscous, the stock, and the reserved porcini liquid and bring to a boil. Reduce the heat to medium low and cook at a brisk simmer, partially covered, for 18 to 20 minutes, or until the liquid is absorbed and the couscous is tender. Stir in the sliced porcini mushrooms and the parsley. Taste for salt and pepper and serve.

NOTE: Fresh mushrooms contain a good bit of water. To clean them, put in a colander and run quickly under a spray of cold water. Place in a clean kitchen towel and pat dry. The mushrooms are ready to use.

POLENTA WITH FENNEL MARMALADE

SLOW-COOKED FENNEL IN OLIVE OIL TRANSFORMS INTO A DELICIOUS, LIGHTLY CARAMELIZED
vegetable sauce. Serve the fennel over warm polenta—for a warm and comforting dish.

YIELD: 6 TO 8 SERVINGS

FOR THE FENNEL MARMALADE

3 large fennel bulbs,
  trimmed of stalks and
  fronds

$1/4$ cup extra-virgin olive oil

3 to 4 large garlic cloves,
  sliced paper thin

$1/2$ cup water

Kosher salt and freshly
  ground black pepper

FOR THE POLENTA

4 cups water or chicken
  stock (see page 335) or
  low-sodium canned

Kosher salt and freshly
  ground black pepper

1 cup stone-ground cornmeal

2 to 3 tablespoons coarsely
  chopped fresh Italian
  parsley, for garnish

For the fennel marmalade, discard any bruised layers of fennel and the core. Cut into julienne strips between $1/4$ and $1/2$ inch wide. Soak in a bowl of cold water for 15 minutes.

Heat the oil in a large nonstick skillet over medium-low heat. Add the garlic, reduce the heat to low, and cook for 5 to 6 minutes, or until the pieces are pale yellow. Scoop out the garlic with a slotted spoon and reserve.

Increase the heat to medium-high and add the fennel to the skillet. Sauté for 2 to 3 minutes. Add the water and salt and pepper to taste and cover the skillet. Simmer over medium heat, stirring occasionally, until golden brown on all sides. Uncover the pan. Add the reserved garlic, toss to mix, and reduce any liquid left in the pan. The fennel can be prepared up to several hours ahead and reheated before serving.

Warm a serving platter in a low 180°F oven.

For the polenta, in a 3 to 4-quart saucepan, bring the water or stock to a rolling boil. Add salt and pepper to taste and reduce the heat to a simmer. Slowly sift the cornmeal through your fingers into the water while stirring constantly with a wooden spoon or whisk. This should take about 1 minute. Continue whisking and return to a boil. Simmer, whisking constantly until the cornmeal begins to thicken, 1 to 2 minutes. Reduce the heat to the barest simmer, cover the pan, and cook slowly, stirring every 8 to 10 minutes, until the polenta is smooth and thick and comes away from the side of the pan, about 20 to 25 minutes. Pour the polenta onto the warm platter and spread to the edge. Spoon the fennel marmalade in a mound in the center of the polenta. Sprinkle with the parsley and serve warm.

RISOTTO WITH PORCINI, HERBS, AND TRUFFLE OIL

A SPECIALTY OF NORTHERN ITALY, RISOTTO IS FAMOUS FOR THE CREAMY TEXTURE THE RICE develops as it slowly cooks. As all rice retains its warmth, I particularly enjoy this rich and satisfying dish in the colder months. If desired, drizzle with a bit of truffle oil for a luscious finish.

YIELD: 6 TO 8 SERVINGS

$3/4$ ounce dried porcini mushrooms

1 tablespoon unsalted butter

$1/4$ to $1/3$ pound shiitake mushrooms, trimmed, rinsed, and thinly sliced

2 tablespoons extra-vigin olive oil

1 medium red onion, finely chopped

1 garlic clove, finely chopped

2 cups imported rice, preferably Italian Arborio

$1/3$ cup dry white wine

$5 1/2$ to 6 cups chicken stock (see page 335), heated to simmering

$1/2$ cup chopped fresh mixed herbs, such as basil, chives, and parsley

$1/3$ cup freshly grated Parmigiano-Reggiano

Kosher salt and freshly ground black pepper

Truffle oil (optional)

Soak the porcini mushrooms in a small bowl of lukewarm water for 30 minutes Place the mushrooms in a clean bowl, reserving the liquid. Strain the reserved liquid through a fine sieve lined with cheesecloth into a small bowl. Repeat this procedure back and forth three or four times, discarding the sandy residue left in the strainer each time. Slice the mushrooms thin and set aside.

Heat the butter in a large flameproof saucepan over medium heat. Sauté the shiitake mushrooms for 3 to 4 minutes until tender. Set aside with the porcini. Add the oil and cook the onion and garlic for several minutes until tender but not brown. Stir in the rice and cook about 1 minute. Add the wine and cook, stirring, until most of the wine has evaporated.

Add $1/2$ cup of the simmering stock and cook, stirring, at a gentle simmer. When most of the liquid is absorbed, add an additional $3/4$ cup of stock. Repeat, adding more stock, until the rice is half cooked, 12 to 15 minutes. Return the porcini and shiitakes to the pot. Add an additional $1/2$ cup of stock, stirring as the liquid absorbs into the rice. Continue this process, adding more stock, $1/2$ cup at a time, until the rice is tender, 22 to 25 minutes.

Taste the rice for doneness. It should be creamy yet slightly toothsome to the bite. Add the mixed herbs and cheese and stir to mix. Taste for salt and pepper. Remove from the heat and serve immediately with a drizzle of truffle oil, if desired.

Wine Suggestion: Roanoke Vineyard Ryhme and Meter Chardonnay

ROASTED STRIPED BASS FILLETS WITH CAPERS AND CROUTONS

ROASTING LARGE FILLETS OF FIRM WHITE FISH SUCH AS STRIPED BASS, TOPPED WITH tomatoes, capers, and croutons, makes for festive, elegant, and striking dinner party fare.

YIELD: 8 SERVINGS

2 garlic cloves, finely chopped

Kosher salt and freshly
   ground black pepper

2 striped bass fillets (about
   $3\frac{1}{2}$ to 4 pounds), with skin

1 bunch scallions (white and
   pale green parts), trimmed
   and cut into 1-inch pieces
   on the diagonal

$\frac{1}{4}$ cup finely chopped
   flat-leaf Italian parsley

1 cup diced ripe Roma
   tomatoes (3 to 4)

$\frac{1}{4}$ cup capers

2 tablespoons extra-virgin
   olive oil

$1\frac{1}{2}$ cups toasted croutons
   (see page 335)

$\frac{1}{4}$ cup niçoise olives

Roasted baby carrots
   (optional) (see page 221)

Preheat the oven to 400°F. Lightly oil an ovenproof platter large enough to hold the fillets in one layer. Place the greased platter in the oven while preheating.

Meanwhile, rub the garlic and salt and pepper to taste into the flesh side of the fish and set aside. Combine the scallions and parsley in a bowl and set aside.

When ready to cook the fish, remove the platter from the oven and place the fish, skin side down, on the sizzling platter to crisp the skin. Reduce the oven temperature to 375°F.

Scatter the scallion-parsley mixture over the fish and then scatter the tomatoes and capers on top. Sprinkle the olive oil over the fillets. Bake for 15 minutes. Remove the platter from the oven and scatter the croutons and olives over the fish. Return the platter to the oven and bake for 3 to 5 minutes longer, until the fillets are springy to the touch. Surround the fillets with roasted baby carrots, if desired, and serve.

Wine suggestion: Macari Vineyard Reserve Chardonnay

STRIPED BASS IS an anadromous fish, meaning that it lives in the ocean but breeds in fresh water. It can be legally caught off Long Island's Atlantic Coast from July 1 to early December. It is a favorite of Hamptons' sports fishermen, and is a favorite of mine too.

PECONIC BAY SCALLOPS
WITH TOMATO-VINEGAR SAUCE

THIS CLASSIC BUT CONTEMPORARY RECIPE HAS ORIGINS IN PROVENCE.

YIELD: 4 TO 6 SERVINGS

$1^1/_2$ pounds bay scallops,
   tough muscle removed

Kosher salt and freshly
   ground black pepper

3 tablespoons extra-virgin
   olive oil, divided

2 leeks, rinsed well, soaked,
   and thinly sliced

2 to 3 garlic cloves, finely
   chopped

$^3/_4$ cup dry white wine

3 tablespoons tarragon vinegar or white wine vinegar

3 medium ripe tomatoes,
   peeled (see note on page
   57), seeded, and chopped

$^1/_4$ teaspoon tomato paste

Kosher salt and freshly
   ground black pepper

Fresh parsley or tarragon
   sprigs, for garnish
   (optional)

Rinse the scallops quickly and pat dry with paper towels. Sprinkle with salt and pepper to taste and set aside.

Warm 2 tablespoons of the oil in a saucepan over medium-low heat. Add the leeks and sauté for 3 to 4 minutes, stirring until tender. Add the garlic and sauté a few seconds longer. Add the wine, turn the heat to high, and bring to a boil. Reduce the heat to medium and simmer briskly until the wine is reduced by half. Add the vinegar and cook for 2 to 3 minutes longer. Add the tomatoes and tomato paste. Sprinkle lightly with salt and pepper; then simmer for 12 to 15 minutes. Taste to adjust the seasonings if necessary. The sauce can be made up to two days ahead to this point. Refrigerate in a suitable container. Bring to room temperature before reheating.

Heat the remaining tablespoon of oil in a nonstick skillet over medium-high heat. Let the pan heat for 1 to 2 minutes. Add the scallops and quickly sauté for about $1^1/_2$ minutes, turning once and being careful not to overcook. Ladle the sauce evenly in the center of six salad plates and divide the scallops over the sauce. Garnish with fresh sprigs of parsley or tarragon, if desired.

Wine suggestion: Peconic Bay Winery Dry Riesling

THE SMALL BAY or calico scallops are either dredged or hand-gathered from deep cold waters by divers close to shore or during a defined season. The season for bay scallops on the East End of Long Island begins the first Monday in November.

FLOUNDER FILLETS
WITH PANKO BREADCRUMBS

COAT THE FISH WITH PANKO, COARSE JAPANESE BREADCRUMBS, TO GIVE THE FISH EXTRA CRUNCH.
Measure out your ingredients and place on a tray. The actual cooking time takes mere minutes.

YIELD: 3 TO 4 SERVINGS

4 flounder fillets
(about 1 pound)

4 to 5 tablespoons panko
breadcrumbs

Kosher salt

$1/4$ teaspoon paprika

1 teaspoon fresh thyme
leaves or $1/4$ teaspoon dried

2 tablespoons canola oil

2 tablespoons unsalted
butter

Freshly ground black
pepper

$1/3$ to $1/2$ cup freshly
squeezed lemon juice

1 lemon, scored and thinly
sliced, for garnish
(optional)

Rinse the fillets and pat dry with paper towels. Place the panko in a small bowl and season with salt, paprika, and thyme and stir to mix. Spread the panko mixture on a large shallow plate and dredge the fillets on both sides in the seasoned panko.

Heat the oil and butter in a large heavy skillet over medium-high heat. When hot, add 2 or 3 fillets at a time, one layer deep. Cook each side until lightly golden, 2 to 3 minutes. Carefully turn with a wide spatula and cook $1/2$ to 2 minutes longer. Season with freshly ground pepper and keep warm. You may have to do this in two batches.

Discard any excess fat in the skillet. Add the lemon juice, scraping the pan with a wooden spatula to deglaze the pan juices. Pour the warm sauce over the fillets and serve immediately. Garnish with lemon slices, if desired.

POACHED MONKFISH WITH
FRESH TOMATO TARRAGON SAUCE

IN LATE SUMMER AND FALL, MANY FARM STANDS WILL OFFER "SAUCE TOMATOES" AT A BARGAIN price. These tomatoes may have slight bruises on the skin as well as soft spots. I have even found some heirloom sauce tomatoes that were perfectly fine at one-third the cost of regular heirlooms. I saved those for slicing and the more damaged ones for making a sauce such as the one below.

YIELD: 6 SERVINGS

2 tablespoons extra-virgin olive oil

1 tablespoon unsalted butter

3 large shallots, finely chopped

2^1/$_2$ cups peeled, seeded, and diced tomatoes (see note on page 57)

^{1}/$_4$ cup dry white wine

Kosher salt and freshly ground black pepper

1 tablespoon capers in brine, rinsed

1 tablespoon finely chopped flat-leaf Italian parsley

1 tablespoon chopped fresh tarragon leaves

1^1/$_2$ pounds monkfish fillet, cut into 1^1/$_2$-inch cubes

Place the oil and butter in a 10 to 12-inch sauté pan over medium heat, and when the butter foam subsides, add the shallots. Sauté for 1 to 2 minutes, until tender. Add the tomatoes, wine, and salt and pepper to taste and bring to a boil. Reduce the heat to medium and simmer and cook for 5 to 7 minutes, until the wine evaporates by half. Add the capers, parsley, and tarragon and stir to mix. Taste to adjust the seasonings if necessary. The sauce can be prepared several hours ahead. Return the saucepan to medium heat and simmer the sauce when ready to cook the fish.

Add the fish to the sauce in the pan, spooning the sauce over the fish to coat, and simmer for 7 to 8 minutes, until the fish is springy to the touch. Serve on warm plates with the sauce spooned over it.

MONKFISH, known abroad as lotte, is a delicious fish with a sturdy texture; hence, it is referred to as the poor man's lobster in the United States. A Dutch sauté pan with straight sides about 2-inches high is my pan of choice to prepare this sauce and ultimately the cubes of fish.

BOBBY VAN'S RESTAURANT
Bridgehampton

SOME OLD-TIME REGULARS STILL THINK THEY CAN HEAR THE TINKLING OF A piano tune or the chit chat of actors, musicians, artists, and writers who haunt the eponymous restaurant of classical pianist Bobby Van.

Bobby Van's classic steakhouse is a lively, fun, and social Mecca of a place with the celebrity factor continuing today. Joe Phair, formerly a restaurateur in Ireland, purchased the restaurant in 1996 and runs it with his son, James, who is the general manager. The restaurant, offering an eclectic menu, is open seven days a week throughout the year for lunch and dinner. Bobby Van's center door is flanked by floor-to-ceiling window walls that open to the street in summer, giving the effect of a sidewalk café. Glass window panes allow light to pass through a divider that separates the inviting thirty-foot walnut bar area from the comfortable restaurant. Bar customers at the southern end of the bar can gaze at photographs of James Jones, Truman Capote, and John Knowles while nibbling on sliders. The colorful bar menu is written on the chalkboards above the mirrored bar and local art sits above the shelves of spirits. High ceiling fans made of sail cloth sewn into fishing poles are in constant motion over the grass papered walls of the dining room, and curved woven-back bamboo-framed bistro chairs surround the crisp white-on-white tabletop settings.

John Stella is the executive chef of Bobby Van's. He and his kitchen staff have been together for more than ten years, making for efficiency of kitchen and service. In 1987 the talented chef started out as a pantry cook in Oakdale, Long Island. John worked summer jobs at Bobby Van's in 1995, 1996, and 1997. Off season included a stint in a family-operated food business. His connection to the impressive Myriad Restaurant Group headed by Drew Neiporent and Robert DeNiro allowed him to get invaluable experience at Tribeca Grill. John then went to South Beach where he worked mornings cutting meat at Smith and Wolensky and evenings as sous chef at the China Grill. John returned to Bobby Van's as sous chef and was named executive chef in 1999. Steak and pasta were mainstays on the menu when John first started at Bobby Van's; he has since brought a level of sophistication and creativity to the menu. In season John brings in produce from local farms and local fish from commercial draggers in Shinnecock Bay.

BOBBY VAN'S LOBSTER LAVASH WRAP

ALTHOUGH PRICEY, COOKED LOBSTER MEAT IS AVAILABLE AT YOUR FAVORITE FISH STORE. FOR 1½ pounds of lobster meat from the shell, you will need six 1¼-pound lobsters.

YIELD: 6 SERVINGS

1½ pounds cooked
   lobster meat, cubed

⅓ cup finely diced carrot

⅓ cup finely diced celery

⅓ cup finely diced onion

1½ cups light mayonnaise

2 teaspoons Old Bay seasoning, or more to taste

Kosher salt and freshly
   ground white pepper

6 lavash wraps*

1 bunch arugula, washed
   and spun dry

Sweet chili sauce*

In a bowl, mix the lobster meat with the carrot, celery, onion, mayonnaise, Old Bay, and salt and white pepper to taste.

Arrange the lavash on a counter and arrange a layer of arugula over the bottom third of the bread. Divide the lobster meat equally and spread the mixture over the arugula. Roll up each wrap toward the unfilled portion and secure closed with bamboo skewers. The wraps can be prepared ahead to this point and refrigerated covered in a suitable container. When ready to serve, slice in half on the diagonal between the skewers and serve with a drizzle of the sweet chili sauce.

* NOTE: If you are unable to find lavash wraps, you may substitute plain square roll-ups or tortillas available at supermarkets. Sweet chili sauce is available at Asian grocers or online (See Sources, page 339).

COR-J SEAFOOD
Shinnecock Bay

ON SUNNY DAYS, THE LIGHT REFLECTING ON THE WAVES IN SHINNECOCK BAY behind Cor-j Seafood market in Hampton Bays looks like fireflies dancing on the water. When you enter the sprawling one-story stucco building, you will find "cutters" in their long rubberized aprons and high boots gutting, cleaning, and filleting fish that is so fresh the air is perfumed by the scent of the sea.

The proprietor of Cor-J Seafood, Jim Coronesi, was born and raised in Oyster Bay, Long Island. Jim started digging clams with tongs from a boat at the legal age of sixteen. After high school he immersed himself into the life of the sea, working and experiencing the business end at an oyster farm in Greenport. He took courses in marine science at Suffolk Community College at night and went on to work for Marine Life in Woodbury, where he became the lobster buyer. He started a little business on the side selling fish at retail out of a row boat station in Hampton Bays. He then leased Smitty's Lobster House, which eventually became Cor-J, a play on Coronesi and Jim. Jim is in business today with his partners, Danny Coronesi, his son, and Greg Morgaze.

Customers can find a pristine array of local fish such as fluke, flounder, weakfish, bluefish, sea bass, tuna, haddock, cod, halibut, monkfish, skate, and porgies. They also dry sea scallops, which can be opened in their shells right at the market upon request—yielding their roe, a delicious and rare delicacy.

The local Peconic bay scallops, a fine, smaller-than-a-penny delicacy harvested from clean waters, are sensational raw, making them the perfect choice for ceviche (fish "cooked" in acidic juices). The first Monday in November officially opens the bay scallop season, which continues through March.

Most fish are regulated by size or quotas. "Regulation," said Jim, "is necessary or there would be nothing left." Striped bass, for example, is a regulated species. You need a license to harvest and to sell this "queen of the sea."

Jim and his partners purchased Tully's, formerly retail seafood and take-out shop just around the bend from Cor-J. They continue to offer prepared seafood dishes to take out or eat in with an outdoor clam and oyster bar to soak in the fresh sea aromas.

CRESCENT DUCK FARM
Aquebogue

I GOT SUCH A KICK OUT OF SEEING THE EGGS CRACK OPEN AS I PATTED THE sweet little furry bodies of the barely hatched tiny ducklings. Doug Corwin of Crescent Duck Farm escorted me into the hatchery and was delighted by the experience.

Doug is a Corwin on his great grandfather's side and a Hallock on his great grandmother's side. These are two names that represent generations of North Fork families going back to the 1600s. In 1908, great grandfather Corwin, descendant of a family of carpenters, decided to do something on the property that was left to him. "With twenty or thirty acres," said Doug, "which was sandy and hilly and not good for crops, he decided to grow ducks."

The duck industry was thriving at the time here on Long Island. The industry began in 1873 when a sea captain brought nine Peking ducks over from China. As I understand it some of the ducks were eaten, but obviously enough remained to begin the Long Island duck industry. Duck farms were prevalent on both the North and South Fork of Long Island in the nineteenth and twentieth centuries. Today most are gone, leaving behind a few historic farm houses.

"Crescent Duck farm is a self-sustaining city in Aquebogue," said Doug. "We do our own breeding, our own hatching, and our own harvesting (processing). There are 160,000 ducks at any given time on 140 acres of land where they wander around in big open barns between the feeders and the waterers. We own our own feed milling operation and have our own feed corn, wheat, and soybean grown for us to make our own feed. Our ducks consume over 230 tons of feed a week. We also provide feed for other poultry farms; any low corn you see growing locally is all coming to us. We have an inter-relationship with dirt farmers on the twin forks. We buy corn and straw from them, which keeps us all active in farming and helps keep the local economy going."

Doug had a great deal to say about the family legacy. "With two sons in their twenties and other family members in the business, we're preserving to keep the industry going. We've never sold any development rights. We're looking to grow not to retrench. This is a business that has staying power—and that's a good thing!"

SPICED DUCK BREASTS WITH SHALLOT SAUCE

LONG ISLAND DUCKS ARE FAMOUS FOR THEIR PEKING HERITAGE, AND I'M DELIGHTED THAT THEY are harvested so close to home. The agreeably spiced duck breasts served with a sweet shallot sauce are the perfect choice for duck lovers, like me.

YIELD: 4 TO 5 SERVINGS

FOR THE DUCK

1 teaspoon ground star anise

2 teaspoons ground coriander

1 teaspoon ground cumin

1 teaspoon freshly ground white pepper

Pinch of cayenne

1 whole duck breast

Kosher salt and freshly ground black pepper

FOR THE SHALLOT SAUCE

1 tablespoon unsalted butter, divided

3 to 4 large shallots, thinly sliced

Kosher salt

1/4 cup dry white wine

1/3 cup chicken stock (see page 335) or low-sodium canned

1 tablespoon thyme leaves

Thyme sprigs, for garnish (optional)

For the duck, combine the star anise, coriander, cumin, white pepper, and cayenne and stir to mix. Remove the duck breasts from the package and cut each in half through the skin that separates each whole breast, yielding 4 halves. Rinse the duck and dry with paper towels. Place on a work platter and season with salt and black pepper. With a sharp knife, score the skin, making 3 or 4 diagonal slits across the fat but being careful not to cut into the breast meat. Rub the spice mixture evenly into the duck skin.

Heat a heavy skillet over medium-high heat for 2 to 3 minutes. Sear the duck breasts, skin side down, in the pan to render some of the fat and crisp the skin. Reduce the heat to medium and cook until the skin is golden brown and crispy, 6 to 7 minutes. Turn the duck over and continue to cook for about 4 minutes longer for medium rare, the appropriate doneness for duck breasts. Transfer the duck, skin side down, to paper towels to absorb excess moisture.

For the shallot sauce, pour off all but 1 tablespoon of fat from the skillet and add 1/2 tablespoon of the butter to the fat and heat over medium high. When the foam subsides, add the shallots, sauté for 2 minutes, and season with salt to taste. Add the wine and cook until it evaporates. Add the remaining butter and the stock and bring to a boil. Reduce the heat to medium and simmer for 5 to 7 minutes longer. Add the thyme leaves and stir to mix.

To serve, cut the duck breasts into 1/4-inch slices and fan them out in a semi-circle on the plate. Spoon the shallot sauce evenly over the duck and garnish with thyme, if using.

Wine suggestion: Raphael First Label Merlot

WOLFFER ESTATE VINEYARDS
Sagaponack

ROMAN ROTH IS FROM ROTTWEIL, GERMANY, A REGION IN THE VICINITY OF the Black Forest. As a young man Roman fantasized about the creative part of the wine business. "You create a product that celebrates." He did an apprenticeship at the Kaiserstuhl, a wine region in Boden on the right side of the Rhine, opposite Alsace.

Christian Wolffer, founder of Wolffer Estate Vineyards, was looking for a winemaker. When Christian and Roman met, they were in sync with what their vision for the winery would be. Christian's words to Roman made an impact: "Buy whatever you need to buy and do whatever you have to do to make the best wine on Long Island." That was in the spring of 1992.

"Wolffer is in a unique position because it is a boutique winery and able to reach most of their customers personally. As a result it can make a more distinctive wine than the more commercial wineries and have the ability to make a more rustic or traditional wine despite being in the New World. What sets it apart is its red and its barrel-fermented Perle Chardonnay," he continued. For Roman, "a great wine should be concentrated and elegant. The varieties that inspired Wolffer Estate wines are the grapes originating from France, which basically consist of the classic Burgundy and Bordeaux."

One of the greatest benefits to winemaking is the soil. Wolffer's distinction is that the Merlot and Cabernet Franc grapes love the Bridgehampton soil. The winery is 2.6 miles from the Atlantic Ocean, which provides a moderating sea breeze, another huge advantage.

"Long Island is so unique and special as compared to other areas of the United States when it comes to wine," said Roman. "It's set up to show individuality," and then he quoted the wine writer Peter Sichel: "It takes great location, great soil, great climate, money and skill—also pride and passion to make great wines."

The entire team at Wolffer takes pride in the wine and brings individuality to the process. The setting is undoubtedly one of the most picturesque in the Hamptons. The saffron-hued Tuscan-style mansion at Christian Wolffer's Estate Vineyard in Sagaponack sits majestically on fifty rolling acres of vineyard. In addition to producing some of the area's finest and award-winning wines, Wolffer Estate holds special wine tasting musical events throughout the year.

Christian Wolffer set the standard and direction for the winery, which is a tribute to his vision. Christian Wolffer died December 31, 2008, and his presence will be greatly missed at Wolffer Estates and in the Hamptons.

CHICKEN WITH DRIED PORCINI AND RED WINE

THIS IS A SUCCULENT CHICKEN DISH WITH THE WOODSY AROMA OF PORCINI MUSHROOMS. Porcini mushrooms, or Italian wild mushroom, are sold dried and are available in Italian and gourmet markets and some supermarkets. It is necessary to reconstitute them before using. They tend to be pricey, but a little goes a long way.

YIELD: 4 SERVINGS

1 chicken (about 3½ pounds), cut into eight pieces

1 ounce dried porcini mushrooms

¼ cup all-purpose flour

4 tablespoons extra-virgin olive oil

2 tablespoons unsalted butter

6 to 8 fresh sage leaves

½ cup dry red wine

1 cup warm chicken stock (see page 335) or low-sodium canned

3 medium tomatoes, peeled (see note on page 57), seeded, and puréed

Kosher salt and freshly ground black pepper

Chopped fresh parsley, for garnish (optional)

Remove any excess fat from the chicken. Rinse the chicken pieces well and dry thoroughly on paper towels. Transfer to a work platter.

Soak the porcini mushrooms in a small bowl of warm water to barely cover for 15 to 20 minutes. Place the mushrooms in a clean bowl, reserving the broth. Strain the reserved broth through a strainer lined with cheesecloth into a small bowl. Repeat this procedure back and forth three or four times to discard the sandy residue left in the strainer each time. Reserve the broth and reconstituted mushrooms.

Tap the flour in a sieve over the chicken pieces to dust them. Heat the oil with the butter in a 12-inch skillet over medium heat and when the butter is completely melted, add the chicken pieces in two batches, being careful not to crowd the pan. Cook the chicken gently until golden brown, about 10 to 12 minutes. Pour off the excess fat from the skillet, leaving about 1 to 2 tablespoons in the skillet. Reduce the heat to medium low and add the sage leaves and wine, letting the wine evaporate slowly for about 10 minutes.

Add the strained mushroom broth, chicken stock, and mushrooms to the chicken in the skillet. When the mushroom broth is reduced by half, about 15 minutes, add the tomatoes and season to taste with salt and pepper. Let simmer for about 10 minutes longer, until the chicken is cooked through. Check for doneness. Serve warm garnished with parsley, if desired.

Wine suggestion: Wolffer Estate Cabernet Franc

BRAISED CHICKEN WITH 20 GARLIC CLOVES

THIS IS A DISH FOR ALL SEASONS, YET FALL SEEMS THE APPROPRIATE TIME FOR THIS BRAISED, light, and tasty comfort food.

YIELD: 4 TO 5 SERVINGS

1 (3 to 3¹/₂-pound) chicken, cut into eight pieces

Kosher salt and freshly ground black pepper

¹/₂ cup all-purpose flour

2 to 3 tablespoons extra-virgin olive oil

2 tablespoons unsalted butter, divided

20 garlic cloves, peeled

4 to 5 ribs celery, trimmed and cut into 1¹/₂ inch slices on the diagonal

1¹/₂ tablespoons chopped fresh rosemary leaves

1 tablespoon chopped fresh sage

1 tablespoon chopped fresh thyme

1 tablespoon chopped fresh parsley leaves

3 sprigs parsley

2 or 3 inner ribs celery, with leaves

1 to 1¹/₂ cups chicken stock (see page 335) or low-sodium canned

8 to 10 slices from 1 crusty baguette, toasted and sliced on the diagonal

Rinse the chicken well and pat dry with paper towels. Sprinkle with salt and pepper all over and dust with the flour.

Heat the oil over medium heat in a heavy 12-inch skillet. When hot but not smoking, add the legs and thighs, skin side down, and sauté until the pieces are golden brown, about 4 minutes on one side and 3 minutes on the other. Remove from the pan and set aside. Put the remaining chicken pieces, skin side down, in the skillet and sauté for 3 minutes on one side and 2 to 3 minutes on the other.

Return the dark meat chicken to the skillet. Add the butter and toss with the chicken until melted. Transfer the chicken to a colander to drain. Pour off all but 2 tablespoons of fat from the pan and add the garlic cloves, celery, rosemary, sage, thyme, and parsley and stir to mix. Season with salt and pepper and sauté for 4 to 5 minutes, stirring occasionally, until the garlic cloves begin to lightly color.

Return the chicken pieces to the pan and deglaze the juices with about ¹/₄ cup of water. Tie the parsley sprigs and celery stems together with twine. Add to the pan with the stock. Simmer, partially covered, for about 20 minutes for the white meat and 3 to 5 minutes longer for the dark meat.

Serve the chicken with the vegetables and juices over the toasted bread slices.

BRINED ROASTED TURKEY
WITH LEMON AND HERBS

FRESH HERITAGE TURKEYS ARE AVAILABLE IN THE HAMPTONS AT ART LUDLOW'S TURKEY FARM in Bridgehampton and North Sea Farm in Southampton. Ordering a month or more ahead is a must.

YIELD: 12 TO 14 SERVINGS

FOR THE BRINE

2 quarts cold water, divided

$\frac{1}{2}$ cup kosher salt

$\frac{1}{4}$ cup sugar

$\frac{1}{2}$ cup freshly squeezed
orange juice

$\frac{1}{4}$ cup freshly squeezed
lemon juice

2 tablespoons cracked
black pepper

FOR THE TURKEY

1 (14 to 16-pound) prepared
fresh turkey

1 large garlic clove, halved

$\frac{1}{4}$ cup freshly squeezed
lemon juice

$\frac{1}{2}$ cup mixed fresh herbs,
such as sage, rosemary,
and thyme

1 large onion, quartered

Herb branches (from the
mixed herbs)

Kosher salt and freshly
ground black pepper

For the brine, pour 1 quart of the water into a large saucepan and add the salt, sugar, orange juice, lemon juice, and pepper. Bring to a boil. Remove from the heat and add the remaining 1 quart of water. Let chill completely before brining the turkey.

For the turkey, remove the giblets from the turkey. The giblets and the neck may be used for turkey stock, if desired. Rinse the turkey inside and out and pat dry with paper towels. Tuck back the wing tips and place the turkey in a large garbage bag. Pour in the cooled brine and tie the garbage bag closed. Place another garbage bag over the tied end and tie the bag tightly at the other end. Place in the refrigerator for 24 hours, turning the turkey several times in the refrigerator to redistribute the brining liquid. It may be necessary to have someone help with this task.

Preheat the oven to 325°F.

Remove the turkey from the refrigerator and place in a clean sink. Open and remove the bags, discarding the brine. Rinse the turkey very well and pat the inside and outside dry with paper towels. Massage the turkey with the garlic halves; then combine with the lemon juice and mixed herbs and slide the mixture under the skin into the breast and thighs as well as possible. Stuff the cavity with the quartered onion and herb branches. Truss the turkey by crisscrossing a length of kitchen twine around the tail to cross over the top of the legs and then pulling the twine along the lower portion of the breast and hooking it through the joint of the wings to tie the neck flap tightly closed. Place the turkey on a rack in a roasting pan and season all over with salt and pepper.

FOR THE NATURAL SAUCE

2 shallots, finely chopped

1^1/$_3$ cup dry red wine

2 cups chicken stock
(see page 335) or low-
sodium canned

Kosher salt and freshly
ground black pepper

Roast the turkey for 3^1/$_2$ to 4 hours, basting with drippings every 30 minutes, until an instant thermometer inserted into the inner thigh below the leg joint (do not touch the bone) registers 165°F. If the skin begins to brown too quickly, tent with a sheet of heavy-duty aluminum foil. To test for doneness, prick the thigh meat down to the joint and press gently for juices to run clear. The turkey will continue to cook when removed from the oven. Let rest for 15 to 20 minutes so the internal juices redistribute throughout. Transfer to a carving board.

For the natural sauce, spoon off the excess fat from the pan drippings. Add the shallots to the roasting pan and sauté over medium heat until translucent, 3 to 4 minutes. Stir in the wine and bring to a boil. Reduce the liquid by half and add the chicken stock. Season with salt and pepper to taste and cook at a brisk simmer to thicken slightly, 15 to 20 minutes. Transfer the sauce to a saucepan and keep warm while the turkey is carved.

NOTE: I'm a firm believer in brining anything from boneless chicken breasts to almost any size turkey. The larger the turkey, however, the more challenging it will be to handle, not to mention refrigerate. But if you can handle it, you are guaranteed to enjoy a moist and tender bird whenever you prepare it.

Wine suggestion: Shinn Estate Vineyards Cabernet Franc

THE GRAPES OF ROTH

THE DREAM OF BECOMING A WINEMAKER FOR ROMAN ROTH WAS VERY REAL. As a successful, award-winning winemaker at Wolffer Estate Vineyard in Sagaponack, New York, Roman had another dream that was slowly evolving, that of making wines on a small scale under his own label, The Grapes of Roth, crafting his own brand. "The model for the wines," said Roman, "is artisanal or *garagist*, meaning on a small scale to ultimate quality."

Over the years he planted two significant varieties, Merlot and Riesling. "I felt that either one of these," said Roman, "could make special wines on a consistent basis for years to come. The grape is grown on a vineyard in Jamesport on the North Fork. Jamesport has the warmest climate on the East End where the Merlot grape ripens especially well. The Riesling grape is from a vineyard in Greenport on the North Fork and as a result is influenced by both the Long Island Sound and the Atlantic Ocean. It is perfect for the Riesling to have a cooler sea breeze."

Roman has special relationships with the growers to ensure that the best grapes possible come into the cellar. "One must create ideal conditions in the vineyard to keep perfectly trimmed vines to avoid disease pressure from high humidity then to execute the process to perfection in the winery so that the flavors express the way they grow in the vineyard without over manipulating," said Roman.

Roman Roth is indeed a perfectionist. Robert Parker's Wine Advocate gave Grapes of Roth 92 points for the 2002 Merlot, which made it the highest rated wine in New York State. He was recognized at the April 2003 East End Food & Wine Awards, (judged by the American Sommelier Society), where he was named "Winemaker of the Year".

An addendum: A friend of Roman's, in a playful moment, came up with the label The Grapes of Roth, needless to say, a play on words on John Steinbeck's *Grapes of Wrath*. Roman Roth is a resident of Sag Harbor, as was John Steinbeck in his late years. The name clicked and it was clear this was the choice of name for Roman's artisanal wines.

BRAISED SHORT RIBS
WITH CARROTS AND FENNEL

FOR SLOW-BRAISED RECIPES SUCH AS THIS, I PREFER TO USE ENAMEL-OVER-IRON CASSEROLE Dutch ovens such as Le Creuset. When you prepare the food ahead of time, the casserole can stay in the refrigerator overnight and then be reheated and served directly from the casserole. Whatever pot you choose to use, prepare the recipe one day ahead for the meat to absorb the rich flavorful sauce.

YIELD: 4 SERVINGS

4 tablespoons extra-virgin olive oil, divided

1 large onion, finely chopped

2 to 3 garlic cloves, finely chopped

4 carrots, thinly sliced on the diagonal

1 large fennel bulb, trimmed and thinly sliced

Kosher salt and freshly ground black pepper

3 to 4 tablespoons flour, for dusting

Paprika

8 short ribs (about 4 pounds)

2 cups dry red wine

3 to 3^1/$_2$ cups beef or chicken stock (see page 335) or low-sodium canned

4 to 5 (1-inch strips) orange zest

Juice of 1 orange

Chopped parsley or chives, for garnish

Put 3 tablespoons of the oil in a heavy 12-inch skillet over medium heat and heat until the oil begins to ripple. Add the onion and sauté for 3 to 4 minutes until translucent, stirring occasionally. Add the garlic and sauté for 30 to 40 seconds longer. Stir the carrots and fennel into the onion and garlic. Cook over low heat, partially covered, for 10 to 12 minutes, stirring occasionally, until the vegetables are tender but firm. Season with salt and pepper to taste. With a slotted spoon transfer the vegetables to a Dutch oven large enough to hold the meat and vegetables, over medium-low heat; do not drain the skillet.

Meanwhile, in a small bowl, combine the flour with equal amounts of salt, pepper, and paprika. Dust the short ribs on all sides with the seasoned flour. Heat the remaining 1 tablespoon of oil over medium high in the same skillet the vegetables were cooked in. When hot, add the ribs a few at a time without crowding the pan and sear on all sides until golden brown. Transfer the ribs as they are done to the Dutch oven. Deglaze the skillet with the wine, scraping the bottom with a wooden spoon, and bring to a boil. Simmer briskly until the wine is reduced by half. Add the stock and bring the mixture to a boil. Cook at a brisk simmer for 2 to 3 minutes.

Sprinkle the orange zest and orange juice over the ribs and pour in the reduced pan juices. Adjust the heat under the Dutch oven and cook, partially covered, at a gentle simmer for 1^1/$_2$ to 2 hours, until the ribs are fork tender.

The ribs can be prepared up to several hours ahead or overnight to this point. Allow them to cool completely before covering and placing in the refrigerator.

When ready to serve, skim off as much surface fat as possible (refrigeration helps this process). Bring to room temperature and then simmer over medium-low heat for 20 to 25 minutes or until heated through. Garnish with the parsley and chives and serve with polenta (see page 314), if desired.

Wine suggestion: The Grapes of Roth Merlot

ESTIA'S LITTLE KITCHEN
Sag Harbor

ESTIA'S LITTLE KITCHEN, A SMALL COUNTRY RESTAURANT ON THE BRIDGE/SAG Turnpike in Sag Harbor, is known for its cozy atmosphere and flavorful dishes. The restaurant is under the direction of chef/owner Colin Ambrose, who has recently signed on as executive chef/part owner and creative director of the East End's oldest steak house, The Old Stove Pub in Sagaponack.

Colin's love of food and entertaining led him to work his way through college in restaurants and pubs, where he developed a style that reflects his spirited restaurant fare. While dinner is served every Friday and Saturday night year round, in season the restaurant will open for dinner Thursday through Sunday from May 15 through October 15. Estia's Little Kitchen is a very popular place for breakfast and lunch throughout the year. From fresh-squeezed orange juice and omelets to homemade pasta and classic fish and vegetable dishes to the use of chiles in such dishes as braided steak Axteca, tortilla soup, spicy turtle rolls and posole, with local ingredients from the farm and sea, whenever possible, are Colin's specialty of the house. In addition, Colin Ambrose's wine list features wines from neighboring vineyards Wolffer Estate and Channing Daughters.

The "Little Kitchen" can be chartered for private parties and weddings for up to 36 people or barbecues on the outside grounds for up to a hundred people.

ROASTED PORK LOIN WITH BRAISED FENNEL AND TOMATO

COLIN AMBROSE, EXECUTIVE CHEF AND OWNER OF ESTIA'S LITTLE KITCHEN, A COUNTRY roadside restaurant in Sag Harbor, prides himself on his use of locally grown sustainable food.

YIELD: 4 TO 6 SERVINGS

1 large onion, sliced

2 fennel bulbs

2½ pounds center-cut pork roast, untrimmed

Sea salt and freshly ground black pepper

2 ripe red tomatoes, cored and cut into small dice

2 to 3 long thin slices prosciutto

½ cup extra-virgin olive oil, divided

1 ripe yellow tomato, cored and cut into small dice

2 tablespoons freshly squeezed lemon juice

Preheat the oven to 375°F.

Arrange the onion slices and the top stalks of the fennel, reserving the fronds for the garnish, in the bottom of a roasting pan. Season the pork loin with sea salt and pepper and place over the vegetables. Top with the diced red tomatoes. Arrange the prosciutto slices over the tomatoes. Pour 2 tablespoons of the olive oil over the prosciutto and tent with a folded sheet of foil, shiny side in. Roast the pork for 45 minutes. Remove the foil and top with the diced yellow tomato. Return to the oven and roast 35 to 40 minutes longer or until the internal temperature reaches 150°F on an instant thermometer. Remove from the oven and let rest.

While the pork roasts, cut each fennel in half through the core; then cut out and discard the core. Cut the fennel into thin slices and then separate the layers to achieve thin fennel sticks. Soak the fennel in a bowl of cold water to refresh, about 15 minutes. Drain and pat dry with a clean kitchen towel. Pour the remaining 2 tablespoons of oil in an ovenproof sauté pan over medium heat and add the fennel. Toss to coat in the oil and sauté for about 5 minutes, stirring occasionally. Place in the oven and cook for 12 to 14 minutes. When tender, remove from the oven, dress with the lemon juice, and season lightly with sea salt. Divide the fennel centered on warm dinner plates.

With a sharp carving knife, slice the roast into thin slices and place overlapping slices over the fennel. Garnish with chopped fennel fronds and serve.

PUMPKIN CREAM ROLL

THIS SPECIAL OCCASION CAKE, APPROPRIATE FOR THANKSGIVING AND THE WINTER HOLIDAYS, can be prepared up to two days ahead or frozen for up to one month.

YIELD: 10 TO 12 SERVINGS

FOR THE CREAM ROLL

3 large eggs

$^2/_3$ cup granulated sugar

1 cup canned pumpkin purée

1 to 2 teaspoons freshly squeezed lemon juice

$^3/_4$ cup all-purpose flour

1 teaspoon baking powder

1 teaspoon ground cinnamon

$^1/_2$ teaspoon ground allspice

$^1/_2$ teaspoon freshly grated nutmeg

$^1/_2$ teaspoon salt

FOR THE FILLING

1 cup heavy whipping cream

$^1/_4$ cup confectioners' sugar, plus more for serving

$^1/_2$ teaspoon vanilla extract

For the cream roll, tear a length of wax paper to fit an 11 x 17-inch jelly-roll pan leaving a slight overhang. Grease one side of the paper with softened butter or vegetable oil. Place the paper, greased side down, to adhere to the pan and then lightly grease the exposed side.

Preheat the oven to 375°F.

With an electric mixer, beat the eggs and sugar on medium-high speed for 7 to 8 minutes until thick ribbons form when dropped from the beater. Fold in the pumpkin purée and lemon juice.

In a separate bowl, sift the flour, baking powder, cinnamon, allspice, nutmeg, and salt and fold into the pumpkin mixture. Pour the batter into the prepared pan, gently smoothing to edges of the pan. Bake for 16 to 18 minutes, or until the cake springs back gently to the touch and begins to pull away from the sides of the pan. Allow the cake to cool in the pan for 10 minutes.

To remove the cake from the pan, spread a clean, slightly damp kitchen towel (not terry cloth) on a work surface. Hold onto the sides of the jelly-roll pan and carefully tilt and lower the pan toward the towel to invert. Lift off the pan and carefully remove the wax paper and discard. Starting at one long side, roll up the cake in the towel. Arrange the cake seam side down on the jelly-roll pan and let sit for 10 minutes.

For the filling, chill a mixing bowl and beaters for 10 minutes. Whip the cream until it begins to firm. Continue to beat, gradually adding the confectioners' sugar until stiff peaks form, being careful not to overbeat. Fold in the vanilla.

Unroll the cake (do not be concerned if it cracks a bit,

just push in from outside edges to close any gaps). With a rubber spatula, evenly spread the cream onto the cake, leaving a 1-inch border of exposed cake along the edge opposite you. Starting at one long side and using the kitchen towel as a guide, roll the cake to enclose the filling. Transfer the cake, seam side down, to a platter and refrigerate, lightly covered with plastic wrap, 3 to 4 hours until firm, or overnight. When the cake is firm, trim off the unattractive ends with a serrated bread knife to expose the rolled layers.

To serve, sift confectioners' sugar over the cake roll. Slice the cake and serve.

APPLE GALETTE

A GALETTE IS SIMPLY AN OPEN TART COOKED IN A FREE-FORM STYLE RATHER THAN MOLDED into a quiche pan or flan ring. The choice of fruit is flexible. Use apples, pears, nectarines, or peaches in season. It makes an ideal dessert for company.

YIELD: 8 TO 10 SERVINGS

Pastry dough for a 12-inch crust (see page 337)

5 to 6 Golden Delicious apples

$^{1}/_{4}$ cup sugar

3 tablespoons butter, cut into small dice

5 tablespoons apricot preserves

1 tablespoon Calvados, brandy, or cognac

Whipped cream or vanilla ice cream (optional)

The apple galette was introduced to the culinary world by the indefatigable master of the culinary arts, Jacques Pepin, over thirty years ago. The apple galette was prevalent in major food magazines and took on many forms and shapes, using a myriad of fruits as well as savory fillings. My own approach was to be true to the classic, and I'm forever grateful to Jacques for this basically simple and very appealing dessert.

On a lightly floured surface, roll out the dough to $^{1}/_{8}$-inch thick. Drape the dough over a rolling pin and transfer to a large baking sheet. Prick the bottom of the pastry with the tines of a fork and refrigerate until firm, at least 30 minutes or longer.

Preheat the oven to 400°F.

Peel and core the apples and slice $^{1}/_{4}$ inch thick. (If using peaches or nectarines, do not peel. Wash and dry them very well and slice $^{1}/_{4}$ inch thick.) Arrange the apple slices on the dough beginning at the outside edge, approximately 1 inch from the border in concentric circles, overlapping the slices to imitate the petals of a flower.

Sprinkle the apples with the sugar and dot with the butter. Fold the dough over the edge of the apples. Lightly brush the pastry edge with water. Place in the oven and bake for 65 to 75 minutes, until the galette is well browned and crusty.

About 15 minutes before the galette is done, place the apricot preserves in a small saucepan and bring to a simmer. Stir to dissolve over low heat for a few minutes. Remove from the heat and stir in the Calvados. Keep warm.

When the galette is done, slide onto a large cutting board and drizzle the thinned apricot preserves over the top. The galette can be prepared ahead and refrigerated, tented with plastic wrap. Cut the galette into wedges and serve lukewarm or at room temperature with a dollop of whipped cream or vanilla ice cream, if desired.

ROASTED CARAMELIZED PEARS

PEARS DEVELOP A CONCENTRATED, COMPLEX FLAVOR WHEN ROASTED. SERVE THE SAUCE
warm to maximize its comforting flavor. Select gracefully shaped pears with their stems if possible.

YIELD: 6 TO 8 SERVINGS

Juice of 1 lemon

6 to 8 Bosc pears, with stems
    attached

1½ cups sugar

1 tablespoon freshly
    squeezed lemon juice

1 cup water

⅓ cup heavy whipping cream

Fresh berries, for garnish
    (optional)

Preheat the oven to 450°F.

Fill a large bowl with water and squeeze the juice of 1 lemon into it. Peel the pears. Carefully core each one and cut a slice from the base so that they stand. Place in the lemon water.

In a large ovenproof skillet, combine the sugar, lemon juice, and water. Cook over medium heat, without stirring, until the mixture is lightly caramelized 15 to 18 minutes. Remove from the heat.

Drain the pears and pat dry with paper towels. Transfer to the caramel and carefully coat by turning them with 2 wooden spoons. Stand the pears up in the pan and transfer to the oven. Roast for 45 minutes, basting occasionally with the caramel, until tender and golden brown. Keep the basting spoon in a dish of warm water to keep it from getting sticky.

Using the wooden spoons, carefully transfer the pears to a rack over a sheet of foil, and allow them to drain. Place the skillet over medium heat and return the caramel to a simmer. Whisk in the cream. The pears and sauce may be completed to this point up to one day ahead. Tent with plastic wrap and refrigerate.

When ready to serve, transfer the pears to a serving dish and bring the pears and sauce to room temperature. Reheat the sauce before serving and drizzle over the pears. Garnish with fresh berries, if desired.

MILK PAIL
Water Mill

HALSEY IS ONE OF THE MOST RECOGNIZED NAMES ON THE EAST END OF LONG Island. Tom Halsey settled on the East End in the 1640s. If you ask a Halsey how they are related to one another, the answer would probably be, "Well, I'm a third cousin once removed."

The original Halseys were potato farmers. John Halsey's father grew potatoes from the 1920s until the 1970s. John (descendant of the original Tom Halsey) and Evelyn Halsey of the Milk Pail Country Store and Orchard in Water Mill took a different route. They grow apples.

John Halsey had cows as a boy growing up, and he continued with his dairy farm, selling raw milk to Schwenk's processing plant in East Hampton. John bought back the dairy products, which consisted of milk, butter, and cheese, for the farm stand that he and Evelyn set up in 1969 on Onmontauk Highway between Water Mill and Bridgehampton. Evelyn Halsey came up with the idea of a retail store, so in 1972, after ten generations of potato farming, John and Evelyn Halsey moved in a different direction and founded the Milk Pail Country Store and Orchard on Route 27 (Montauk Highway) in Water Mill. In the fall of that year, Evelyn and John brought seventy-five bushels of apples to the retail store from Vermont, where Evelyn got her first taste for apple growing from her parents' commercial apple orchard. With the store and Evelyn's family connection, they thought, why not sell apples? They brought in just three varieties, Macintosh, Cortlands and Northern Spy from Vermont. When they realized how successful selling apples would be, they sold the cows and made a commitment to the apple business. John went on to buy a few apple trees from the nursery at Cornell.

As they began to produce apples for retail, they noticed a trend towards local produce. The Halseys connected with the consumers, backing up their products with facts and quality. Starting with forty trees, they went on to plant four hundred trees in 1980. In 1983, they opened their orchard for consumer picking and expanded the store, providing their own farm-pressed apple cider, not-to-be missed apple donuts, and delicious Vermont cheeses. (The Milk Pail's apple cider is unpasteurized, using ultraviolet light to protect it.)

Through the 1980s and 1990s, the Halseys continued to plant more varieties of apples.

The orchard has grown to fifteen thousand trees producing twenty-six apple varieties on twenty acres. The first varieties of apples come in late August, and the last varieties generally come in around about the middle of November. The farm itself has sixty-five acres. Ten of those acres are devoted to fifty different varieties of bright orange pumpkins of varying sizes, along with gourds and winter squash. These colorful varieties are abundantly displayed on carts in front of the familiar country store when driving past in early autumn.

John and Evelyn's two daughters, Amy and Jennifer, are the eleventh generation and very much a part of their farm family tradition. Amy Halsey earned a floriculture and plant science bachelor's degree from SUNY Cobbleskill in 1994. Her training included an internship in Holland, and today she runs her own state-of-the-art greenhouse operation. Amy grows hundreds of varieties of annual and perennial plants. She also works with private clients. Jennifer Halsey Dupree earned a bachelor of science degree from Cornell University in 1997, specializing in pomology, the study of growing and marketing fruit. She grows yellow, white, and donut peaches on three and a half acres of the family farmland. Her fruit is available at the Milk Pail and other local farm stands from late July through August.

The Milk Pail Country Store, the U-Pick Orchard, Amy's unique flowers, and Jennifer's juicy peaches are a family tradition on the East End of Long Island.

HARVEST GRAPE TART

THE VINEYARDS ON THE EAST END INSPIRED THIS TIMELY GRAPE TART.

YIELD: 8 TO 10 SERVINGS

Pastry dough for a 12-inch
  crust (see page 338)

2 pounds dark seedless
  wine grapes

2 egg whites, lightly beaten

$^1/_4$ cup plus 3 tablespoons
  sugar, divided

$^1/_2$ cup pine nuts,
  lightly toasted

2 tablespoons unsalted
  butter, cut into small dice

$^1/_3$ cup grape jelly

1 tablespoon Kirsch or Grand
  Marnier

Whipped cream or vanilla
  ice cream (optional)

On a lightly floured surface, roll out the dough to $^1/_8$-inch thick. Drape the dough over a rolling pin and transfer to a large baking sheet. Prick the bottom of the pastry with the tines of a fork and refrigerate until firm, at least 30 minutes.

Preheat the oven to 400°F.

Stem and rinse the grapes, and pat dry with paper towels. Set aside.

Beat the egg whites in a small bowl and add $^1/_4$ cup of the sugar and the pine nuts. Spread the mixture evenly over the dough to within $1^1/_2$ inches of the edge. Arrange the grapes close to each other over the pine nuts. Sprinkle the remaining 3 tablespoons of sugar over the top and dot with the butter. Fold the dough over the edge of the grapes. Lightly brush the edge with water.

Bake the tart on the middle rack of the oven for 40 to 50 minutes, until the fruit is tender and the pastry is golden brown and crusty.

About 15 minutes before the tart is done, place the grape jelly in a small saucepan, bring to a simmer, and cook over low heat for 2 to 3 minutes. Remove from the heat and stir in the Kirsch or Grand Marnier.

When the tart is done, slide onto a large cutting board and drizzle the jelly mixture over the top to glaze the fruit. The tart can be prepared ahead up to this point and refrigerated, tented with plastic wrap. Cut the tart into wedges and serve with a dollop of whipped cream or vanilla ice cream, if desired.

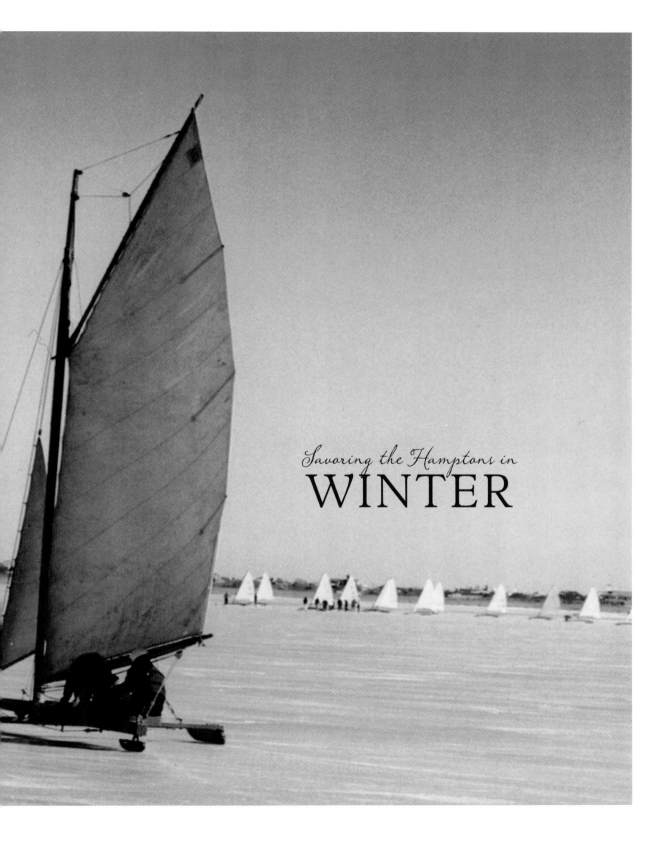

Savoring the Hamptons in
WINTER

I love winter in the Hamptons—the mid-winter holidays are busy with festive parties, and friends and neighbors are more apt to get together to share last-minute potluck dinners. One of my favorite things to do when the temperature dips and snow falls is to have friends over for an evening of good food and conversation in front of the fire. At moments like these, it's as if winter itself becomes the life of the party.

During a terrific snowstorm some years ago, some neighbors trudged over in knee-high boots to join us for an impromptu, one-pot meal—a must menu for any last-minute hostess and certainly useful when the roads to the stores are impassable. With nearly a foot of snow on the ground, no one was venturing out that night.

I'm almost never without homemade chicken stock in the freezer, and fresh herbs and a wedge of Parmesan in the refrigerator. As I explored my cupboard, I knew I would find a box of Arborio rice, the Italian-style rice for risotto, and recalled the wonder of the creamy fusion of rice and seasonings the first time I ate it in Northern Italy. "Great!" I thought. I still had a butternut squash that I picked up at the Green Thumb farm a few weeks before. We settled in front of the fireplace with one of my favorite risottos and a glass of wine. The flickering flames of the fireplace warmed our bodies and the sheer pleasure of just being together warmed our hearts.

This American scene could have played out in any number of regions across the country—any with the right latitude for snow, of course.

Those particular much-loved neighbors have since moved, and while I miss them, I was not surprised by their departure. The Hamptons is as well known for its transient population as it is for its potatoes. Many East Enders have left family behind elsewhere, or in this mobile society we live in, members of local families have left. As a result, our sense of community is different than it was even fifty years ago—it is built not so much spent in one place, but on the love and dedication to the place while living there. It is a sense of community, of belonging somewhere, that gives any place its distinct character and creates its local flavor.

POTATO AND ONION TORTILLA

THE EAST END OF LONG ISLAND IS POTATO COUNTRY, SO I COULDN'T RESIST INCLUDING this flavorful potato omelet. Considered one of Spain's national dishes, it is a familiar offering at tapas bars here and abroad. Prepare ahead and serve at room temperature for maximum flavor.

YIELD: 8 TO 10 SERVINGS

$^1/_3$ cup extra-virgin olive oil

$^1/_3$ cup vegetable oil

2 russet potatoes (about 1 to $1^1/_2$ pounds), peeled and thinly sliced

1 Spanish onion, peeled and thinly sliced

Kosher salt and freshly ground black pepper

6 large eggs

Heat the oils in a 9 or 10-inch nonstick skillet over medium heat. Add a layer of potato slices alternating with a layer of onion slices and season each layer with salt and pepper to taste. Cook slowly, lifting and turning the mixture occasionally with 2 large spoons, until the potatoes are barely tender yet slightly crisp, and the onion slices are golden brown, 10 to 12 minutes. Place a colander or large sieve over a bowl and drain the potatoes and onions, reserving 3 tablespoons of the oil.

Meanwhile, in a large bowl, beat the eggs until foamy and season with $^1/_2$ teaspoon salt and 6 to 8 grinds of pepper. Add the cooked potato mixture to the beaten eggs, pressing the potatoes down gently into the liquid until completely submerged.

Heat the reserved oil in the skillet and when hot, slide the potato and onion mixture into the skillet, rapidly spreading it out in the skillet with a heatproof rubber spatula. Reduce the heat to medium and shake the pan back and forth occasionally to prevent sticking. Reduce the heat to medium low and continue to cook, pulling in the side with the spatula until the eggs are set along the edges. When the eggs are well set and the omelet is well detached from the bottom of the pan, about 5 to 7 minutes, cover the skillet with a plate and invert the omelet onto the plate. If the skillet is dry, add an additional 1 tablespoon of oil and return the pan to the heat. Carefully slide the uncooked side back into the skillet and cook for 3 to 4 minutes longer. Slide onto a serving dish and bring to room temperature; then cut into wedges for serving.

EAST END DUCK PÂTÉ

WHEN PREPARING A WHOLE DUCK AT HOME, BE SURE TO USE THE LIVER FOR THIS APPETIZING pâté. Fresh herbs and verjus, unfermented grape juice, lend a clean yet piquant flavor to this simple no-bake version of a classic terrine.

YIELD: ABOUT ³/₄ CUP PÂTÉ

2 tablespoons extra-virgin olive oil

2 tablespoons unsalted butter, divided

2 shallots, finely chopped

Kosher salt and freshly ground black pepper

1 large duck liver (about 3 ounces), trimmed of membrane

Flour, for dusting

2 tablespoons verjus

1 hard-cooked egg, coarsely chopped

1 tablespoon finely chopped fresh parsley

1 tablespoon fresh thyme leaves

Toast points or crackers, for serving

In a 9 or 10-inch nonstick skillet, heat the oil and 1 tablespoon of the butter over medium heat. When the butter foam subsides, add the shallots and sauté, stirring for 1 minute. Season to taste with salt and pepper. Transfer to the work bowl of a food processor fitted with the steel blade and allow to cool completely.

Rinse the liver and pat dry with paper towels. Dust both sides of the liver with flour. Heat the remaining tablespoon of butter over medium heat in the same skillet the shallots cooked in, and when the butter foam subsides, add the liver. Sauté the liver for about 3 minutes, until crisp and brown. Turn and cook for 2 minutes longer on the other side. Season with salt and pepper to taste. Pour the verjus over the liver and cook until the liquid evaporates, scraping the bottom of the skillet to deglaze the pan juices. Cut the liver into pieces and allow to cool thoroughly.

When the liver has cooled, add with the pan juices to the shallots in the food processor. (If the liver and pan juices are added while hot, the mixture will curdle.) Add the egg, parsley, and thyme to the work bowl. Process until the mixture is thoroughly blended to a smooth paste, scraping down the sides as needed. Taste to adjust the seasonings as necessary. Using a rubber spatula, transfer the contents to a covered crock or small soufflé dish. The pâté can be prepared up to two days ahead. Refrigerate covered. Serve at room temperature with the toast points or crackers.

POLENTA SQUARES WITH BLUE CHEDDAR AND SAGE

POLENTA IS A REMARKABLE FOIL FOR CHEESE OF ALL KINDS. MELTED BUTTER WITH MECOX Bay Dairy blue Cheddar is added to the cooked polenta and then it is cut into squares when ready to broil or grill.

YIELD: 24 SQUARES, 6 TO 8 SERVINGS

2$^{1}/_{4}$ cups water

$^{1}/_{2}$ teaspoon kosher salt

$^{1}/_{2}$ cup yellow stone-ground polenta

1 tablespoon extra-virgin olive oil

2 tablespoons unsalted butter

$^{1}/_{3}$ pound blue cheese, crumbled

2 to 3 tablespoons fresh sage chiffonade (see note on page 104)

$^{1}/_{4}$ cup grated Parmigiano-Reggiano cheese

Bring the water to a rolling boil in a wide saucepan. Add the salt and reduce the heat to a simmer. Gradually add the polenta in a thin stream to the hot water, whisking vigorously to prevent lumps. Cook the polenta, stirring constantly in the same direction with a wooden spoon for about 10 minutes as the polenta thickens. Continue to stir the polenta occasionally for another 6 to 8 minutes until the polenta pulls easily away from the side of the pan. Add the olive oil and stir to mix.

Melt the butter in a small skillet over medium heat and stir in the crumbled blue cheese until the cheese is thoroughly softened. Stir in the sage. Spoon the cheese mixture into the polenta and stir to mix thoroughly.

Rinse an 8-inch square glass baking dish with cold water and pour off any excess. Pour the polenta mixture into the dish and smooth the top to an even layer. Cover with plastic wrap and refrigerate for several hours or overnight.

Preheat the oven to 450°F.

Turn the polenta onto a parchment-lined baking sheet and cut into 1-inch squares. Sprinkle the Parmigiano-Reggiano evenly over each square and then separate the squares slightly. Bake for 4 to 5 minutes.

Preheat the broiler. Adjust the rack to 3 to 4 inches from the heat source and broil the polenta squares for 1 to 2 minutes, until the squares are bubbly and golden brown. Watch carefully so as not to burn the squares. Serve warm.

LEEK AND GOAT CHEESE CROSTINI WITH POMEGRANATE

CATAPANO FARMS CHÈVRE ADDS A CREAMY TANG TO THIS COLORFUL CANAPÉ—
perfect for the mid-winter holidays.

YIELD: 20 TO 24 CANAPÉS

2 large or 3 medium leeks

2 tablespoons extra-virgin olive oil

3 ounces chèvre cheese, softened

1½ to 2 tablespoons snipped fresh chives

Kosher salt and freshly ground black pepper

1 day-old narrow baguette, cut into 24 thin slices, toasted

Seeds from ⅓ pomegranate or whole chive stems, for garnish (optional)

Cut the large green tops of the leeks at an angle, exposing the light green upper parts. Discard any bruised outer layers and then, holding your knife at a 45-degree angle, cut through the dark green layers to expose the light green layers within. Hold the leek at the base, insert your knife just above the root end, and make lengthwise cuts in but not through the leeks. Rinse away the sand between the leaves under a spray of cold tap water and then soak in a bowl of clean water for 10 to 15 minutes. Drain and squeeze the leeks dry with a paper towel. Holding on to the root end, cut crosswise into thin slices.

Heat the oil in a 10 to 12-inch nonstick skillet over medium heat. Add the leeks and cover with a square of wax paper and cover the pan with the lid tightly. Sweat over low heat for 7 to 8 minutes, until the leeks are tender and then let cool.

Meanwhile, mash the softened cheese in a bowl with a fork. Stir in the cooled leeks, the chives, and salt and pepper to taste.

About 2 hours before ready to serve, spread the leek mixture on the toasted crostini slices. Arrange on a platter and sprinkle the pomegranate seeds or chives over the crostini.

NOTE: The leek mixture can be prepared two to three days ahead for the flavors to develop. When ready to serve, be sure to bring the topping to room temperature so that the mixture spreads easily on the toasts.

TUNA TARTARE

TOM SCHAUDEL, AUTHOR, CHEF AND RESTAURATEUR, IS KNOWN FOR HIS WAY WITH NEW AMERICAN cooking and his seafood specialties. He owns Amano in Mattituck on the North Fork, and several restaurants in Nassau County and is the author of *Playing with Fire: Whining and Dining on the Gold Coast.* He invites readers to meet all the neurotics, the psychotics, the allergic, the affected, and the afflicted. By Tom's calculations he has fed two million people in the course of this career and thanks the 1,999,915 who have been wonderful—eight-five made it into this book.

YIELD: 6 TO 8 SERVINGS

FOR THE RED GINGER VINAIGRETTE

3 tablespoons rice wine vinegar

$^1/_3$ cup plus 2 tablespoons canola oil

1 teaspoon pure sesame oil

$2^1/_2$ teaspoons soy sauce

$1^1/_2$ tablespoons pickled ginger

FOR THE TARTARE

1 pound sushi-grade yellowfin tuna, diced

2 tablespoons finely diced red bell pepper

2 tablespoons finely diced yellow bell pepper

$^1/_2$ teaspoon red pepper flakes

1 tablespoon black sesame seeds

1 tablespoon white sesame seeds

Kosher salt and freshly ground black pepper

Fried wonton crisps or crackers, for serving

Fresh chervil or parsley leaves, for garnish

For the vinaigrette, whisk together the vinegar, canola oil, sesame oil, and soy sauce in a mixing bowl. Fold in the ginger and stir to mix.

For the tartare, cut the tuna into slices, stack the slices and finely dice. Put the tuna in a mixing bowl with the bell peppers, red pepper flakes, sesame seeds, and salt and pepper to taste. Add $^1/_2$ cup of the vinaigrette, reserving the rest for another use, and carefully stir to mix without mashing the tuna. The tartare can be prepared ahead up to this point. Refrigerate, covered, in a suitable container.

When ready to serve, transfer the tuna tartare to a serving bowl and bring to room temperature. Spread the tuna tartare on wonton or cracker crisps and top with a chervil or parsley leaf.

THE LIVING ROOM AT C/O THE MAIDSTONE
East Hampton

JAMES CARPENTER CAME TO THE EAST END WITH HIS BUDDY SEAN DOTY IN THE nineties when Sean was executive chef at Savannah's in Southampton. Sean hired James to be his sous chef. The boys met at Johnson & Wales University, became good friends, and worked together in Atlanta, Georgia. Through Sean, James was exposed to the teachings of Gunter Seeger, one of the first chefs who valued working directly with farmers to custom request ingredients in season.

After two years at Savannah, James left to work as sous chef with Kevin Penner at Della Femina in East Hampton. When Kevin left to go with the Kreisler Corporation and its restaurants on the East End, James was made executive chef at Della Femina. He continued on at Della Femina until family obligations drew him and his wife, Liza, to Harrisburg, Pennsylvania, where he opened a café. After a while, Liza, who is a sommelier, was ready to plant roots somewhere else, and James decided that they should return to the East End. He was executive chef at the American Hotel run by the iconic Ted Conklin, founding father of Slow Food on the East End, before moving on to the newly established The Living Room at c/o The Maidstone Restaurant and Inn in East Hampton.

James Carpenter met with Jenny Ljuneberg (pronounce juneberg), Swedish proprietor of the Maidstone and innkeeper of four boutique hotels in Stockholm. Jenny enticed Carpenter to come on board with his concept of slow food and his knowledge of local purveyors. She supplied him with a Swedish sous chef, who was instrumental in implementing Scandinavian touches, such as curing their own salmon for gravlax and, with James, taking readily available local ingredients and familiar products on the East End to put a Swedish spin on dishes that work for the American palate.

SWEDISH TART FLAMBÉ

EXECUTIVE CHEF JAMES CARPENTER OF THE LIVING ROOM AT C/O THE MAIDSTONE IN EAST
Hampton contributed this decidedly delicious tart. The tart isn't flambéed as noted in the title, but,
as Chef James points out, it has "just a lovely caramelized surface when the tart is baked." The tart
makes a wonderful dinner party first course served with a bit of lightly dressed greens such as mâche
or mesclun. I made this tart with Shawondasee, a semi-hard artisanal cheese with a sweet-nutty flavor, which is produced by Mecox Bay Dairy in Bridgehampton.

YIELD: 8 SERVINGS

FOR THE
CRÈME FRAÎCHE MIXTURE

$^1/_2$ cup crème fraîche
(see page 338)

$1^1/_2$ tablespoons Dijon
mustard

1 egg yolk

$^3/_4$ cup grated semi-hard,
subtly flavored cheese

FOR THE TART

1 frozen puff pastry sheet
(from 1 ($17^1/_4$-ounce)
package frozen puff
pastry sheets), thawed

2 tablespoons finely
chopped red onion

3 ounces smoked salmon,
cut into small pieces

2 tablespoons snipped
fresh chives

For the crème fraîche mixture, in a mixing bowl combine
the crème fraîche, Dijon mustard, egg yolk, and cheese. Stir
to thoroughly mix. The mixture can be prepared up to one
day ahead and refrigerated in a suitable container.

For the tart, preheat the oven to 400°F. Roll out the puff
pastry sheet on a lightly floured board and drape over a 9-
inch fluted tart pan with a removable bottom. Allow the
pastry to fit into the bottom of the pan. Trim the pastry edge
to one-half inch over the top; fold over the edge and press
into the fluted edge of the pan. Prick the pastry bottom all
over with the tines of a fork. Cover the pastry with a square
of parchment paper and weigh down with pie weights or
dried beans. Bake for 16 to 18 minutes. Remove parchment
paper and weights. If the bottom crust looks a bit raw,
return to the oven for 2 to 3 minutes longer; then let cool for
about 15 minutes.

Spoon the crème fraîche mixture into the cooled pastry.
Scatter the chopped onion over the top and cover the surface with the smoked salmon. Return the tart to the oven
and bake for 18 minutes, until puffed and golden brown. Cut
into wedges for serving with a sharp pizza cutter, garnish
with fresh chives, and serve warm or at room temperature.

NOTE: Packages of frozen puff pastry contain two sheets.
I suggest doubling the recipe above to make two tarts.
When doubling the recipe for the crème fraîche mixture,
use one extra large egg yolk.

CREAM OF CELERY SOUP

THIS CONTEMPORARY UPDATE IS A FRENCH CLASSIC, USING POTATOES TO THICKEN THE SOUP rather than egg yolks and cream. Puréeing the soup makes it creamy. However, you can keep the vegetables whole for a chunky texture.

YIELD: 6 TO 8 SERVINGS

1 leek

2 tablespoons unsalted butter

2 tablespoons vegetable oil

1 large bunch celery (about 4 cups chopped), washed, trimmed, and leaves discarded

2 medium Yukon Gold potatoes, peeled and coarsely chopped

6 cups chicken stock (see page 335) or low-sodium canned

Kosher salt and freshly ground black pepper

Splash of dry sherry or cognac, for serving (optional)

Toasted Croutons, for garnish (see page 335)

Cut the large green tops of the leek at an angle, exposing the light green upper parts. Remove any bruised outer leaves and trim away the heavy dark green tops. With a sharp knife, make lengthwise cuts away from the root end, but not through the leeks. Rinse away the sand between the layers under cold running water and then soak in a bowl of clean water for 10 to 15 minutes to get rid of any excess sand. Squeeze the leek dry with a paper towel and then thinly slice.

Heat the butter and oil in a large saucepan over medium-low heat until the butter is melted. Add the leek, celery, and potatoes and sauté for 4 to 5 minutes, tossing occasionally to prevent the vegetables from sticking to the bottom of the pan. Cover the vegetables with a square of waxed paper; then cover the pan and sweat over low heat for 7 minutes.

Remove the waxed paper and discard. Add the stock and salt and pepper to taste to the saucepan and cover with the lid. Bring to a simmer over medium heat, reduce the heat to medium low, and cook for 35 to 40 minutes. Purée the soup in a blender or a food mill. You might need to do this in batches and if blending, be careful you don't fill the blender too full. Rinse the saucepan of any vegetable bits. Return the puréed soup to the saucepan. Taste the soup to adjust the seasonings if necessary. Prepare the soup up to two days ahead and refrigerate in a suitable container.

To serve, if the soup was refrigerated, bring to room temperature. Bring to a simmer over medium heat to reheat. Remove from the heat and splash a bit of sherry or cognac into the soup, if desired. Stir to mix and serve hot with toasted croutons.

ROOT VEGETABLES AND FARRO SOUP

WINTER ROOT VEGETABLES COMBINED WITH FARRO MAKE FOR A DELICIOUS ADDITION TO your winter soup fare. Farro is a healthy Italian whole-grain wheat with a nutty flavor.

YIELD: 4 TO 6 SERVINGS

2 tablespoons extra-virgin olive oil

1 tablespoon unsalted butter

2 leeks, trimmed, washed very well, and thinly sliced

3 carrots, trimmed, peeled, and sliced

2 to 3 parsnips, trimmed, peeled, and sliced

2 turnips, trimmed, peeled, and diced

2 to 3 garlic cloves, finely chopped

Kosher salt and freshly ground black pepper

6 cups chicken stock (see page 335) or low-sodium canned

1/2 cup farro, soaked*

2 tablespoons coarsely chopped fresh sage leaves

Heat the olive oil and butter in a large saucepan over medium heat. When the butter foam begins to subside, add the leeks, carrots, parsnips, turnips, and garlic and stir to mix. Reduce the heat to low. Cover with a square of wax paper; then cover the pot to sweat the vegetables for 6 to 7 minutes over very low heat. Uncover the pot and discard the wax paper. Season the vegetables with salt and pepper.

Pour the stock over the vegetables and bring to a boil over medium-high heat. Add the soaked and drained farro and stir into the vegetables. Reduce the heat to medium and cook at a brisk simmer for about 45 minutes, until the vegetables and grains are tender. Add the sage leaves and adjust the seasonings as necessary. The soup can be fully prepared up to two days ahead. Refrigerate in a suitable container and reheat before serving.

* NOTE: The grain farro, as it is known in central Italy, is also known as spelt, an ancient red wheat grain. Usually available in health food and specialty food markets, farro can be difficult to find. You may substitute wheat berries, which are more readily available at supermarkets and natural food stores. To use farro or wheat berries, rinse under running water about five seconds and then transfer to a medium saucepan and soak in water to cover for several hours or overnight. Use as directed in the recipe.

THE PLAZA CAFÉ
Southampton

AT AGE FOURTEEN, SOUTHAMPTON-BORN DOUG GULIJA WAS LEARNING HOW TO MAKE hollandaise and pâte à choux, among other classic culinary preparations, under a Burgundian chef at the Old Mill restaurant in Southampton in summer. Natives will remember Jan Berkowski's place, the Old Mill restaurant in Water Mill. While the Old Mill is long gone, Doug's restaurant, The Plaza Café of Southampton, is doing well. In 1973, Doug entered the culinary program at Johnson & Wales in Providence, Rhode Island. After meeting Jacques Torres, the pastry chef at Le Cirque at the time, and experiencing the high level of food there, Doug was convinced of his decision to become a chef.

After Doug did a stint abroad and then returned to the states, he moved to Long Island to work with the distinguished chef Mirko Zagar of Mirko's in Water Mill. From there he took over as executive chef at the former Monterey Seafood grill in East Hampton. In 1997 in a bold move, Doug opened The Plaza Café in December, when most restaurants were beginning to plan a lengthy winter break. It didn't take long for his reputation to spread.

At The Plaza Café, local farmers and fishermen line up at the back door to sell their wares: farm fresh produce, local poultry and fish, and baskets of eggs. Doug plans the menu according to the availability of ingredients. The strength of the restaurant is its seafood, with his signature dish being the seafood shepherd's pie. There is a strong emphasis on wine at the restaurant dating from the time he worked in Paris. "Long Island wines are a natural match for the seafood dishes prepared at The Plaza Café," said Doug. He relishes the relationships forged over the years with many of the wineries that pioneered the unique style of wine that the North and South Forks have come to be known for.

FISHERMAN'S SEAFOOD CHOWDER

DOUG GULIJA, OWNER OF THE PLAZA CAFÉ, SERVES HIS CHAMELEON SEAFOOD CHOWDER, which can incorporate numerous seasonal fish to the chowder base.

YIELD: 2 QUARTS CHOWDER (10 TO 12 SERVINGS)

- 2 slices applewood-smoked bacon, cut into pieces
- 1 large red or Walla Walla onion, finely chopped
- 3 celery ribs, trimmed, rinsed, diced
- 3 carrots, peeled and diced
- 2 fennel bulbs, trimmed and thinly sliced
- 2 garlic cloves, chopped
- $^3/_4$ tablespoon fresh thyme
- $^1/_4$ teaspoon dried oregano
- $^1/_4$ teaspoon ground cumin
- $^1/_4$ teaspoon red pepper flakes
- 3 bay leaves
- Kosher salt and freshly ground pepper
- 1 cup dry white wine
- 2 cups tomato juice
- 1 (8-ounce) jar clam juice
- 1 (28-ounce) can crushed plum tomatoes, with juice from can
- 2 pounds Yukon Gold potatoes, peeled and diced
- 2 quarts shucked clams with their juice (about 24 quahog chowder clams)
- $^1/_2$ pound cod, monkfish, or striped bass, cut up

Cook the bacon in a heavy 12-inch skillet over medium heat until the bacon begins to turn brown, about 6 minutes. Add the onion, celery, carrots, fennel, and garlic and sauté for 8 to 10 minutes to caramelize slightly. Season the vegetables with the thyme, oregano, cumin, red pepper flakes, bay leaves, and salt and pepper to taste and blend into the mixture. Add the wine and bring to a boil over medium-high heat. Reduce the heat to medium and cook at a brisk simmer until the liquid evaporates. Stir in the tomato juice, clam juice, and crushed tomatoes and simmer for 15 minutes. The chowder can be prepared up to this point and refrigerated for two days ahead or frozen up to one month.

If the chowder is prepared ahead and refrigerated or frozen, bring to room temperature before cooking. Return the soup to a 5 to 6-quart saucepan over medium heat. Add the diced potatoes, bring to a brisk simmer, and cook for 15 minutes. Add the clams and their juice and simmer 6 to 7 minutes longer. Add the fish and cook for 3 minutes longer. The potatoes should be cooked by the time all the fish is cooked. Taste for doneness and adjust seasonings with salt and pepper. Serve in hot soup bowls.

Wine suggestion: Lenz Winery Gold Label Chardonnay

LENZ VINEYARDS
Peconic

WHEN VISITORS COME TO THE VINEYARD FOR TASTINGS, RATHER THAN TELLING YOU what *he* tastes, Fry wants to know what you think and wants tasters to really think about what each wine is giving in the glass. As Fry states, "It's a matter of integrity." His wines are very much alive in the glass and have a real energy, a quality that comes from ripe fruit and great acidity and balanced pH.

Fry admires the wines of Trimbach, Alsace, as being particularly honest wines. Lenz produces elegant sparkling wines, and while Fry does a secondary fermentation in the *methode champenoise* for these wines, he says that he doesn't see Champagne as being a particular model. "Champagne is very closed and secretive. I like it to be funky and Burgundian, even a little cheesy," by which he means to have a creamy, buttery quality.

As for Merlot, Fry says his influence is Burgundian, "which is a little weird. Fifteen years ago I would have said Bordeaux, when they were making funky, reductive wines. Now they are making these simple wines in the California mode. Burgundies are more complex and even barnyardy, mushroomy with a *sous bois* quality. I don't look for clean, happy, fruity wines. That works for my Cabernet Sauvignon, because I can't get it as ripe. But Merlot, I can get that fully ripe and complex."

Fry believes that pH balance is central to how a wine turns out and effects how the wine will age over time. Vineyard management is also a key to his winemaking. As Fry says, "I pick when it's ripe, and only then." Sam McCullough has been the vineyard manager at Lenz for years, and his philosophy dovetails with Fry's. Low crop yield is also an integral part of the plan.

Fry has just released the 2002 Merlot, which was bottled in 2004 and has been patiently aging in the Lenz cellars. Once the consumer does pop the cork, Fry does not agree with decanting his wines. He wants the wine to evolve in the glass. "It's fun to watch. The wines will change with the food over time. Why let that happen in the decanter when you can taste that transformation in the glass."

FENNEL, APPLE, AND ENDIVE SALAD
WITH BLUE CHEDDAR VINAIGRETTE

THE AROMATIC CRISPNESS OF FENNEL COMBINED WITH APPLE SLICES AND ENDIVE BLEND TO create a salad with complexity, texture, and taste that is dressed with Mecox Bay Dairy blue Cheddar and Catapano goat's milk yogurt.

YIELD: 6 TO 8 SERVINGS

FOR THE DRESSING

4 ounces blue Cheddar cheese or blue cheese

2 tablespoons white wine vinegar

2 tablespoons fresh lemon juice

1 tablespoon Dijon mustard

Freshly ground black pepper

$^1/_2$ cup goat's milk yogurt

$^1/_4$ cup cold water

$^1/_2$ cup extra-virgin olive oil

FOR THE SALAD

$^1/_2$ cup walnut halves

2 Granny Smith apples

2 tablespoons freshly squeezed lemon juice

1 large fennel or 2 medium fennel bulbs

1 large head Belgian endive

For the dressing, crumble the cheese in a blender or work bowl of a food processor. Add the vinegar, lemon juice, mustard, pepper, yogurt, and water. Blend to mix, scraping down the sides as necessary. Gradually add the oil through the opening in the blender cover or the feed tube of the food processor and blend to mix. Taste to adjust the seasonings if necessary. Spoon the mixture into a jar with a lid or a small pitcher. The dressing may be prepared up to one day ahead, refrigerated until ready to use.

For the salad, preheat the oven to 375°F.

Arrange the walnut halves on a baking sheet and toast for 6 to 7 minutes, until lightly browned and crisp. Store at room temperature.

Peel, core, and halve the apples; then thinly slice. Place them in a bowl and toss with the lemon juice. Cut the fennel lengthwise, removing the core, and separate strips into thin slices. Soak the fennel in a bowl of ice water to cover for 10 to 15 minutes; drain and pat dry. Toss gently with apples and set aside. Separate the endive into spears. Wash, spin-dry, and wrap in paper towels to absorb the moisture.

To assemble the salad, fan 4 or 5 endive spears on a salad plate. Divide the apple and fennel mixture evenly among six to eight salad plates in a mound at the core end of the spears. Drizzle the dressing over the salad and top with a sprinkle of toasted walnuts. Serve at room temperature.

APPLE AND WALNUT SALAD WITH CELERY ROOT RÉMOULADE

CELERY ROOT RÉMOULADE, A CREAMY SAUCE OF SHREDDED CELERY ROOT, MAYONNAISE, and mustard makes a spectacular presentation when combined with the seasonal flavors of salad greens, apples, and walnuts.

YIELD: 8 SERVINGS

FOR THE RÉMOULADE

1 large celery root, peeled

2 to 3 tablespoons lemon juice

1/4 cup mayonnaise

1 tablespoon whole-grain Dijon mustard

Kosher salt and freshly ground black pepper

FOR THE SALAD

2 heads Belgian endive

2 bunches arugula

1/2 cup walnuts, toasted

2 red apples

FOR THE RASPBERRY VINAIGRETTE

2 shallots, finely chopped

2 tablespoons raspberry vinegar

6 tablespoons extra-virgin olive oil

2 tablespoons heavy cream, whipped

For the rémoulade, rinse the celery root and pat dry with paper towels. Thinly slice; then stack the slices and cut into a fine julienne. Sprinkle the strips of celery root with the lemon juice. Bring a medium saucepan of salted water to a boil over high heat. Blanch the celery root for 1 minute. Drain, rinse under cold water, and dry very well. Let cool completely.

Combine the mayonnaise and mustard in a medium bowl. Add the celery root and toss to mix until well coated. Season to taste with salt and pepper. The rémoulade can be prepared up to two days ahead, refrigerated in suitable container.

For the salad, wash the endive and the arugula separately in a salad spinner and spin dry. Wrap in paper towels to absorb excess moisture and refrigerate up to one day ahead. Lightly toast the walnuts and chop coarsely; set aside. When ready to serve, core and thinly slice the apples.

To prepare the vinaigrette, combine the shallots and vinegar in a small bowl. Whisk in the oil and fold in the whipped cream.

For serving, divide the arugula among each of eight salad plates. Place 2 or 3 endive spears on each plate with the arugula. Slice any remaining endive and divide among the plates. Dress the greens with the vinaigrette. Mound a spoonful of celery root rémoulade over the greens and garnish with apple slices and walnuts.

STUFFED SWEET DUMPLINGS

SWEET DUMPLING SQUASH IS A SMALL, SWEET-TASTING SQUASH. IT HAS MOTTLED GREEN and ivory striped skin and looks like a miniature tureen.

YIELD: 6 TO 8 SERVINGS

6 to 8 ($^1\!/_2$-pound) sweet dumpling squash

3 tablespoons vegetable oil

1 medium red onion, finely chopped

$^1\!/_4$ cup chopped celery or celery leaves

Kosher salt and freshly ground black pepper

2 tablespoons minced fresh ginger

2 cups finely chopped and peeled tart apples

$^1\!/_4$ teaspoon ground allspice

$^1\!/_2$ cup plain breadcrumbs (see page 335)

1 to 2 tablespoons melted butter

Preheat the oven to 400°F. Lightly grease a shallow baking dish, such as a glass or ceramic oven-to-table dish, and line with aluminum foil. Lightly grease the foil.

Cut a thin slice from the bottom of each squash so they stand upright when stuffed. Place the squash in the prepared pan and pour a small amount of water around the base of the squash. Bake about 30 minutes or until the flesh is tender when pierced with a knife. When cool enough to handle, slice the tops off of the squash to make a lid; reserve the tops. Scoop out the flesh and purée in a blender. The squash can be prepared ahead and refrigerated, covered.

Meanwhile, heat the oil in a large skillet over medium heat. Add the onion, celery, and salt and pepper to taste. Sauté, stirring occasionally, until the onion is tender but not brown, 3 to 4 minutes. Add the ginger, apples, and allspice to the skillet and sauté, stirring often, 6 to 8 minutes. Remove from the heat and transfer to a mixing bowl. When slightly cool, add the squash purée and breadcrumbs and stir to mix. Taste to adjust the seasonings if necessary. The stuffing can be prepared up to one day ahead and refrigerated in a suitable container.

When ready to serve, preheat the oven to 350°F. Bring the stuffing and squash shells to room temperature. Fill the bottom half of the shells with stuffing and drizzle about $^1\!/_2$ teaspoon melted butter over the top. Tent with foil, shiny side down, and bake for 20 to 25 minutes, until heated through. Serve as a side dish or main vegetable course.

BRUSSELS SPROUTS WITH HAZELNUTS AND THYME

THE UNIQUE SPIRALED ROWS OF SPROUTS, VISIBLE AT FARMERS' MARKETS AND FARM STANDS in late fall, has found more devotees since cooking methods have improved for this cold-weather crop.

YIELDS: 6 TO 8 SERVINGS

1/3 cup hazelnuts, toasted

1 pound Brussels sprouts

2 teaspoons kosher salt

1 tablespoon extra-virgin olive oil

6 tablespoons unsalted butter

1 tablespoon fresh thyme leaves

Freshly ground black pepper

Place the hazelnuts on a baking sheet and toast until lightly browned, 6 to 7 minutes. Wrap the warm hazelnuts in a clean kitchen towel and rub to loosen the skins as well as possible. Remove from the towel and chop coarsely.

Trim the ends of the Brussels sprouts and remove and discard any discolored outer leaves. Cut an X in the base of each sprout. Bring a large pot of water to a boil over high heat. Add the salt, oil, and Brussels sprouts. Boil until bright green, stirring occasionally, about 10 minutes. Drain and cool quickly under a spray of cold water to stop the cooking; then pat dry in a clean kitchen towel. The Brussels sprouts can be prepared up to one day ahead to this point.

When ready to serve, melt the butter in a 10 to 12-inch heavy skillet over medium-high heat until golden brown, about 1 1/2 minutes. Add the Brussels sprouts and thyme and stir to heat through, 4 to 5 minutes. Season with salt and pepper. Transfer to a warm serving dish and garnish with toasted hazelnuts.

PECONIC BAY WINERY
Cutchogue

WELL BEFORE THEY PURCHASED A VINEYARD AND WINERY, PAUL AND URSULA Lowerre loved the wines of Bordeaux and Burgundy.

As a couple, the Lowerres once rented a house in Bordeaux, but a trip out to the Napa Valley for their tenth wedding anniversary was a real turning point in their personal involvement. Ursula explains that while in the West Coast wine country, she read about the similarity of Long Island wines to those of Bordeaux and casually mentioned to Paul that "if someone were smart, they would buy land on the East End and grow grapes."

In 1999 they purchased Peconic Bay Winery, and along with a top team of professionals, have been making top quality wines ever since. Ursula credits having the "three best people out there: Charlie Hargrave, our vineyard manager, General Manager Jim Silver, and Winemaker Greg Gove. He really is a magician out there. We just let him do his thing."

Paul explains that Peconic Bay wines are "scrupulously under-manipulated. What you get in the bottle is very much an expression of what comes in from the field. Charlie Hargrave has spectacular vineyard management, and is on a mission to do as little as possible. The land on Oregon Road turned out to be an accidental joy. It is the highest point around, and produces fruit of exceptional quality. It is now the site of our principal merlot plantings."

Overall, they make wines with great acidity and little oak. There is a touch of oak in the La Barrique Chardonnay, but always in balance with the fruit. In considering the question of whether to adjust the winemaking style to compensate for the fact that most wines are made to drink right away, Paul Lowerre countered, "The vintage Merlot and Chardonnay, for example, are made in a way that the fruit presents itself." That said, Paul explained, "they recently introduced the nonvintage table wine, Nautique, which is meant to be consumed immediately." The Lowerre's daughter, Lavinia, came up with the idea for the Nautique brand, which is meant to appeal to a wider audience.

Because the Lowerres are based in Manhattan, otherwise known as the greatest wine market in the country, the proximity to the East End is a real and lasting benefit. Lowerre also points out the unique beauty of the North Fork as an immense draw and benefit.

BUTTERNUT SQUASH RISOTTO

WHEN PURCHASING BUTTERNUT SQUASH, SELECT ONES WITH LONG NECKS, WHICH YIELD MORE solid flesh. Peel and discard the hard rind with a chef's knife. Slice the squash horizontally into 1½-inch sections down to the base and then cut into cubes. The base mostly contains seeds.

YIELD: 6 SERVINGS

6 to 6½ cups chicken or vegetable stock (see page 335) or low-sodium canned

1 tablespoon extra-virgin olive oil

1 tablespoon unsalted butter

2 to 3 shallots, finely chopped

2 to 3 garlic cloves, finely chopped

1 butternut squash (about 2½ to 3 pounds), peeled, halved, seeded, and cubed

Kosher salt and freshly ground black pepper

½ cup dry white wine

2 cups Arborio or Carnaroli rice

1 teaspoon chopped fresh sage leaves

2 to 3 tablespoons freshly grated Parmigiano-Reggiano cheese

Pour the stock into a large saucepan and bring to a boil over high heat. Reduce the heat to low and keep warm at a bare simmer.

Heat the oil and butter in a large 4- to 5-quart saucepan over medium heat. When the butter melts, add the shallots and sauté for 1 to 2 minutes or until the shallots are translucent. Add the garlic and sauté for 40 to 50 seconds longer, being careful not to brown the garlic. Add the squash and season with salt and pepper; stir to mix. Add the wine and cook at a brisk simmer, stirring until the wine evaporates. Add ½ cup of the simmering stock. Cover the squash with a square of wax paper to sweat; then cover the pan and cook for 6 to 7 minutes. Remove the cover and wax paper.

Add the rice to the squash and stir to mix. Add another ½ cup of the simmering stock. Cook, stirring continuously with a wooden spatula, until the liquid is absorbed. Add the remaining stock, about ½ cup at a time, allowing the stock to be absorbed before adding more and stirring continuously, until the rice is creamy yet tender and firm to the bite, 25 to 30 minutes. Add the sage and stir to mix. Taste for seasonings and remove from the heat. Stir in the grated cheese and serve at once on warm plates. Pass additional grated cheese at the table, if desired.

NOTE: For ease of cutting the hard rind of the butternut squash, microwave on high for 3 minutes to soften the rind.

Wine suggestion: Peconic Bay Vineyards La Barrique Chardonnay

KALE WITH CURRANTS

KALE IS PARTICULARLY RICH IN VITAMIN C WITH A PLENTIFUL DOSE OF CALCIUM. AT MOST farmers' markets on the East End of Long Island, you are more likely to find the red Russian variety with flat blue-green leaves that are somewhat more tender than the commonly available ruffled grey-green leaves, which are fairly tough.

YIELD: 4 TO 6 SERVINGS

1/4 cup currants

1/4 cup freshly squeezed orange juice

1 bunch kale (about 1 pound), tough stems and ribs removed

1 tablespoon extra-virgin olive oil

1 tablespoon unsalted butter

Kosher salt and freshly ground black pepper

In a small bowl, soak the currants in the orange juice for 15 minutes until plump.

Rinse the kale leaves under cold running water. Stack the leaves and slice crosswise into 2-inch-wide strips. Place in a saucepan of boiling salted water over medium-high heat and cook for 7 to 10 minutes, depending on the variety. The kale can be cooked up to 2 hours ahead. Refrigerate or keep at room temperature.

Heat the oil with the butter in a 10 to 12-inch skillet over medium heat. When the butter foam subsides, add the kale and cook for about 2 minutes, tossing with tongs to coat. Pour in the currants and orange juice and season with salt and pepper to taste. Simmer for 2 to 3 minutes longer until the liquid evaporates. Serve warm or at room temperature.

SPAGHETTINI WITH CHERRY TOMATOES AND PANCETTA

BAKING CHERRY TOMATOES IN THE OVEN FOR JUST 5 MINUTES INTENSIFIES THEIR SWEETNESS, adding to the overall flavor of this satisfying winter pasta dish. This recipe easily doubles, making enough to serve four to six.

YIELD: 2 TO 3 SERVINGS

FOR THE SAUCE

$1/2$ pound ripe cherry tomatoes

3 tablespoons extra-virgin olive oil

$1^1/2$ ounces pancetta, sliced $1/4$-inch thick and diced

2 garlic cloves, finely chopped

Kosher salt and freshly ground black pepper

$1/8$ teaspoon red pepper flakes

8 to 10 large fresh basil leaves, and cut into chiffonade (see note page 104)

FOR THE PASTA

1 to 2 tablespoons kosher salt

$1/2$ pound spaghettini

3 to 4 tablespoons coarsely chopped flat-leaf Italian parsley, for garnish

For the sauce, preheat the oven to 375°F.

Rinse the cherry tomatoes, pat dry with paper towels, and transfer to a baking sheet. Bake for 5 minutes. Remove from the oven and let cool.

Heat the oil with the pancetta in a 10 or 11-inch non-stick skillet over medium heat and cook until the pancetta begins to crisp slightly, 5 to 6 minutes. Add the garlic and sauté briefly, about 20 seconds; do not allow to brown. Add the tomatoes and sauté, stirring occasionally, about 5 minutes. Season with salt and pepper and the red pepper flakes and cook for 5 minutes longer. Add the basil and stir to mix. Remove from the heat.

For the pasta, bring a large pot of cold water to a boil over medium-high heat. Add the salt and all the pasta at once. Cover the pot and return the water to a boil. Uncover and cook the pasta until al dente, 9 to 12 minutes, or according to the package directions. Drain and return the pasta to the pot.

When ready to serve, warm the sauce over low heat. Spoon the sauce over the pasta in the pot and toss to mix so that all the strands are well coated. Transfer to warm plates, sprinkle with the parsley, and serve at once.

FUSILLI WITH FENNEL, SAUSAGE, AND BROCCOLI RABE

THE INGREDIENTS FOR THIS PASTA ARE FELICITOUSLY PAIRED. FUSILLI, SHORT, TWIST-SHAPED pasta, is appropriate for this hearty sauce. Pork and chicken sausages are locally made by several East End Italian specialty markets: Village Prime Meat in Quogue, Scotto's in Hampton Bays, and Villa Italian Specialty in East Hampton.

YIELD: 4 TO 6 SERVINGS

1 large bunch broccoli rabe

1 fennel bulb

1 to 1¼ pounds Italian sweet sausage

2 tablespoons extra-virgin olive oil, divided

5 garlic cloves, sliced paper thin

⅛ to ¼ snipped dried hot chile

1 cup chicken stock (see page 335) or low-sodium canned

Kosher salt and freshly ground black pepper

1 pound fusilli

Kosher salt and freshly ground black pepper

⅓ cup freshly grated Parmigiano-Reggiano or Pecorino cheese, plus extra cheese for the table

Trim the broccoli rabe, discarding the heavy stems. Separate the leaves and florets and soak in cold water for 10 to 15 minutes. Trim and discard the feathery fronds and any outer bruised parts of the fennel bulb. Halve the fennel and discard the core. Cut the bulb into vertical slices about ¼ inch thick. Soak in a separate bowl of cold water for 10 to 15 minutes. Drain the broccoli rabe and the fennel and dry separately in clean kitchen towels; set aside.

Remove the casing from the sausage, breaking the links into bite-size pieces. Heat 1½ tablespoons of the olive oil in a 12-inch skillet over medium heat. Add the sausage and sauté until crispy brown on both sides, 4 to 5 minutes. Remove from the pan and drain all but 1 tablespoon of drippings from the pan.

Sauté the fennel in the reserved drippings over medium heat until lightly golden, 8 to 10 minutes. Add the garlic slivers and hot chile and sauté until the garlic is pale golden, about 1 minute. Add the sausage and broccoli rabe and stir to mix. Pour in the chicken stock and bring to a boil. Reduce the heat to medium and simmer, partially covered, for 5 to 6 minutes, or until the broccoli rabe and fennel are tender. Season with salt and pepper to taste. The sauce can be prepared up to an hour ahead. Reheat over low while cooking the pasta.

Bring a large pot of water to a rolling boil over medium-high heat and add 1 to 2 tablespoons of kosher salt. Add the pasta all at once. Cover and immediately return to a boil; then boil uncovered for 9 to 12 minutes, until al dente or firm to the bite. Drain the pasta, reserving $1/3$ cup of hot pasta water.

Stir the reserved pasta water and the pasta into the skillet. Toss to mix thoroughly. Sprinkle with the cheese and serve at once on warm plates. Drizzle a bit of the remaining $1/2$ tablespoon of oil over each serving and pass extra grated cheese at the table, if desired.

BAY SCALLOPS WITH HONEY AND THYME

THE FIRST MONDAY OF NOVEMBER OFFICIALLY OPENS THE BAY SCALLOP SEASON WITH SCALLOPS that are a little smaller than a penny and come from Peconic Bay on the East End of Long Island. Of the varied species of scallops along the eastern seaboard, it has been documented that none can compare to the delectably sweet Peconic Bay scallop. A colorful julienne of vegetables serves as a backdrop for this savory bay scallop treat. Bay scallops are generally avalable through the winter season.

YIELD: 6 SERVINGS

2 tablespoons extra-virgin olive oil

2 carrots, peeled, cut into julienne strips

1 leek, washed very well and cut into julienne strips

1 yellow bell pepper, cut into julienne strips

Kosher salt and freshly ground black pepper

2 tablespoons unsalted butter

1 pound bay scallops, side muscle removed

2 tablespoons local honey

2 teaspoons fresh thyme leaves

$1/2$ cup vegetable, fish, or chicken stock (see page 335) or low-sodium canned

Warm six luncheon or salad plates in a 200°F oven.

Heat the oil in a 12-inch skillet over medium heat and sauté the carrots, leek, and bell pepper for 5 to 6 minutes, until they have a slight crunch. Season the vegetables with salt and pepper. Divide evenly among the warm plates.

In the same skillet, melt the butter over medium high until it browns slightly. Be careful not to burn the butter. Add the scallops and sauté for $1^1/2$ minutes total, turning once. With a slotted spoon, divide the scallops evenly over the vegetables.

Add the honey and thyme to the same skillet over medium-high heat and stir to deglaze the pan juices. Add the stock and season with salt and pepper. Bring to a boil over high heat, stirring. Reduce the liquid by one-third. Drizzle the sauce over the scallops and serve at once.

ATLANTIC COD WITH POTATOES AND ROASTED GARLIC

COD IS SO POPULAR IN THE NORTHEAST, IT IS ALMOST SYNONYMOUS WITH THE WORD FISH. This Catalan-inspired dish from Spain is a simple but sophisticated one-dish meal.

YIELD: 4 TO 6 SERVINGS

8 to 10 whole garlic cloves, unpeeled*

Extra-virgin olive oil, for roasting

1 pound russet potatoes, peeled and sliced $1/4$ inch thick

4 to 5 tablespoons extra-virgin olive oil, divided

Kosher salt and freshly ground black pepper

$1^3/_4$ to 2 pounds cod fillets

1 red bell pepper, cut into julienne strips

2 ripe plum tomatoes, peeled (see note on page 57), seeded, and diced

12 to 14 black niçoise olives, pitted

1 bay leaf

Several sprigs fresh thyme

$1/4$ cup dry white wine

Preheat the oven to 375°F.

Place the garlic cloves in a small ceramic dish and pour in just enough olive oil to barely cover. Cover the dish with foil and roast for 50 to 60 minutes or until tender. Remove from the oven and, when cool enough to handle, slip the garlic from their skins. Set aside.

Meanwhile, in a saucepan of boiling, salted water, cook the potatoes for 7 to 8 minutes. Drain and pat dry. Coat the bottom of an ovenproof serving dish or casserole dish with 1 tablespoon of the extra-virgin olive oil. Layer the potato slices to completely cover the bottom. Drizzle about 1 tablespoon of olive oil over each layer of potatoes and sprinkle lightly with salt and pepper. Arrange the cod fillets on top and drizzle with additional olive oil and season with salt and pepper. The entire dish can be prepared up to several hours ahead. Refrigerate, covered, until ready to bake.

When ready to cook, place the roasted garlic, bell pepper, tomatoes, olives, and bay leaf around and over the fish. Drizzle with a bit more oil and season with salt and pepper. Top with the sprigs of thyme and drizzle with the wine. Bake for 16 to 18 minutes, until the fish is firm to the touch and opaque. Before serving, discard the bay leaf. Serve at once, spooning the juices from the baking dish over the fish.

* NOTE: If there isn't enough time to roast the garlic cloves, place the unpeeled cloves in the water with the potatoes and cook together.

Wine suggestion: Shinn Estate Vineyard Sauvignon Blanc Semillon

ROASTED SALMON FILLET WITH SWISS CHARD

TO HEIGHTEN THE MILD FLAVOR OF FARM-RAISED SALMON, TOP IT WITH A SAVORY SEASONED crust, bake, and serve on a bed of Swiss chard—an agreeable accompaniment.

YIELD: 6 SERVINGS

1 large bunch Swiss chard (about 2 pounds)

2 pounds center-cut salmon fillet

2 shallots, finely chopped, divided

1 to 2 tablespoons grated fresh ginger

1 heaping tablespoon whole-grain Dijon mustard

2 teaspoons fresh thyme leaves

1 to 2 teaspoons kosher salt

Freshly ground black pepper

1 tablespoon extra-virgin olive oil

1 teaspoon lemon juice

Remove the stems from the chard. Wash and spin dry the leaves and stems separately. Stack the leaves and cut crosswise into 2-inch-wide strips. Trim the stem ends and cut into 1½-inch lengths.

Preheat the oven to 450°F. Cut the salmon into 6 equal fillets and place in a lightly greased baking pan. Combine one shallot, the ginger, mustard, thyme, salt, and pepper in a small bowl and stir to mix. Spread the mixture evenly over each salmon fillet to coat and marinate about 20 minutes. Roast the fillets for 8 to 10 minutes, or until springy to the touch.

When ready to serve, heat the oil in a nonstick skillet over medium-high heat. Add the other shallot and sauté for about 1 minute or until translucent. Add the Swiss chard. Toss to coat and sauté for 3 to 4 minutes, until the leaves are wilted and the stems are tender. Season with salt and pepper to taste and stir in the lemon juice. Divide the mixture among four to six warm dinner plates.

Serve the roasted salmon over the sautéed chard along with roasted or boiled new potatoes, if desired.

ROASTED CHICKEN WITH HERBS AND SHALLOTS

PLACE A BUNDLE OF FRESH HERBS IN THE CAVITY OF THE CHICKEN AND ROAST OVER CARROTS and shallots. The aroma and flavors are hedonistic.

YIELD: 4 TO 5 SERVINGS

1 (3$\frac{1}{2}$ to 4-pound) chicken

1 lemon, halved

Sprigs of fresh herbs, such as flat-leaf Italian parsley, rosemary, thyme, and sage

4 to 5 large garlic cloves, peeled and crushed

2 tablespoons extra-virgin olive oil

$\frac{1}{2}$ teaspoon paprika

Kosher salt and freshly ground black pepper

3 to 4 carrots, peeled and sliced on the diagonal

10 to 12 shallots, peeled and left whole

$\frac{1}{2}$ cup dry white wine

Preheat the oven to 400°F.

Trim the chicken of excess fat. Remove the giblets and reserve for another use. Rinse the chicken inside and out then pat dry with paper towels. Tuck the wing tips under.

Rub the lemon halves over the chicken, squeezing gently as you rub. Place the herb sprigs in the cavity along with the lemon halves and crushed garlic cloves. In a small bowl, combine the olive oil, paprika, and salt and pepper to taste and rub over the chicken.

To truss the chicken, cut a length of kitchen string about 4 feet long, crisscross the string under the drumsticks, bringing the string up and around the end of the drumsticks and pulling the string taut. Bring the string along both sides of the body under the curve of the legs, pulling into the crevice of the wings; tie the two ends into a secure knot at the neck.

Place the chicken in a roasting pan breast side up. Scatter the carrots and shallots around the chicken. Roast 20 minutes; then turn breast side down. Baste and continue to roast another 20 minutes. Return the chicken to breast side up, basting with the pan juices, and continue to roast about 15 minutes longer, or until the skin is nut-brown and an instant thermometer inserted into the thickest part of the thigh registers 165°F. Transfer to a carving board.

Set the roasting pan over medium-high heat and bring the pan juices to a boil, skimming the fat that rises to the surface. Add the wine, stirring to deglaze the pan juices. Reduce the heat and simmer to keep warm.

Carve the chicken into 8 pieces and serve with the roasted carrots, shallots, and warm pan juices.

NOTE: If the thigh and leg show a touch of pink when the chicken is carved, return them to the roasting pan with the pan juices and vegetables and simmer over medium-low heat for 3 to 5 minutes longer.

Wine suggestion: Channing Daughters Winery L'Enfant Sauvage Chardonnay

ARISTA OF PORK

"ARISTA," MEANING "THE BEST" IN GREEK, WAS EXCLAIMED BY THE GREEK DIGNITARY VISITING Florence, Italy—the culinary center of the West in the middle ages—when served a delicious pork roast with garlic, rosemary, and black pepper—a Florentine specialty.

YIELD: 6 TO 8 SERVINGS

3$\frac{1}{2}$ to 4 pounds center-cut pork loin

2 tablespoons fresh rosemary leaves

6 to 8 garlic cloves, cut into thin slivers

2 to 3 teaspoons kosher salt

1 tablespoon freshly ground black pepper

1 tablespoon extra-virgin olive oil

Have your butcher bone and tie the pork loin. Reserve the bones.

Preheat the oven to 350°F.

With kitchen shears, snip the rosemary leaves. Combine the rosemary, garlic, salt, and pepper in a small bowl. Make several slits in the pork with the tip of a sharp paring knife. Insert the herb mixture into the slits and then rub any remaining herb mixture over the meat. This preparation can be done up to a day ahead. Refrigerate, covered, in a suitable container. Bring to room temperature before continuing.

Place the oil in a shallow roasting pan that can hold the roast snugly. Put the bones on the bottom of the roasting pan and place the meat on top of the bones, fat side up. Roast about 1$\frac{1}{2}$ hours, until a thermometer inserted into the meat reaches 155°F, basting with the pan juices occasionally.

Transfer the roast to a carving board when done and let rest for 8 to 10 minutes. Discard the string and carve into thin slices for serving. Serve warm. Leftover arista is delicious served cold the next day.

EAST END ROAST DUCK
WITH APPLE AND PRUNE STUFFING

MANY POLISH FAMILIES ON THE EAST END OWNED DUCK FARMS, WHICH ARE MOSTLY GONE now. As in all cultures, recipes were handed down from mother to daughter (and sons), and in translation or in new lifestyles, some of that information was forgotten. This is precisely the reason for documenting what can be saved.

YIELDS: 4 SERVINGS

1 (5 to 5 1/2-pound) fresh duck

1 large Granny Smith apple, peeled, cored, and diced

1/2 cup pitted prunes, diced

1 whole garlic clove, halved

2 tablespoons extra-virgin olive oil

1 tablespoon thyme leaves

Kosher salt and freshly ground black pepper

Remove the giblets, neck, and liver from the duck cavity; reserve the giblets and neck for stock and the liver for pâté, if desired. Remove excess fat from around the neck and cavity to render, if desired. Leave the loose duck skin around the cavity for ease of enclosing the stuffing. Rinse the duck and pat dry with paper towels, inside and out. Using a long-tined fork, take long shallow running stitches through the surface of the duck skin, being careful not to cut through the fat into the meat. Place the duck on a rack over a pan, cover with a tent of plastic wrap, and refrigerate for up to 48 hours for the skin to dry out.

Up to 2 hours before roasting, stuff the duck with the apple and prunes and secure the opening with toothpicks or metal skewers. Rub the cut side of the garlic halves over the duck, coating the surface. In a small bowl, mix the oil, thyme, and salt and pepper and rub all over the duck skin.

Preheat the oven to 400°F.

Coat a shallow roasting pan with oil and heat over medium low. Put the duck in the pan and brown about 3 to 4 minutes on each side. Remove the duck and pour the accumulated fat into a heatproof bowl. Reduce the oven temperature to 325°F. Place the duck on its side on a rack in the roasting pan and roast for 20 minutes. Turn to the other side and roast for another 20 minutes. Turn breast side down and roast for 30 to 40 minutes longer, or for a total of 1 hour and 30 to 40 minutes, or until an instant thermometer inserted into the thigh without touching the bone reads 180°F. Remove from the pan, pour off any remaining duck fat, and save for cooking.*

Remove the duck and let rest on a carving board. Scoop out the stuffing and set aside. Place the roasting pan on the stove over medium heat and bring the pan juices to a boil, skimming off and discarding the fat. Carve the duck and arrange on a warm serving platter. Garnish with the fruit. Pour over the clear pan juices and serve.

*NOTE: The rendered fat can be used for cooking and is particularly good for sautéing potatoes. Refrigerating the precooked duck is a helpful technique to dry the skin. Although duck is properly cooked at 180°F which would normally dry out poultry, the moisture of the apple and prune stuffing keeps the meat moist. To render the duck fat, put the pieces of fat in a skillet over low heat and let cook slowly for 15 to 20 minutes. Pour off the fat in a glass or ceramic container along with the melted duck fat from roasting and keep refrigerated.

OSSO BUCCO
WITH ROSEMARY AND RED WINE

A DINNER PARTY FAVORITE BEST PREPARED THE DAY BEFORE, OSSO BUCCO IS A SAVORY BLEND of veal shank braised in a broth with herbs and vegetables.

YIELD: 8 SERVINGS

8 (1½-inch-thick) pieces veal shank

Flour, for dusting

Kosher salt and freshly ground black pepper

2 tablespoons canola oil

1 tablespoon unsalted butter

3 onions, coarsely chopped

3 carrots, cut into large dice

1 (12 to 16-ounce) can plum tomatoes with liquid

3 to 4 garlic cloves, finely chopped

1 (750-millimeter) bottle dry red wine

2 to 3 tablespoons chopped fresh rosemary sprigs

2 cups chicken stock (see page 335) or low-sodium canned

Chopped fresh parsley or chives, for garnish

Preheat the oven to 450°F.

Tie each veal shank with kitchen string. Dust with flour, shaking off the excess. Season with salt and pepper.

Heat the oil and butter in a large, heavy skillet. When the butter melts and the foam subsides, brown the veal shanks on both sides until golden; do not crowd the pan. You will have to do 3 or 4 at a time. Remove from the pan and set aside as they are done.

Add the onions to the skillet, adding a little more oil if necessary, and sauté over medium-high heat for 3 to 4 minutes, stirring occasionally. Add the carrots and continue cooking until the onions are slightly caramelized. Transfer the vegetables to a large, heatproof casserole or Dutch oven and place the shanks over them. Add the tomatoes, garlic, wine, and rosemary, crushing the tomatoes with the back of a spoon. Bring to a boil.

Meanwhile, add the stock to the skillet the shanks browned in and bring to a boil to deglaze the pan drippings. Pour over the veal shanks in the casserole. Taste the sauce for salt and pepper. Cover the dish and bake for 1½ to 2 hours, until the meat is tender. Refrigerate in the Dutch oven overnight.

When ready to cook, bring to room temperature and reheat over medium and then transfer the meat to a warm platter. Increase the heat to high and cook until the liquid is reduced and thickened, then pour over the shanks. Garnish liberally with parsley or chives. Serve with spinach noodles, polenta (see page 242), or risotto, if desired.

RACK OF LAMB
WITH ROASTED SHALLOT VINAIGRETTE

CHARLIE TROTTER, EMINENT AWARD-WINNING CHICAGO CHEF, RESTAURATEUR, AND AUTHOR, inspired this brilliant recipe for lovers of rack of lamb. Restaurant chef recipes, however, can be daunting. Here is a workable make-ahead, kitchen-friendly plan to prepare this special-occasion dish at home.

YIELD: 4 TO 6 SERVINGS

FOR THE VINAIGRETTE

3 or 4 peeled shallots

$^1/_2$ cup extra-virgin olive oil

3 tablespoons verjus or white wine vinegar

2 tablespoons chopped fresh chives, plus more for garnish (optional)

Kosher salt and freshly ground black pepper

FOR THE POLENTA

$^1/_2$ cup polenta

Kosher salt and freshly ground black pepper

3 tablespoons unsalted butter, divided

2 tablespoons chopped garlic

FOR THE LAMB

2 frenched racks of lamb (7 to 8 ribs each rack)

Kosher salt and freshly ground black pepper

$^1/_4$ cup extra-virgin olive oil

Fresh thyme leaves from about 10 sprigs

Preheat the oven to 400°F.

For the vinaigrette, place the shallots and the oil in a small ovenproof pan. Cover tightly with foil and bake for 30 to 35 minutes, until the shallots are soft. Let the shallots cool in the oil and then remove with a slotted spoon, reserving the oil. Cut the shallots into thin strips and place in a small bowl. Add the verjus and slowly whisk in the reserved shallot oil. Add the chives and season to taste with salt and pepper. The vinaigrette can be prepared up to two days ahead. Refrigerate, covered, in a suitable container.

For the polenta, bring 2 cups of water to a boil in a medium saucepan over high heat. Slowly whisk in the polenta. Reduce the heat to low and simmer, stirring occasionally until thick and smooth and the polenta pulls away from the sides of the pan, 8 to 10 minutes. Season to taste with salt and pepper.

Melt 2 tablespoons of the butter in a small skillet over medium heat. Sauté the garlic for 1 minute and then with a rubber spatula, add it to the polenta. Taste for seasonings. Spread the polenta on a baking sheet into a 6-inch square about $^1/_2$ inch thick. Cover with plastic wrap and refrigerate for several hours or overnight.

A few hours before serving, cut the polenta into four 3-inch round disks. Heat the remaining 1 tablespoon of butter in a hot, nonstick skillet over medium-high heat. Add the polenta and cook for 2 to 3 minutes on each side, until golden brown and crispy. Blot with paper towels.

Meanwhile, bring the shallot vinaigrette to room temperature.

For the lamb, preheat the oven to 425°F.

Season the lamb racks with salt and pepper and rub with the oil and thyme leaves. Place the racks in a roasting pan and roast for 25 minutes for medium-rare or 30 to 35 minutes for medium. Let the lamb rest for 5 minutes and slice between the bones just prior to serving.

To serve, place a polenta round in the center of each of four warm dinner plates. Arrange 3 lamb chops over the polenta. Drizzle the vinaigrette over the chops and sprinkle chives around the plate for presentation, if desired. Season with freshly ground black pepper and serve.

Wine suggestion: Pellegrini Vineyards Vintner Pride Encore

NICK & TONI'S
East Hampton

JOSEPH REALMUTO IS THE EXECUTIVE CHEF FOR ALL HONEST MANAGEMENT
Company establishments, including Nick & Toni's. He is a man on the move.

Joseph's cooking career began early in life by virtue of his Italian heritage. At age fourteen he joined his older brother and sister working after school running food in a catering business. He's been running ever since. Realmuto graduated from the Culinary Institute of America, interned at several high-end New York City restaurants, and in 1993 was hired as a line cook at Nick & Toni's. He went on to become sous chef at the restaurant and was appointed executive chef in 1996. Through the years, the restaurant garnered many awards and received a three-star review from *The New York Times* in 2001.

The familiarity of Italian cooking is very close to Realmuto's heart. It's simply a food he is comfortable with, and as a devoted locavore, he brings the element of simplicity to all his creations, using local and organic produce. Some of the local produce is even grown on property adjacent to the restaurant and managed by Scott Chaskey of the Peconic Land Trust's Quail Hill Farm (see page 202) in Amagansett. Seedlings are started in green houses at Quail Hill and transplanted in Nick & Toni's garden.

Realmuto has been instrumental as well in sustaining a farmers' market in the vicinity of the restaurant. He's involved with Bridgehampton's private Hayground School's "Young Chefs Program," a chef-led workshop with young students. He maintains relationships with many local farmers and built a greenhouse at the Springs School, a local public school his two children attend. The children have the full devotion of their father, who manages, between his restaurant responsibilities, to take the time to share their lives, cooking healthy and eating locally.

ROASTED LEG OF LAMB
WITH POTATO FENNEL GRATIN

THIS SPECIAL OCCASION RECIPE WAS INSPIRED BY NICK & TONI'S EXECUTIVE CHEF JOSEPH Realmuto's Italian roots, as well as the flavors of Italy.

YIELD: 8 SERVINGS

1 (7 to 8-pound) bone-in leg of lamb, tail and pelvic bones removed, shank bone frenched (have your butcher do this)

3 garlic cloves, thinly sliced, plus 2 garlic cloves, finely chopped

4 to 5 anchovy fillets, cut into quarters

5 sprigs rosemary, cut into 1-inch pieces, plus 2 teaspoons finely chopped rosemary

Kosher salt and freshly ground black pepper

5 tablespoons extra-virgin olive oil, divided

2 large fennel bulbs, trimmed and thinly sliced

1¼ cups chicken stock (see page 335) or low-sodium canned, divided

½ cup dry vermouth

5 medium Yukon Gold potatoes, peeled and thinly sliced

1 large yellow onion, thinly sliced

Trim and discard any excess fat from the lamb. Make 18 to 20 small slits over the entire surface of the lamb and insert a slice of garlic, a piece of anchovy, and a 1-inch piece of rosemary, leaving a tip of the rosemary stem sticking out, of each slit. Season the lamb all over with salt and pepper. Transfer the lamb to a roasting pan, cover loosely with plastic wrap, and refrigerate overnight.

Remove the lamb from the refrigerator 2 hours before roasting to allow it to come to room temperature.

Preheat the oven to 450°F.

Rub the surface of the lamb with 2 tablespoons of the oil and then transfer the lamb, meatier side down, to a 16 x 13-inch roasting pan and roast just until it begins to sizzle, 20 to 25 minutes; maintain the oven temperature.

Meanwhile, heat the remaining 3 tablespoons of oil in a 12-inch skillet over medium-high heat. Add the chopped rosemary, the chopped garlic, the fennel, and salt and pepper to taste and cook, stirring occasionally, until the fennel is lightly golden, 6 to 8 minutes. Stir in ¼ cup of the stock and the vermouth. Reduce the heat to medium and simmer, covered, stirring occasionally, until the fennel is tender, 8 to 10 minutes.

Remove the lamb from the roasting pan to a platter. In the same roasting pan, layer the sliced potatoes with the fennel mixture and sliced onion. Season each layer with salt and pepper. Pour the remaining 1 cup of stock evenly over the vegetables. Place the lamb, meatier side up, over the vegetables in the roasting pan. Pour any accumulated pan juices left in the platter over the lamb and return to

the oven. Reduce the heat to 350°F and cook for an additional 30 to 40 minutes or until a meat thermometer inserted into the thickest part registers 135°F for medium rare. Check the potato-fennel mixture for doneness and remove from the oven. Transfer the lamb to a carving board, cover with foil, and let rest for 20 minutes before carving. If the potatoes are not completely tender, return to the oven and continue to roast until knife tender. Slice the lamb and serve with the potato-fennel gratin.

NOTE: Several do-ahead steps can be executed for this delectable company dish. Season the lamb and refrigerate overnight. Prepare the vegetables for the gratin up to one day ahead and refrigerate in suitable containers.

Wine suggestion: Raphael Vineyard Port

ROASTED FILET OF BEEF
WITH SPINACH AND SWEET PEPPER STUFFING

FILET OF BEEF IS A FAVORITE CUT OF MEAT TO SERVE AT DINNER PARTIES. THE COLORFUL AND savory stuffing makes an elegant dish for the winter holidays.

YIELD: 8 SERVINGS

1 whole beef filet, trimmed (about 3 pounds)

1 pound spinach, stems trimmed and discarded (use baby spinach if available)

2 red bell peppers

Kosher salt and freshly ground black pepper

3 tablespoons extra-virgin olive oil

$^1/_4$ cup finely chopped shallots

2 cups dry red wine

Butterfly the filet by cutting lengthwise down the center but not through the meat. The thin tail end can be reserved for use in a sauté or stir fry or can be tucked under itself and then tied securely with kitchen string to form a roll of even thickness.

Wash the spinach in several changes of lukewarm water to rid it of any sand; then soak in a bowl of clean water for 10 minutes. Lift the spinach into a large saucepan and cook with the water that clings to its leaves. Cover the pan and bring to boil over high heat. Reduce the heat to medium and cook at a brisk simmer for about 2 minutes. Drain the spinach and squeeze dry, leaving some moisture in the spinach. Coarsely chop the spinach and set aside. (If using baby spinach, leave whole.)

Roast the bell peppers by grilling or broiling them until the skins are charred all over. Transfer to a paper bag to steam. Peel and seed the peppers in a sieve over a bowl. Cut into $^1/_2$-inch-wide strips. This procedure may be done several days ahead, and the peppers may be refrigerated in a suitable container.

Open the butterflied meat and season with salt and pepper. Place a layer of spinach along one side of the filet; season with salt and pepper. Place a layer of bell pepper strips on top of the spinach and then season with salt and pepper. Roll the filet over to enclose the filling and tie at 2-inch intervals with kitchen string. The filet may be prepared ahead up to this point. Refrigerate, covered, overnight.

Preheat the oven to 400°F

Pour the olive oil into a shallow roasting pan just large enough to hold the filet. Heat over medium-high heat. Season the filet with salt and pepper to taste and sear in the hot oil. Reduce the heat to medium and brown the filet on all sides. Remove from the pan and drain any excess oil. Return the filet to the roasting pan and surround it with the shallots. Pour the red wine into the pan and roast in the oven until the filet is crusty brown on the outside and pink within, 25 to 30 minutes, or until an instant thermometer inserted into the thickest part of the meat registers 125°F to 135°F for rare to medium rare. Place the filet on a cutting board and let stand, loosely covered with foil, 10 to 12 minutes before carving.

Meanwhile, reduce the pan juices by half over high heat. Transfer to a small saucepan and keep warm until ready to serve.

Slice the filet and transfer to a warm serving platter. Pour the pan juices over the roast and surround with whole roasted baby carrots, if desired.

NOTES: I prefer not to strain out the shallots from the reduced pan liquids; as they add great flavor and texture to the sauce.

Wine Suggestion: Roanoke Vineyard Blend I

PEAR TARTE TATIN

TRADITIONALLY, TARTE TATIN, A FRENCH CLASSIC, IS MADE WITH APPLES. USING SWEET, RIPE pears is a delicious twist on the classic. When I serve it at a dinner party, I accompany it with pear sorbet—a very pleasing addition.

YIELD: 8 TO 10 SERVINGS

5 to 6 ripe Comice or Anjou pears

3 to 4 tablespoons freshly squeezed lemon juice

6 tablespoons unsalted butter

$\frac{1}{2}$ cup sugar

Tarte Tatin Pastry Dough (see page 337)

Pear sorbet, vanilla ice cream, or freshly whipped cream (optional)

Peel and core the pears; then cut in half vertically. Put into a mixing bowl and sprinkle with lemon juice. Toss gently to coat. Set aside.

Melt the butter in a heavy cast-iron skillet. Add the sugar and stir into the butter to coat the bottom of the pan. Cook over medium to medium-high heat until the mixture turns a light caramel color, 3 to 4 minutes, watching carefully as the sugar cooks. Remove from the heat.

Preheat the oven to 425°F.

Place the pear halves in the caramel, cut side up, with the narrow ends of the pear meeting at the center and close together to make them fit. Slice any extra pear into wedges and insert between the pear halves to make a tight fit. Pour the accumulated pear juice from the bowl over the pears. Return the skillet to the heat and cook until the sugar turns a deep caramel color. Gently move the pan back and forth over the heat so the pears do not stick and the sugar does not burn. Remove from the heat and allow to cool for 15 to 20 minutes or until ready to top with the pastry.

Meanwhile, roll out the prepared pastry to a 12-inch round and place on a baking sheet. Chill in the refrigerator for 30 to 60 minutes before baking. Lift the pastry with the aid of a rolling pin and then lower to cover the pears completely. Trim the excess pastry to about 1 inch beyond the edge of the pan, and with your fingers, push the pastry inside the edge, forming a border around the pears. Prick the pastry gently with a fork and brush lightly with water.

Place the skillet on middle rack of the oven and bake for 20 minutes. Reduce the heat to 375°F and bake for 20 minutes longer. Turn off the oven and allow the tart to sit in the oven for 10 to 15 minutes longer with the oven door open. Remove from the oven and unmold as soon as the skillet is cool enough to handle, about 30 to 40 minutes.

To unmold, run a kitchen table knife around the edge of the tart to loosen. Place a serving plate over the skillet and invert. The pear tart may be prepared up to a day ahead. Tent with plastic wrap and refrigerate. Cut into wedges for serving and serve with pear sorbet, vanilla ice cream, or whipped cream, as desired.

HOT SPICED APPLE CIDER

WHETHER SERVED FROM MUGS AT AN ICEBOATING EVENT OR FROM A LARGE HAMMERED copper pot simmering on the kitchen stove at a winter party, the hot mingled flavors of cider, honey, spices, apples, and oranges will warm a crowd.

YIELD: 18 TO 20 SERVINGS

2 gallons fresh
  unpasteurized apple cider

1 tablespoon honey

1 lemon, sliced and seeded

9 or 10 whole cloves

3 small cinnamon sticks

2 apples, peeled, cored, and
  thinly sliced

2 navel oranges, sliced and
  seeded

Pour the cider into a large saucepan and stir in the honey and lemon slices. Tie the cloves and cinnamon sticks in cheesecloth and add to the pot. Bring to a boil over medium-high heat. Reduce the heat and simmer for 20 minutes. Prepare the cider up to several hours ahead to this point.

When ready to serve, add the apple and orange slices and keep the cider warm over very low heat. Set a tray of mugs on the counter next to the kitchen stove and provide a ladle for guests to help themselves.

TY LLYWD FARM
Jamesport

THERE IS A LITTLE FAMILY-OWNED FARM IN JAMESPORT ON THE NORTH FORK called Ty Llywd (pronounced Tee Klew-id). The owners, David and Liz Wines, are rarely visible. Patrons know to drive past the house, circle the big tree, and go to the smaller building to pick up their farm fresh eggs and produce, where an "on your honor" system is in place.

The Ty Llywd farm is small, simple, and real in the best sense of the word. The house was built by David's maternal uncle in 1870, and it's been in the family along with thirty acres ever since. Liz came over from Wales as a young woman to work as a nanny. "In the Welsh tradition, your farm is given a name, not just a number," said Liz. "'Ty Llywd' in Welsh means brown house." David and Liz met at a local church in 1973, married in 1974, moved into the house, which has been in David's family for generations, and resumed farming.

They started with potatoes and cauliflower, which were the typical North Fork crops, but soon found that there was a shrinking market for these large-scale crops. So, they bought one hundred chickens, diversified their produce varieties, and decided to focus on the retail market.

Liz expanded the chicken operation to one thousand chickens—mostly Red DeKalbs and a few White Leghorn roosters. The chickens are free-range and are fed a mix of natural feed that includes alfalfa meal, fish meal (for protein), argonite (for calcium), corn grain, and home-grown wheat and soy beans. Liz goes into the hen houses each morning, gathers up the eggs that were just laid, brings them to her hand-operated sorter, boxes them, and they're usually sold out by the afternoon. You can be sure you are getting fresh eggs.

David has expanded his crop varieties to include about ten kinds of potatoes, including tender fingerlings, delicate rosas, red skin, and the sweetest sweet potatoes. The emphasis is on seasonal crops, and the Wines are adamant about selling only what they grow.

The farming lifestyle is alive and well at Ty Llywd. They raise a pig each year, butcher it in early winter, and eat the meat for the remainder of the year. Of their three children, Christopher chose to remain on the farm and is indispensable. This is a self-sustaining, hard working family that truly loves the land, and the North Fork is all the better for it.

ICE SAILING ON MECOX BAY

BECAUSE OF ITS PROXIMITY TO THE ATLANTIC OCEAN, MECOX BAY IS ONE OF THE most beautiful bays in the Northeast. Through diligent dredging, an inlet is kept open between the bay and the ocean each year from mid-December through the end of March. From high on a dune at Cameron or Flying Point Beach in Water Mill, you can see the still waters of the bay rushing back and forth to the great ocean. Tidal activity and sand, sand, sand can fill in the cut during this period. But then the dredgers come back to clear the way to keep the bay fresh. Though there isn't any commercial fishing in Mecox Bay, as there is in nearby Shinnecock Bay, the blue waters bring to mind the availability of fresh local shellfish I'm always tempted to try, such as bay scallops from Peconic Bay, so sweet they hit the tongue like bite-sized candies, or a pan roast of local littleneck clams.

In a cold winter, the bay water can freeze to at least four to five inches thick, and the iceboats are retrieved from barns and garages and hauled out onto the ice. Cold defying enthusiasts bundle up for leisurely sails or participate in the races organized by one of several iceboating clubs. Iceboats have a heavier sail than regular sailboats and a T-bat structure with three runners that are razor sharp. Smaller boats can have as little as twenty-five foot sails—imagine a Currier and Ives painting.

Local families—such as the Halseys, the Coopers and the Tallmadges—sail similar-sized boats, and the racing is very competitive. When the weather is right, Tom Halsey brings his work van down to the bay and sets up an enormous cooker in back to "bubble up" the family apple cider. The cauldron can stay hot for hours, and the steamy cider rife with spices is known to "perfume" the air clear across the bay. This is a big drawing card—good advertising for Tom's brother John Halsey, proprietor of The Milk Pail and the apple orchard and farm in Water Mill. Another sailor cooks up frankfurters and sauerkraut in the back of his van, frankfurters and apple cider, an unusual combination, but nevertheless a treat for those hearty souls.

Though I have never been on an iceboat, I've watched the boats rip across the bay, making me feel every bit a part of the Mecox Bay experience.

FALLEN CHOCOLATE SOUFFLÉ
WITH BERRY SAUCE

THE FATHER AND SON-IN-LAW TEAM OF OYSTER POND BERRY FARM IN ORIENT ON THE NORTH Fork of Long Island supplies fresh berries to the East End through the year. Ron Apostle and Tom Stevenson grow an amazing variety of berries: strawberries, blueberries, blackberries and red, yellow, orange, and black raspberries. The berries are frozen in the off season. I have cooked them into sauces or microwaved them for a few seconds to have with my morning cold cereal mix. Here, sugarless individual soufflés are unmolded over a pool of strawberry or raspberry purée with a dollop of ice cream or crème fraîche for a festive winter do-ahead dessert.

YIELD: 8 SERVINGS

FOR THE SAUCE

1 quart frozen or fresh strawberries or raspberries

$1/2$ cup sugar

$1/2$ cup freshly squeezed orange juice

Grated rind of 1 lemon

$1/2$ teaspoon vanilla extract

1 teaspoon Kirsch or framboise

FOR THE SOUFFLÉ

6 ounces semi-sweet chocolate

$1/2$ cup heavy cream

4 egg yolks

6 egg whites

$1/4$ teaspoon cream of tartar

Vanilla ice cream or yogurt, or crème fraiche (see page 338) (optional)

For the sauce, if using strawberries, hull them and rinse. Cut into pieces and put in a saucepan. If using raspberries, add to the saucepan whole. Add the sugar, orange juice, and rind. Simmer over low heat for 15 to 20 minutes, until the fruit is soft and the mixture is slightly thickened. Add the vanilla and stir to mix. Purée in a blender or food processor. Add the liqueur and process to mix. Transfer to a covered container and refrigerate up to several days ahead until ready to use.

For the soufflés, butter eight custard cups very well and dust lightly with sugar. Refrigerate cups until ready to use.

Preheat the oven to 350°F.

Break up the chocolate and put in a heavy saucepan. Add the cream and stir to mix over low heat until the chocolate melts to a thick cream. Remove from the heat and transfer to a mixing bowl, scraping the side of the pan with a rubber spatula. When the chocolate cools, whisk the egg yolks into the chocolate mixture one at a time and mix well.

In bowl of an electric mixer or with hand beaters, beat the egg whites at low speed until foamy, add the cream of tartar, and then beat at medium speed until firm, but not dry, peaks form.

Fold one-third of the beaten egg whites into the chocolate mixture and stir gently to mix. With a large rubber spatula, fold in the remaining egg whites until well incorporated. Carefully spoon the mixture into the prepared custard cups, filling to the rim. Place the filled cups on a jelly-roll pan and bake for 20 to 22 minutes, until well puffed and slightly firm to the touch.

Remove from the oven when done and cool at room temperature. The soufflés will fall. Place the custard cups in the refrigerator for several hours or overnight. When ready to serve, spoon a puddle of the sauce on eight dessert plates. Using a knife, cut around the inside of each cup and invert the soufflés onto the puddle of sauce. Garnish with a scoop of ice cream or frozen yogurt or a dollop of crème fraîche, if desired. The fallen soufflé will have the consistency of a light, moist chocolate cake.

CARAMEL APPLE MOUSSE

THE APPLES COOK TO A THICK PURÉE AND, WITH THE HELP OF EGGS, BAKE INTO A DELICIOUS mousse sweetened with a swirl of caramel.

YIELD: 8 SERVINGS

FOR THE CARAMEL

$^3/_4$ cup sugar

$^1/_4$ cup water

FOR THE MOUSSE

$2^1/_2$ pounds sweet-tart apples, such as Cortland, Jonagold, or Empire

6 tablespoons unsalted butter

$^1/_2$ cup sugar

$^1/_4$ cup apricot preserves

4 large eggs

Crème Chantilly, for garnish

Preheat the oven to 350°F. Position the oven rack in the middle.

For the caramel, in a small saucepan dissolve the sugar and water over medium heat. Cook at a brisk simmer for several minutes until the mixture turns a deep amber caramel color. Using potholders, quickly pour the caramel into a 6-cup ring mold, rotating the mold to coat the bottom and sides as well as possible. Place the mold in the refrigerator to harden the caramel.

For the mousse, peel, seed, and coarsely chop the apples. Heat the butter and sugar in a heavy saucepan over medium heat until the butter is melted. Add the chopped apples, stirring to mix. Partially cover and simmer, stirring occasionally with a large wooden spoon, until the mixture is almost a purée but still a bit chunky. If any liquid remains in the pan, continue to cook until the mixture is dry, stirring frequently. Remove from the heat and stir in the apricot preserves. Transfer to a mixing bowl and stir until completely cool.

Lightly beat the eggs with a whisk until combined and then gradually pour into the cooled apple mixture. Using a rubber spatula, transfer the mousse into the caramel-lined mold.

Line a baking pan with a kitchen towel and pour lukewarm water into the pan about two-thirds full. Place the mold in the water bath and bake on the middle rack of the oven until golden brown and it pulls away from the side of the mold slightly, 1 hour to 1 hour and 15 minutes. Remove from the oven and let the mousse sit in the water bath for about 10 minutes. Remove from the water bath and run a knife blade around the inside edge of the pan. When cool enough to handle, place a serving platter over the mousse and invert the mold. Let rest for 5 to 10 minutes longer inverted on the plate and then carefully remove the mold. The mousse can be prepared up to one day ahead. Refrigerate, tented with plastic wrap overnight, and bring to room temperature before serving. Garnish with a dollop of Créme Chantilly.

NOTE: Some of the caramel will stick to the mold. Return the mold to the water bath, add 3 to 4 tablespoons of water to the caramel and stir over heat for a few minutes to soften and then pour over the mousse.

REFERENCE RECIPES

DUCK CONFIT

Duck confit is available in some supermarkets and specialty food stores. If, however you are an adventurous duck lover, here is a recipe to prepare your own duck confit. I'm a fan of duck confit and find it a fine accompaniment to a variety of salads. (See recipes on pages 125 and 216.)

YIELD: 4 SERVINGS

4 whole duck legs

$^{1}/_{2}$ cup packed light brown sugar

$^{1}/_{4}$ cup kosher salt

1 garlic clove, peeled and smashed

4 black peppercorns

3 sprigs fresh thyme

2 whole cloves

2 bay laurel leaves

2 (7-ounce) containers rendered
　duck fat, as needed

Trim excess fat from the duck legs and place in a bowl; set aside.

Combine the brown sugar, salt, garlic, peppercorns, thyme sprigs, cloves, and bay leaves in a bowl large enough to hold the duck legs. Place the duck in the mixture and liberally rub the mixture all over the duck. Cover the bowl with plastic wrap and refrigerate for 48 hours, turning the legs once after 24 hours.

Meanwhile, place the duck trimmings in a heavy cast-iron skillet with 2 teaspoons of cold water. Over very low heat cook the duck fat for about 1 hour, or until most of the fat is rendered and pieces of the fat become cracklings. Let cool and pour the fat through a fine strainer into a bowl. Cover and refrigerate. (When roasting ducks, collect the fat in the roasting pan; it can be strained into a bowl and then cover and refrigerate. If necessary, duck fat can also be purchased.)

Remove the duck legs from the bowl and wipe with a clean damp cloth.

Preheat the oven to 275°F.

In a 5-quart ovenproof saucepan, melt the rendered duck fat over medium-low heat. Add the duck legs. Cover the saucepan with heavy-duty foil, poking a few holes in the foil to allow the steam to escape. Put the covered saucepan in the preheated oven and simmer the duck legs very gently for 4 to $4^{3}/_{4}$ hours until tender, or when a bamboo skewer inserted into the legs show no resistance. Remove the duck legs to a glass or crock-like bowl. Strain the duck fat into a separate bowl and let cool completely. Pour the cooled fat over the duck legs to completely cover. Add the containers of rendered fat, if needed, to ensure the duck legs are covered. Cover the bowl and refrigerate. The legs are best used about one month or later from the time they cooked in the rendered fat.

BASIC PASTA

YIELD: 2/3 POUNDS, 4 SERVINGS

1³/₄ cups all-purpose flour
2 extra large eggs
1 tablespoon extra-virgin olive oil
Pinch of kosher salt

Place the flour in a mound on a large wooden board. Make a deep well in the center of the mound. In a bowl, beat the eggs together. Add the oil and salt. Pour into the well and carefully stir with a fork until well blended. When a heavy paste has formed, mix in as much flour as needed until the mixture becomes crumbly. Toss the mixture back and forth with the your hands to make a soft dough that is no longer sticky, adding more flour if necessary. Gather the dough into a ball and set aside. With a pastry scraper, clean the board by scraping away any dry bits of dough then sift the remaining flour on the board through a sieve back onto your board before you begin to knead.

With clean hands, knead the dough very gently with the heel of your hand by folding, turning, and pressing on a lightly floured surface. It is not necessary to use a lot of pressure. Continue kneading gently until the dough is smooth and supple, about 3 to 4 minutes. Any remaining flour should be passed through a sieve again and kept to coat the dough as you knead and thin the pasta in the machine.

Clamp a pasta machine to a table and adjust the rollers to the widest setting.

Divide the dough in half and work with one piece at a time. Set the remaining half aside, covered with plastic wrap. Lightly flour the dough and flatten the dough with your fingertips. Pass through the rollers. The dough will be unevenly textured at this point. Lightly flour one side of the dough only, tapping off any excess. Fold the dough into thirds, floured side out, and press down to flatten. Pass through the rollers, open side first to push out the air. Repeat 6 or 7 more times, folding in thirds each time and passing open side first until the dough is smooth and elastic. At this point, the dough is ready to thin in the machine.

Place the pasta into the widest setting (first notch) and roll the pasta through. Go to the next notch, decreasing the gap between the rollers and placing the pasta to roll through again. Continue to decrease the notch after each rolling of the pasta until you reach the last notch to thin the pasta. Let the pasta dry on clean towels for about 10 minutes and then cut on the roller for fettucine, angel hair, or spaghetti.

ROASTED GARLIC

1 garlic head
Extra-virgin olive oil

Preheat the oven to 350°F.

Rub off the outer papery skin of the garlic. Using a large sharp knife, cut off a slice of the top of the head to expose the tips the cloves. Arrange the head upright in an oiled baking dish and drizzle with a little olive oil. Place 3 to 4 tablespoons of water in the dish. Cover with foil and bake for 1 hour to 1 hour 15 minutes, until the garlic is completely tender. The garlic can be roasted ahead and refrigerated in a suitable container for up to one week.

HOMEMADE CROUTONS AND BREADCRUMBS

The reason I make homemade croutons and breadcrumbs is that my husband brings home fresh crusty Italian bread or a French baguette almost daily, and so day- or two-day-old bread accumulates in my house. I use croutons in salads and soups and to add crunch to a fish recipe such as roast stripe bass fillets with capers and croutons.

1/2 to 1 loaf day-old crusty bread

Preheat the oven to 375°F.

For croutons, cut the bread into 1/2-inch-thick slices. Stack two slices at a time and cut the slices into 1/2-inch cubes. Place the cubed bread onto a baking sheet and bake until golden brown, 5 to 7 minutes, turning once. When the croutons come to room temperature, they are ready to use. Store any extras in a wax paper–lined cookie tin in a cool dark cupboard. Croutons are bigger and will retain moisture and therefore become stale if not used within a week.

For breadcrumbs, make the croutons per the directions above. Then put the croutons in the workbowl of a food processor and process the cubes into crumbs as fine or as coarse as you like. Transfer the crumbs to a glass screw top jar and store in a cool dark cupboard. Because the bread crumbs are dried and ground up fine, they dry perfectly through and can last indefinitely.

CLASSIC CHICKEN STOCK

Its simply liquid gold.

YIELD: 8 TO 10 QUARTS

3 to 4 pounds chicken backs, necks, and giblets

10 to 12 quarts cold water

2 carrots, trimmed

2 ribs celery, trimmed

Greens from 1 or 2 leeks

2 bay leaves

3 or 4 sprigs flat-leaf Italian parsley

2 or 3 sprigs thyme

1 large unpeeled onion, pierced with 2 whole cloves

10 whole black peppercorns

Rinse the chicken pieces and put into a 12-quart (or larger) stockpot. Cover with the water and bring to a boil over medium-high heat. With a fine-mesh skimmer, skim the froth that rises to the surface. Add 1/2 cup of cold water to stop the cooking and slowly bring back to a boil. Repeat the process of adding water and bringing to a boil two or three more times until the liquid is free of froth. Reduce the heat and simmer, uncovered and without stirring, for about 30 minutes. Do not allow the water to boil at anytime during the cooking process.

Tie the carrots, celery, leek greens, bay leaves, parsley, and thyme with kitchen string into a bundle. Add to the simmering stock with the onion and peppercorns, submerging the vegetables and herbs into the stock. If necessary, skim the stock again, but never stir the stock. Partially cover and simmer for 4 to 5 hours.

With a slotted spoon, lift out and discard the heavy bones and vegetable bundle; then place a chinois or large strainer lined with cheesecloth over a deep bowl. Strain the stock and allow to cool to room temperature. Refrigerate overnight.

After a thorough chilling, the surface of the stock will be covered with a layer of solidified fat. Remove and discard the fat. The stock will keep three to four days in the refrigerator, or divide the stock into quantities of 1 cup or more and freeze. You can also freeze the stock in an ice cube tray. Each cube is approximately a $1/4$ cup.

FISH STOCK

YIELD 1^1/$_2$ QUARTS

3 pounds fish heads and
   trimmings from fresh,
   firm-flesh white fish

2 quarts cold water

1 to 2 ripe tomatoes, coarsely chopped

1 carrot, scrubbed and cut into thirds

1 onion, peeled and quartered

Leek or scallion trimmings

1 bay leaf

6 peppercorns

3 sprigs flat-leaf Italian parsley

Wash the fish trimmings under cold running water and place in a large 8-quart stock pot with the remaining ingredients. Cover the pot and bring to the edge of a boil over medium-high heat; then, with a fine-mesh skimmer, skim and discard the froth that rises to the surface. Briskly simmer, uncovered, for 30 to 35 minutes.

With a fine-mesh strainer, or one lined with moistened cheesecloth, anchored over a large bowl, ladle the stock through the strainer into the bowl. Divide evenly among four pint-size freezer-safe containers and freeze until ready to use.

BASIC PÂTE BRISÉE
SHORT CRUST PASTRY DOUGH

The instructions below are for preparing the short crust pastry by hand or in the food processor.

YIELD: 2 (8-TO 9-INCH) PIECRUSTS

2 cups all-purpose flour

¹/₂ teaspoon salt

Pinch sugar

7 tablespoons cold unsalted butter, cut into pieces

3 tablespoons cold vegetable shortening, cut into pieces

6 tablespoons ice water plus 1 teaspoon, if necessary

HAND METHOD: In a mixing bowl, combine the flour, salt, and sugar. Add the butter and the shortening to the flour with fingertip or a pastry blender until the mixture resembles coarse meal. Make a well in the center and add the ice water, 1 tablespoon at a time, and gently stir the dough with a fork, until you have a rough ball of dough. If the dough feels dry, add more water, 1 teaspoonful at a time. With the heel of your hand, gently push the mass of dough across a floured work area. Gather the dough with a pastry scraper and push out again. You only have to do this 2 or 3 times. Gather the dough once again into a ball and gently flatten into a disk. With a knife, cut an X on the top of the disk. This will relax the gluten in the flour, making the dough easier to roll out. Cover the dough with wax paper and chill for 1 hour before rolling out.

FOOD PROCESSOR METHOD: In the work bowl of a food processor with the steel blade, quickly pulse the flour, salt, and sugar just to mix. Add the butter and shortening and process until the mixture resembles coarse meal. Slowly pour the ice water through the feed tube in a steady stream, processing until all the water is added. The moment the last drop of water has been added, turn off the machine even though the flour mixture in no way resembles a ball of dough. (If the dough is formed into a ball in the food processor the pastry will be overworked.) Transfer the mixture to a lightly floured surface. If any of the dough sticks to the steel blade, slide it off carefully and add to the dough. Gather the dough into a ball and gently flatten into a disk. Cover the dough with wax paper and chill for 1 hour before rolling out.

TARTE TATIN
PASTRY DOUGH

YIELD: 1 (12-INCH) PASTRY DOUGH

2 cups all-purpose flour

¹/₂ teaspoon salt

Pinch sugar

1 stick (8 tablespoons) cold unsalted butter

1 egg yolk

6 tablespoons cold water

Place the flour, salt, and sugar in the work bowl of a food processor fitted with the steel blade. Pulse quickly just to mix. Remove the cover and cut the cold butter into pieces directly into the bowl. Process until the mixture has the consistency of coarse meal. Add the egg yolk and pulse to mix. With the machine running, carefully pour the water through the feed tube in a steady stream. The moment the last drop of water has been added, stop the food processor even though the ingredients have not completely come together. (If a ball of dough is formed, the pastry will be tough.) Turn the dough out onto a lightly floured surface. If any of the dough sticks to the steel blade, slide it off carefully and add to the mass of dough.

With the heel of your hand, gently push the dough across a floured work area. Shape the dough into a ball and push out again one or two more times. Gather the dough once again into a ball and gently flatten into a disk. With a knife, cut an X on top of the disk. This will relax the gluten in the flour, making the dough easier to roll out. Cover the dough with wax paper and chill about 1 hour before rolling out. The dough may also be wrapped securely and placed in the freezer. Freeze leftover dough for a small tart or quiche.

When ready to use, defrost overnight in the refrigerator.

CRÈME FRAÎCHE

YIELD: 2 CUPS

2 cups heavy cream
6 tablespoons active-culture buttermilk

Combine the heavy cream and buttermilk in a saucepan and stir until the mixture is smoothly blended. Heat over medium-low to 65 to 80 degrees or just tepid. Warming the liquids acts as a starter and aids the process of fermentation. Pour into a wide-mouth screw-top jar and cover. Let the liquid stand at room temperature for 48 hours, until the surface has thickened. Remove the cover and stir with a wooden spoon. Refrigerate until ready to use. This simple formula makes a good facsimile of French crème fraîche.

RESOURCES

ARTISANS

Bees' Needs
P.O. Box 3139
Southampton, NY 11969
Email: mgwoltz@
optonline.net

Catapano Dairy Farm
33705 North Road
Peconic, NY 11958
631-765-8042
www.catapanodairyfarm.
com

Mecox Bay Dairy
855 Mecox Road
P.O. Box 411
Bridgehampton, NY 11932
631-537-0335
Email: art@mecoxbaydairy.com
www.mecoxbaydairy.com

**North Fork
Potato Chip Co.**
Martin Sidor Farms
Mattituck, NY 11952
631-734-2243
www.northforkchips.com

Open Minded Organics
David Falkowski
631-574-8889
www.openmindedorganics.
com
Email: davidfalkowski@
hotmail.com

Scotto's Pork Store
25 West Montauk Highway
Hampton Bays, NY 11946
631-728-5677
www.scottosporkstore.com

**The Taste of
the North Fork**
8595A Cox Lane, Unit #3
Cutchogue, NY 11935
631-734-6100
www.atasteofthenorthfork.com

Citarella
2209 Montauk Highway
Bridgehampton, NY 11932
631-726-3636
2 Pantigo Road
East Hampton, NY 11937
631-726-3636
www.citarella.com

Villa Italian Specialties
7 Railroad Ave
East Hampton, NY 11937
631-324-5110
www.villaitalianspecialties.
com

Village Prime Meat Shoppe
495 Montauk Highway
East Quogue, NY 11942
631-653-8071
www.villageprimemeatshoppe.
com

FARMS

Balsam Farms
Town Lane and Windmill Lane
Amagansett, NY 11930
Ian 734-735-8510
Alex 631-255-9417
Email: hamptons-
farmer@balsamfarms.com
www.balsamfarms.com

**Dale & Bette's
Organic Produce**
1726 Bridgehampton Turnpike
Sag Harbor, NY 11963
631-725-5262

Foster Farms
729 Sagg Main Street
Sagaponack, NY 11962
631-537-0070

The Green Thumb
829 Montauk Highway
Water Mill, NY 11976
631-726-1900
www.greenthumborganicfarm
.com

The Iacono Chicken Farm
106 Long Lane
East Hampton, NY 11937
631-324-1107

Jurgeliewicz Duck Farm
P.O. Box 68
Moriches, NY 11955
631-878-2000

Milk Pail
(Halsey's Farm and Milk Pail)
1346 Montauk Hwy. & 757
Mecox Rd.
Water Mill, NY 11976
631-537-2565
www.milk-pail.com

North Sea Farms
1060 Noyac Road
Southampton, NY 11968
631-283-0735

Oysterponds Farm
24850 Main Road
Orient, NY 11957
631-323-2463
www.oysterpondsfarm.com

Pike Farms
82 Sagg Main Street
Sagaponack, NY 11962
631-537-5854
Email: jjpikfarms@
yahoo.com
www.pikefarms.com

Quail Hill Farm
Old Stone Highway
Amagansett, NY 11930
631-267-8492

Round Swamp Farm
184 Three Mile Harbor Road
East Hampton, NY 11937
631-324-4438
www.roundswampfarm.com

Sang Lee Farms
25180 Country Road 48
Peconic, NY 11958
631-734-7001
www.sangleefarms.com

Satur Farms LLC
3705 Alvah's Lane
Cutchogue, NY 11935
631-734-4219
www.saturfarms.com
e-mail: info@saturfarms.com

Stuart Seafood Market Ltd.
41 Oak Lane
Amagansett, NY 11930
631-267-6700
www.stuartsseafood.com

Ty Llwyd Farm
5793 Sound Avenue
Riverhead, NY 11901
631-722-4241

**Cor-J Seafood
Corporation**
36 Lighthouse Road
Hampton Bays, NY 11946
631-728-5186

Crescent Duck Farm
10 Edgar Avenue
Aquebogue, NY 11931
212-929-3118

RESTAURANTS

The 1770 House
143 Main Street
East Hampton, NY 11937
631-324-1770
www.1770house.com

**A Mano Osteria
& Wine Bar**
13550 Main Road
Mattituck, NY 11952
631-298-4800
www.amanorestaurant.com

Almond
1970 Montauk Highway
Bridgehampton, NY 11932
631-537-8885
www.almondrestaurant.com

American Hotel
49 Main Street
Sag Harbor, NY 11963-3012
631-725-3535
www.theamericanhotel.com

Beacon
8 West Water Street
Sag Harbor, NY 11963
631-725-7088
www.beaconsagharbor.com

Bobby Van's
2393 Montauk Highway
Bridgehampton, NY 11932
631-537-0590
www.bobbyvans.com

Café Max
85 Montauk Highway
East Hampton, NY 11937
631-324-2004
www.unhampton.com

Della Femina Restaurant
99 North Main Street
East Hampton, NY 11937
631-329-6666
www.dellafemina.com

Estia's Little Kitchen
1615 Bridgehampton-Sag
Harbor Turnpike
Sag Harbor, NY 11963
631-725-1045
www.estiaslittlekitchen.com

**Fishbar | Montauk
Seafood Restaurant**
467 East Lake Drive
Montauk, NY 11954
631-668-6600
www.freshlocalfish.com

Fresno
8 Fresno Place
East Hampton, NY 11937
631-324-8700
www.fresnorestaurant.com

**The Jedediah Hawkins
Inn / Luce & Hawkins
Restaurant**
400 South Jamesport Avenue
Jamesport, NY 11947
631-722-2900
Email:
info@jedediahhawkinsinn
.com
www.jedediahhawkinsinn
.com

**The Living Room c/o
Maidstone**
207 Main Street
East Hampton, NY 11937
631-324-5006
www.themaidstone.com

Nick & Toni's
136 North Main Street
East Hampton, NY 11937
631-324-3550
www.nickandtonis.com

North Fork Table & Inn
57225 Main Road
Southold, NY 11971
631-765-0177
www.northforktableandinn
.com

The Plaza Cafe
61 Hill Street
Southampton, NY 11968
631-283-9323
www.plazacafe.us

Starr Boggs
6 Parlato Drive
Westhampton, NY 11978
631-288-3500
www.starrboggs.com

Stone Creek Inn
405 Montauk Highway
East Quogue, NY 11942
631-653-6770
www.stonecreekinn.com

VINEYARDS

Bedell North Fork, LLC
36225 Main Road, RT 25
Cutchogue, NY 11935
631-734-7537
www.bedellcellars.com

Channing Daughters Winery
1927 Scuttle Hole Road
P.O. Box 2202
Bridgehampton, NY 11932
631-537-7224
Email:
info@channingdaughters.com
www.channingdaughters.com

The Grapes of Roth
P.O. Box 114
Sag Harbor, NY 11963
631-725-7999
Email:

info@thegrapesofroth.com
www.thegrapesofroth.com

The Lenz Winery
P.O. Box 28
Peconic, NY 11958
631-734-6010
e-mail: office@lenzwine.com
www.lenzwine.com

Lieb Family Cellars
35 Cox Neck Road
Mattituck, NY 11952
631-298-1942
www.liebcellars.com

Macari Vineyard
150 Bergen Avenue
Mattituck, NY 11952
631-298-0100
www.macariwines.com

Paumanok Vineyards
1074 Main Road (Route 25)
Aquebogue, NY 11931
631-722-8800
Email: info@paumanok.com
www.paumanok.com

Peconic Bay Winery
P.O. Box 818
Cutchogue, NY 11935
631-734-7361
www.peconicbaywinery.com

Pellegrini Vineyards
23005 Main Road
Cutchogue, NY 11935
631-734-4111
e-mail:
wine@pellegrinivineyards.com
www.pellegrinivineyards.com

Raphael Vineyards
39390 Main Road, Route 25
Peconic, NY 11958
631-765-1100
Email: general-
info@raphaelwine.com
www.raphaelwine.com

Shinn Estate Vineyards and Farmhouse
2000 Oregon Road
Mattituck, NY 11952
631-804-0367
www.shinnestatevineyards
.com

Wolffer Estate Vineyard
139 Sagg Road
Sagaponack, NY 11976
631-537-5106
www.wolffer.com

INDEX